NORMA FAIN PRATT

MORRIS HILLQUIT

A Political History of an American Jewish Socialist

CONTRIBUTIONS IN POLITICAL SCIENCE, NUMBER 20

GREENWOOD PRESS
WESTPORT, CONNECTICUT • LONDON, ENGLAND

Library of Congress Cataloging in Publication Data

Pratt, Norma Fain.
Morris Hillquit: a political history of an American Jewish socialist.

(Contributions in political science; no. 20 ISSN 0147-1066)
Bibliography: p.
Includes index.
1. Hillquit, Morris, 1869-1933. 2. Socialists—United States—Biography. 3. Socialists, Jewish—United States—Biography. 4. Jews in the United States—Biography. I. Series.
HX84.H5P7 335'.0092'4 [B] 78-55349
ISBN 0-313-20526-4

Library of Congress Catalog Card Number: 78-55349
ISBN: 0-313-20526-4
ISSN: 0147-1066

First published in 1979

Greenwood Press, Inc.
51 Riverside Avenue, Westport, Connecticut 06880

Printed in the United States of America

10 9 8 7 6 5 4 3 2 1

To my parents,
Abraham and Jean Fain

Contents

Preface

It is possible to follow the historical course of the birth, maturation, and decline of socialism in America through examining Morris Hillquit's lifelong activities in the movement. Hillquit (1869-1933) not only played an extremely important role in molding American socialism's ideologies and policies but his impact was of exceptional duration. Unlike such leaders as Eugene V. Debs, Daniel De Leon, and William Haywood, Hillquit's influence on socialist politics continued long after World War I. He was an active participant until his death in 1933.

What is especially interesting—and what is explored in this work—are the complexities and seeming contradictions of Hillquit's life. His is a fascinating and unique American biography—the life of an impoverished immigrant who personally fulfilled the American dream of middle-class success yet neither abandoned his social responsibilities nor rejected his earliest ideals of justice and equality. As an immigrant Jew, he took part in the development of the socialist and labor movement among New York Jews. As an intellectual, a Marxist theorist, he wrote one of the first histories of socialism in the United States as well as books on socialist theory and hundreds of articles which appeared in the socialist and non-socialist press. He was a politician whose interests encompassed the local, national, and international scene. The vitality and diversity of his political career was impressive. Furthermore, Hillquit was a lawyer whose legal practice included civil rights cases and labor law. He defended radicals of all political persuasions, including anarchists Johann Most and Alexander Berkman with whom he disagreed ideologically. From 1914 until his death, he was the leading attorney and negotiator for the International Ladies Garment Workers' Union, one of the American Federation of Labor's most radical unions.

Hillquit, a controversial figure in his own time, has remained so among historians. To some of his contemporaries, his wealth and his cultivated way of life seemed to contradict the socialist aspiration he espoused. Moreover, he was condemned for his gradualist and non-revolutionary Marixism and for his desire to create a mass-based socialist party which included not only the working class but the middle class as well, especially the intellectuals. Leon Trotsky unkindly called him the perfect leader for successful dentists.

Hillquit's identity as a Jew was equally controversial and problematic. Many Jewish socialists, for instance, regarded him as an asssimilationist disloyal to the Jewish community for he did not practice either a religious or a secular form of Judaism. Throughout his life he claimed to be loyal to the international working class and to the United States. Ironically, Hillquit's critics among midwestern socialists considered him a foreigner, a Jewish immigrant centered in New York City who did not truly represent the American Socialist Party since he was not an indigenous product of America's political soil.

This book is not a conventional biography; I am not concerned primarily with Hillquit's personal development. Rather it is more accurate to call this study a political history since I reconstruct Hillquit's public life and deal with his ideas on socialism and with his career as a politician, trade unionist, and lawyer. Although the narrative is in chronological order, I do not examine all aspects of his life. Instead, I focus upon those concepts, strategies, and tactics which evoked critical comment within the radical movement. Also I attempt to engage some of the fundamental issues which have preoccupied historians in their evaluation of the left in America. Indirectly, through an examination of Hillquit's political life, I am concerned with why the Socialist Party of America and socialism in general failed to strike deeper roots in American society.

The available sources have determined, in part, the nature of this work. It would have been helpful to examine Hillquit's personal and inner life. Unfortunately, the overwhelming number of his letters and writings are concerned with public matters and are written in an impersonal style—including his autobiography. The Morris Hillquit Papers, a collection compiled by Hillquit and his family during his life and given to the State Historical Society of Wisconsin by his daughter Nina in 1952, is the single most important source of information about his life. The papers contain a few letters which offer glimpses into his private affairs and his feelings. It is possible he did not write intimate letters but, more likely, he did not collect them. His thoughts, including "unofficial" views on Socialist Party matters remain, for the most part, hidden from the investigator.

Furthermore, the Hillquit Papers lack materials which might illuminate his relationship with the left wing of the Socialist Party or with the Communists. His collected letters are those mainly between himself and right-wing socialists or non-socialist reformers. The papers hold very few clippings from the left-wing press. Thus a left-wing critique of Hillquit is virtually absent from this collection. Clippings from Jewish newspapers and correspondence with Jewish socialists are also missing. As I have discovered, the New York Yiddish press covered Hillquit with great interest. Apparently the interest was not mutual.

In contrast, the Hillquit Papers include a wide array of newspaper clippings from the American conservative and non-socialist press. There are even articles from small towns in the Middle and Far West. The cumulative impression one gets from the clippings is that the American press regarded Hillquit variously as a radical, as a respectable leader of a significant political party, and as a formidable opponent of capitalism. Hillquit wanted to be seen this way.

For those areas which the Wisconsin collection does not consider, I have investigated other Socialist Party collections, particularly those in the Tamiment Library and at Duke University. I have consulted the Yiddish-language press, especially the collections at the Jewish Division of the New York Public Library, YIVO, and the Jewish Labor Bund Archive in New York. The translations from the Yiddish are mine.

Norma Fain Pratt

Los Angeles, California

Acknowledgments

While writing this work I received advice from many people. I particularly want to acknowledge the help of John H. M. Laslett, Professor of History at the University of California, Los Angeles, whose manifold insights into the socialist movement have guided me throughout. Also I wish to thank Bernard Johnpoll for his astute editorial comments.

My debt to archivists and librarians is incalculable. I have a single debt of gratitude to Hillel Kempinski of the Bund Archives in New York. He generously allowed me to share in his enormous fund of knowledge and the collected materials of the international socialist movement. His judicious yet critical judgments and his loyalty to Jewish socialism helped me frame my own interpretations. I wish to thank most warmly Dorothy Swanson of the Tamiment Library for her assistance in providing me with research materials. Although there are too many individuals to name, I am also appreciative of the staffs of the following libraries: University of Wisconsin; Duke University; Columbia University; University of California, Los Angeles; Hebrew University, Jerusalem; the New York Public Library (Jewish Division), and the Research Department of the International Ladies Garment Workers' Union.

I have been fortunate in calling upon the assistance of friends and family. Marsie Scharlatt offered me editorial advice and encouragement. To my husband Kenneth I owe thanks for his scholarly sympathy, his advice in editing, and especially for his interest. Finally, to my children Adam and Oliver, who lived with the creation of a work that altered their lives as it did mine, I express my deepest indebtedness.

MORRIS HILLQUIT

On Becoming a Socialist

Chapter 1

Morris Hillquit, or rather Moishe Hillkowitz, was born in Riga, Latvia, on August 1, 1869. He was the second son of Benjamin and Rebecca, German-speaking middle-class Jews who owned a factory in this commercial Baltic port where the family resided until Hillquit was seventeen.[1] The Jews of Riga were in the minority; they numbered 22,000 in a total population of 278,000 Latvians and Germans. Politically and legally Riga was administered by the Czarist Russian government which excluded Jews from engaging in various kinds of occupations and prohibited them from owning land. The majority of Riga Jews were poor, faithful to Orthodox Judaism, and isolated within their own community.[2]

Hillquit's parents were somewhat different from most other Riga Jews. They were not poor and they did not adhere strictly to orthodox Jewish practices. In fact, their behavior was radical in the sense that they were among the first generation of Eastern European Jews whose contacts with Western European ideas induced them to reject the traditions of the past. It was his parents who instilled in Morris the ambition to become a lawyer or an academic; perhaps they even stirred in him the hope of exchanging the cloistered existence of the religious Jewish community for a life among the gentiles.

In the 1860s and 1870s the Russian monarchy, under whose control the originally Latvian city of Riga was governed, began to advocate programs aimed at assimilating minority groups into a Russian way of life through higher education. The Russians also initiated a policy of absorbing a few Jews into the professions. The Hillkowitz family tried to take advantage of these opportunities in the 1880s.

In 1882 Hillquit was enrolled in a non-Jewish secular school, the Russian-language Alexander gymnasium. Although he originally wanted to attend the only other non-Jewish gymnasium in Riga, the German-language school, the school had filled its Jewish quota. He accepted what was available and as a result learned Russian fluently.[3] There were very few Jewish students at the Alexander gymnasium.

At the age of fifteen, in 1884, the year after Marx's death, Hillquit took his first step toward radicalism by becoming a socialist. He was in his third year at the gymnasium. In his autobiography, *Loose Leaves from a Busy Life,* he failed to explain why he chose socialism or in what ways it expressed his ideological belief. However, he described his brand of socialism at that time as "largely emotional" and his notions about the philosophy and practical program of the movement as "quite vague."[4]

Explanations for Hillquit's original impulse to become a socialist are not difficult to find. He shared this interest in political radicalism with many other Eastern European Jews, especially students, who attended secular gymnasia and universities in the Russian Empire of the 1880s. There were several reasons why Jewish students became radicalized in those years. First, they desired an end to the restrictions placed upon all Jews in the Russian Empire. The ethics of justice and the universalist message of socialism appeared to offer a solution to the termination of minority status and social marginality. Socialism seemed to promise, almost in a messianic way, the future integration of Jews into a broader society.

Second, the desire for egalitarianism was intense among Jewish students because of personal disappointment. The new Russian policy of so-called assimilation had led many people to expect that their education would result in social and economic advancement within the Russian system. Instead, anti-Semitism persisted. Jews continued to be excluded from the civil service and from the professions. In addition, at the beginning of the 1880s an especially virulent outbreak of government-supported pogroms enhanced the sense of anti-Semitism. Most students who turned to socialism as an alternative to the present reality despaired of fulfilling their professional aspirations under Czarism.

Still another reason why socialism attracted students—born out of their particular Jewish experience—was the iconoclastic aspect of this new secular philosophy. The young intellectuals read authors such as Chernyshevski, Buckle, and Spencer, all of whom possessed a strong anti-religious thrust.[5] These authors wrote about personal and societal improvement through rational means and through an understanding of the evolving modern circumstance. Students like young Hillquit were already in the process of divesting themselves of Talmudic traditions. Their concerns were secular. The blend of socialist and scientific readings, made available to them through the socialist movement, armed them with a set of rational arguments with which to oppose the vast majority of their still orthodox brethren.

At fifteen Hillquit had a personal reason for feeling bitter toward the world and for desiring to change it. In 1884 his father lost his factory in Riga. Benjamin Hillkowitz decided to improve the family's financial situation by emigrating to the United States. Leaving his wife, two young daughters, and two sons in Riga, he emigrated with his eldest son Jacob to New York City. Under these insecure circumstances, sometime in his last two years at the Alexander gymnasium, Hillquit became a socialist.

Hillquit's nascent socialist feelings were reinforced and enhanced by dislocation and by personal and perceived poverty. In 1886 Hillquit, his mother, sisters, and younger brother emigrated to New York City. During that year more than 20,000 other Jewish immigrants from Eastern Europe came to the United States settling mainly in New York City.[6] Nina Hillquit, Morris's daughter, described how her father, who was then seventeen, assumed the role of head of the family on the trip to the United States. Offering a rare glimpse into Hillquit family life, she wrote:

> They traveled for three weeks in the steerage with little or no food, making one stop en route in Scotland. The only food the family could afford to buy was potatoes. Morris, their

spokesman, asked the shopkeeper for "pomes" [*sic*] of the earth. Somehow he made himself understood, and a little richer by their purchase, they continued their journey to New York.[7]

Benjamin Hillkowitz remained poor in New York City. There is no record of the kind of work he did. According to Hillquit, his father set up housekeeping in a two-room tenement apartment on the lower East Side where from 1886 the reunited family lived for a few years.[8] In this period the lower East Side was predominately Jewish and the primary area of Jewish immigrant settlement. It was a colorful part of the city with an unhealthy residential density and a congested business population of street peddlers, workshops, and factories.

According to his own account, Morris held a special place within the family circle. Although his older brother Jacob later attended law school, he and the older of Hillquit's two sisters were sent to work to supplement the family income. Hillquit, however, was enrolled in a public high school. "It was the unanimous decision of the family," he wrote, "that I resume my interrupted studies and prepare myself for a professional career." But the continuing pressure of poverty and the fact that he "felt uncomfortable in the role of the drone of the family"[9] persuaded the young Hillquit to leave school and to find work in 1886.

During his seventeenth year Hillquit worked at a series of jobs all of which he either lost because of the seasonal nature of the work or left because he found the conditions distasteful. He was employed for short times as a cuffmaker in a shirt factory, as a waistmaker, and as a picture frame maker in a factory. Poor wages, the insecurity of employment, and boredom were the dominant realities of those months from 1886 through 1888. It is probable that he first contracted tuberculosis in this period. Such was his initiation into American immigrant life.

Almost as soon as he settled in New York, Hillquit was drawn into East Side Jewish radical circles. He was then a small (5′4″), slightly built, frail adolescent with dark hair, dark oval-shaped eyes, and a gentle charming manner. He was immediately attracted to other young Jewish immigrants, mostly former students, now shop workers, who considered themselves intellectuals—a new radical *intelligentsia*. He wrote about them empathetically in his autobiography. "They are persons of high school or college education who had been suddenly plucked from their studies and associations by persecution and discriminations in their cruel native land."[10] Or like him, "their years of preparation of professional careers were of no practical value to them. . . . they felt unhappy and forlorn in their workshops."[11]

For the most part their radicalism was rooted in their experiences in the European socialist and anarchist movements. But emigration and economic hardships in the United States also contributed to their further radicalization. As foreigners in America they were situated far enough outside the society to observe its failings. As frustrated but literate people, they were ambitious enough to want to participate in it. These young intellectuals were interested in finding alternatives to their present circumstances; their solution was to transform them.

There was considerable confusion among Jewish radical intellectuals as to how to alter these circumstances. During his first summer in New York, in 1886, Hillquit discovered a group of Jewish Russian-speaking intellectuals. Members of this group were between the ages of eighteen and twenty-five. They met on the rooftop of an East Side Cherry Street tenement where they sang Russian folksongs, reminisced about their student days, which most of them had now exchanged for work in small garment factories, and held heated discussions on every imaginable subject. "There was not a mooted question in science, philosophy, or politics that was not aired on the roofs in ardent, impassioned, and tumultuous debate," Hillquit recalled. In the winter he met with his friends in the lower East Side cafes where "we could pass many hours talking and occasionally sipping weak tea served in tumblers, Russian style."[12]

He also attended meetings at the newly founded Russian Progressive Union whose members represented "all shades of radical and liberal thought."[13] When he worked several weeks in the shirt factory, Hillquit encountered a special "circle of young Russian intellectuals" who were attracted to shirtmaking because it was not exacting and the surroundings were congenial. He recalled that the shirtwaist workers "spent at least as much time in discussing social and literary topics as in turning out shirts, and the whir of the sewing machines was often accompanied by the loud and hearty sound of revolutionary songs."[14]

The adolescent Hillquit first found acceptance as a person in these intellectual circles. The seventeen-year-old immigrant from Riga had many virtues. He was exceptionally intelligent, contentious, and he had an incisive manner in debate. As part of his gymnasium education he had learned to speak and to read fluent German and Russian. He also knew a little English, French, Latin, and Italian. These qualities were admired by his new friends. It is possible that this early personal success among intellectuals helped determine his lifelong adherence to an intellectual kind of socialism. Despite his later interest in workers and in creating a working-class party, Hillquit always felt most comfortable with radical intellectuals and he could never quite discard the feeling that the socialist movement was first and foremost intellectual. In a sense his later design for the Socialist Party of America, particularly his emphasis on worker education and propaganda, was influenced by his early years among the intellectuals on the rooftops.

Hillquit's tenacious loyalty to the radical movement also was forged in these earliest years. Psychologically his adjustment to the strange and hostile New York environment was rooted in radical politics. As he said, "The fraternity of the roofs . . . was the main link between the idealism of my youth and the sordid realities of my daily occupations."[15] Radicalism was a means by which he was socialized into American life. At least it was one of the first stages in this process. Later, law school and his legal career offered him another kind of socialization.

On his eighteenth birthday in August 1887, Hillquit joined the Socialist Labor Party. He was introduced into the Party by a fellow shirtwaistmaker Louis Miller, the editor of the New York socialist Russian-language weekly *Znamia*.[16] Miller had spent several years in Switzerland and learned his socialism from George Plekhanov who later, in 1898, was to become one of the theoreticians and founders of the Russian Social Democratic Party. "I was . . . deeply impressed with the practical idealism of Social Democracy," Hillquit recalled in his autobiography.[17] The young Hillquit, who had engaged in manual labor for less than a year and had never belonged to either a trade union or a political organization, wanted to apply the general theories of Western European and Russian social democracy to the American circumstances.

The Socialist Labor Party was a good place for such a novice. Founded in 1877, for ten years the SLP had been involved in trade union recruitment and political activism among New York workers. Composed of a set of foreign-language sections, mainly German, French, Czech, Scandinavian, and Bohemian, its membership oscillated between 2,000 and 3,000. Only about 10 percent of the membership was native-born.[18] The Party's principles included Marxist ideas such as the concepts of class war, political action, and trade union militancy. In the ten years of its existence it had functioned in varied ways, that is, as a socialist propaganda group, as a trade union organizer, and as a political party. The Party ran candidates for local, state, and national offices, subsidized citywide federations of trade unions (*gewerkschaften*), and published Party newspapers in the native languages of the immigrant workers. Throughout the 1880s and 1890s the SLP shifted its tactical politics between supporting the existing trade union movements and participating in political activities. As Hillquit observed in his *History of Socialism in the United States* (1903), the SLP followed a pattern of supporting radical reform politics during periods of depression and then deserting politics for trade unionism during periods of high employment.[19]

Hillquit became a member of one of the newest sections, Branch 17. This section was founded by Russian-speaking Jewish socialists only a few months before Hillquit joined. All previous attempts by Jewish immigrants to form radical or even simple trade union organizations in the 1880s were shortlived. A Jewish Workingmen's Association which supported the Henry George campaign for mayor of New York in 1886 collapsed after the candidate failed to be elected.[20] Thus up until the late 1880s New York Jewish immigrant radicals were isolated from any organized native-born intellectuals or workers. Jewish radical groups were primarily educational debating societies. Moreover, although many Jewish radicals in New York were no longer students but factory workers, their influence with Jewish workers was insignificant. There is no evidence that radicals either led strikes or formed unions.

Distinct radical groups among lower East Side Jews began to form just at the time Hillquit arrived on the scene. Previously, most Jewish immigrant radicals were still unsure of their specific ideological identity. Socialists, anarchists, and a wide variation of social experimenters belonged to the same societies,[21] for example, the Russian Progressive Union, where they engaged mainly in theoretical debates on such issues as the role of violence, the trade union, or politics in the coming society.[22] Generally, Jewish radicals professed an eclectic mixture of European ideas to which a strong ethical and moral emphasis was added from their religious background.

The anarchists were the first radicals to formally separate from the others.[23] On October 9, 1886, the Pioneers for Liberty was created in New York. Its acknowledged leader was the German anarchist Johann Most. Composed predominately of Russian Jews, the ideology of this group included a belief in an imminent and violent revolution, the destruction of the State, and a "return" to communalistic forms of cooperative economy. Tactically the anarchists denounced all types of political activism although they accepted the idea that anarchists ought to work within the trade unions to educate the workers.[24]

A group calling themselves Social Democrats formed shortly thereafter, perhaps in response to the anarchist action. The socialists saw a need for both political and trade union action as part of a class struggle. But they did not expect revolution to take place in the immediate future nor did they imagine a future revolution necessarily to be violent. This group applied for admission into the New York Socialist Labor Party. Four months before Hillquit joined the SLP, two Jewish sections were formed, a Yiddish-speaking and worker-oriented Branch 8 and a Russian-speaking and self-education-oriented Branch 17. Hillquit joined the latter group.

The eighteen-year-old Hillquit chose to become a social democrat and a member of the SLP in 1887 as much in the process of rejecting the New York immigrant variety of anarchism as in accepting a socialist ideology. Before he became a member of any formal socialist group, Hillquit distrusted anarchist ideas and the personal motives of the Russian-Jewish anarchists he met when he first arrived in New York. Even in his "green" rooftop days he thought anarchism was inappropriate for the American environment of the 1880s. "The doctrine," he claimed, "made a special appeal to the Russian mind, largely because of the seemingly hopeless political condition of Russia."[25] Conjecturing that "the brutal suppression of Socialist propaganda in most countries of continental Europe had weakened the faith of many in the efficacy of peaceful methods and embittered them," he characterized Russian-Jewish anarchism as "a simple creed and a romantic movement filled with thrilling conspiracies and acts of heriosm and self-sacrifice." He held anarchism in contempt because it was "a movement of reprisal and violence against personal representatives of the capitalist system" while it disdained "peaceful trade union activities and all species of social reform."[26]

Within a year or so of joining the SLP Hillquit became one of the Party's crusaders against anarchism. In April 1890 he wrote a lengthy article, "Sotzializm un anarchizm," in the *Arbeter zeitung*, a Yiddish newspaper he helped to found. Hillquit, the budding Marxist theorist, compared "individualistic" anarchism with "communistic" socialism.[27] In another article written about the same time, Hillquit warned the Jewish workers against confusing the two ideologies. "Most people envision a revolution and . . . fear it and hate the socialists, anarchists and other revolutionaries who want blood letting."[28]

Hillquit chose to become a member of the SLP because he felt that social democrats, like his friend Louis Miller, were sober men and advocates of practical and realistic programs. Hillquit especially appreciated the fact that social democrats understood revolution in terms of "revolutionizing the minds of the passive millions of workers in all advanced countries of the world."[29] Unlike the anarchists, Miller and the other socialists rejected the possibility of "a great social, economic and moral world revolution accomplished by guerrilla warfare, dynamite bombs and theatrical conspiracies."[30]

Hillquit's early and deeply emotional disapproval of anarchism is an important clue to understanding the mature Hillquit's support for the expulsion of William Haywood, leader of the Industrial Workers of the World, from the Socialist Party's National Executive Committee in 1913 and his general opposition to the IWW's anarcho-syndicalist tendencies.

Notes

1. Hillquit never discussed his parents; his father's occupation in Riga and the United States was not recorded. Bernard Weinstein, *Di yidishe yunyons in amerika* (New York, 1929), p. 155, wrote that Hillquit's parents were wealthy in Riga. Melech Epstein, "Hillquit's leben un tetigkeiten oif der yidisher gas," New York *Der tog*, May 9, 1949, mentioned that his father was a teacher. Also see Zalmon Reison, ed., *Leksicon fun yidisher literatur, presse un philogia*, 4 vols. (Vilna, 1926), 1:844, and *Leksicon fun der nayer yidisher literatur*, 7 vols. (New York, 1956), 3:138-40.

2. For a discussion of Riga Jewry see Isaac Lewin, "Riga," in *The Universal Jewish Encyclopedia*, 10 vols. (New York, 1939), 9:164.

3. Nina Hillquit, "Morris Hillquit: Pioneer of American Socialism," transcript, n.d., p. 2, microfilm in the Morris Hillquit Papers, State Historical Society of Wisconsin, 1964.

4. Morris Hillquit, *Loose Leaves from a Busy Life* (New York, 1934), pp. 8-9. This remarkably impersonal autobiography was published posthumously.

5. It is likely that Hillquit did not read Marx in Riga since Marx's works were not available in Eastern Europe in the 1880s. For example, Ber Borochov, founder of the Poale Zion in the late 1890s, remarked that he first read Marx in Russia in the 1890s. See his "Reminiscences," in *Nationalism and the Class Struggle* (New York, 1937), p. 180.

6. Samuel Joseph, *Jewish Immigration in the United States from 1881 to 1910* (New York, 1914), table 29, p. 173.

7. Nina Hillquit, "Morris Hillquit," p. 4.

8. *Loose Leaves*, p. 31.

9. Ibid.

10. Ibid., p. 33.

11. Ibid., pp. 1-2.

12. Ibid.

13. Ibid., p. 15.

14. Ibid., p. 9.

15. Ibid., p. 8

16. Biographic notes on Louis Miller are in *Loose Leaves*, pp. 34-35, and in *Leksicon fun der nayer yidisher literatur*, 5:628-631.

17. *Loose Leaves*, p. 10.

18. Ibid., p. 44.

19. Morris Hillquit, *The History of Socialism in the United States* (New York, 1903), p. 195.

20. Melech Epstein, *Jewish Labor in USA*, 2 vols. (New York, 1950), 1: 148-54.

21. *Loose Leaves*, pp. 6-7.

22. Hillquit's attitude toward immigrant Russian socialists is expressed in a letter from his brother-in-law Phoebus A. Levene, January 24, 1897, Correspondence, Hillquit Papers.

23. For a discussion of Jewish anarchism see Joseph Cohen, *Di yidish-anarchistishe bavegung in amerika* (Philadelphia, 1945).

24. Morris Winchevski's description of Jewish anarchist ideas in England in the 1880s and 1890s is found in his *Gezamelte verk*, 10, *passim.*

25. *Loose Leaves*, p. 4.

26. Ibid.

27. Morris Hillquit, "Sotzializm un anarchizm," New York *Arbeter zeitung*, April 8, 1890.

28. Morris Hillquit, "Vos iz revolutzie," ibid., April 18, 1890.

29. *Loose Leaves*, p. 10.

30. Ibid.

Work among Jewish Immigrants, 1887-1891

Chapter 2

Hillquit and the other Jewish socialists in the Socialist Labor Party were enrolled exclusively in Jewish sections. Hillquit disapproved of the way the Party was structured and would have preferred to join an "American" party, but there was not even an American section of the SLP in 1888. All of its members in New York were organized in special foreign-language sections. The founders believed ethnic groupings would serve at least three purposes: provide immigrant working people with a socialist-fraternal organization, develop effective political and labor resistance within immigrant groups employed in the same industry, and offer immigrant workers insights into American culture—but in their own language.

The Party did not intend to isolate the immigrant. Rather the leaders imagined that within special educational-propaganda units the immigrant socialist would be made aware of the issues which transcended the confines of specific ethnic concerns. Once this was accomplished, the immigrant then would be integrated gradually into the broader American scene. The long-range goal of the separate foreign-language sections was "Americanization"—the weaning of the immigrant away from the old ways.

Most Jewish socialists agreed with the SLP's program of ethnic separation. Abraham Cahan, Louis Miller, and Morris Winchevski, Hillquit's comrades of the 1880s and early 1890s, reconciled their Marxist sense of working-class solidarity with their loyalty to the concept of a separate Jewish identity. They wanted the socialist movement in New York to appeal directly to the Jewish immigrant worker by means of the Yiddish language, Jewish culture, and religious ideas. Thus Cahan and the others founded the *Arbeter zeitung* in which to expound a socialist philosophy in the immigrant's idiom. The nineteen-year-old Hillquit acted as the paper's business manager, news correspondent, and resident poet during its earliest months.[1]

The Jewish socialists in the Party thought their Eastern European brethren were ready to hear the message of socialism. It was a realistic expectation. Evidence existed all around them on the lower East Side that Jews had become an urban proletariat. Jewish women and men were employed primarily in the small workshops of the garment industry. Most immigrant Jewish workers suffered intense economic hardship.[2]

Jewish workers were exploited in much the same way as other unskilled workers of the 1890s—low wages, long hours, unhealthy working conditions, job insecurity, and long periods of unemployment. Peculiar to Jewish employment was the fact that most work was done either at home or in small factories under the immediate direction of coreligionists. Often the employer was a relative or a *landsman*.

There were signs that the Jewish immigrant workers in New York City were ready for unionization and perhaps for socialism in the late 1880s. Earlier, in the mid-1880s, Jewish cloakmakers and shirtwaistmakers organized their own unions and between 1885 and 1886 several strikes were called in these and other primarily Jewish needle industries.[3] Unfortunately, in the late 1880s virtually all the unions had disintegated and the apparent militancy of the workers vanished. However, Jewish socialists of the SLP hoped that Jewish workers still possessed a high potential for unionization as well as a strong, albeit nascent, sense of working-class solidarity.[4]

Although Hillquit's first friends in New York were the Russian Jewish intellectuals who introduced him into the SLP, he often felt strange and uncomfortable both with Jewish intellectuals and Jewish workers. In his autobiography he confessed that he did not fully fit in with his Jewish comrades because they came from a Russian-Jewish cultural background and he was "only partly Russian." Germany, he wrote, "was closer to me in spirit, culture and temperament, but I was not a German. Thus I grew up, a bilingual and cosmopolitan, without any marked national trait."[5]

Hillquit could not speak Yiddish, the language of the Jewish proletariat, and he possessed little appreciation of the orthodox Jewish religion which a vast majority of the workers still practiced. He learned Yiddish for the express purpose of communicating with the immigrants but he confessed a certain distaste for the language. He told Cahan, with whom he worked in 1890 on the *Arbeter zeitung*, that "since Yiddish is nothing but a corrupted, illiterate and ungrammatical German, the task of the Yiddish writer was to improve and purify the language with the ultimate aim of converting it into modern German."[6] For his part Cahan regarded Hillquit as "educated, talented, intelligent and refined," but also a person "newly arrived" on the immigrant scene and lacking an understanding of Jewish folk culture. Cahan thought it curious that Hillquit should venture into work among Jewish immigrants.[7]

Hillquit never constructed a careful philosophic view of his Jewishness as a practice or as a state of mind. He did not articulate a coherent program about the function of ethnicity in relation to American social life, trade unionism, and political radicalism. Later in his life, in 1924, the New York *Times* quoted him as saying, "I do not approach political problems from the Jewish point of view."[8]

He did have a point of view. Consciously and unconsciously his attitudes toward the Jewish religion and toward Jewish nationalism and culture significantly tempered the kind of socialist leader he became in America. By the late 1880s the young Hillquit had adopted a view of Judaism which in radical Jewish circles was called internationalism or "cosmopolitanism." It was a socialist theory in which loyalty to the working class took precedence over every other kind of identity—religious or national. The cosmopolitan position rejected a special place for Jewish sentiments, identity, and practices in the socialist movement. It anticipated a future society without class or national barriers. "I cannot find a special corner in my heart for the ghetto," wrote the cosmopolitan Rosa Luxemburg. "I feel at home in the entire world wherever there are clouds and birds and human tears."[9] Leon Trotsky, another outspoken cosmopolitan, was once asked by Vladmir Medem, leader

Morris Hillquit, 1886. *Courtesy of State Historical Society of Wisconsin.*

of the socialist Jewish Labor Bund: "When it comes to classifying yourself you certainly cannot ignore the fact of national allegiance. You consider yourself, I take it, to be either a Russian or a Jew?" Trotsky answered, "No, you are mistaken! I am a social democrat and that's all."[10]

Cosmopolitanism also included a strong rejection of religion in general and the traditional practices of Judaism in particular. Judaism was archaic and obscurantist. When he was in his late teens, Hillquit participated in anti-religious demonstrations in New York during the most sacred Jewish holiday, Yom Kippur. He and other young radicals, including both socialists and anarchists, held a Yom Kippur Ball where they mocked the rituals of the holiday by smoking and feasting. Instead of a sermon, the young radicals gave speeches on the coming of the revolutionary new society without religious superstitions.[11] A letter written to his cousin and brother-in-law Dr. Phoebus Levene further corroborates the young Hillquit's disdain for Jewish ritual. In 1895, at the age of twenty-six, he described the reactions of an orthodox Jewish maid from Riga to the customs of the Levene-Hillquit household. In playfully derisive terms Hillquit told of the maid's disappointment in the family's behavior:

> She comes from a pious ancient Hebrew family and desires to see the rite of our religion conformed with all particulars [*sic*], instead, however, Sophie just mixed all meaty and milky dishes; Kate was engaged in frying a sausage . . . with butter of doubtful origins, your father had just finished not praying . . . This, dear doctor, is the third since Molly and before you come we'll expect to have a half dozen more.[12]

In the corner of this letter, signed "your exaggeration hating sister," the soon-to-be Mrs. Hillquit wrote, "I cannot bear it. It is not so terrible as Morris describes it. We are not half as *treyf* (non-kosher) as he writes."

The cosmopolitans' criticism of Jews encompassed aspects other than religious practices. For example, they held the belief that historically Jews were social parasites—a concept tinged with anti-Semitic feeling. Hillquit once characterized the "unproductive" nature of Jews in the economy by claiming that "in the two thousand years of homeless wanderings among the nations of Europe and Asia, in the centuries of outlawry and persecution, the Jewish people have become known as a race of traders and money lenders." However, "the Jewish workers of America have redeemed their race from the stigma of parasitism."[13]

This charge of parasitism against Jews revealed at least two significant characteristics of the cosmopolitans' mentality. First, they had no real appreciation of Jewish history. Second, their internationalist outlook was founded, in part, on self-hatred which made Hillquit blind to any positive aspects of a Jewish identity.[14]

As a result of anti-religious feelings and of the belief that in the past the Jews had played a socially negative role in European society, Hillquit and other cosmopolitans did not seek ways to preserve a unique Jewish life. He expected patterns of assimilation and acculturation to occur in Jewish communities in the United States and Europe. He was not concerned about a future national identity for Jews.[15] He was not a Zionist and he did not believe that there was a special political solution to the homelessness of the Jews. Once, in describing Lassalle's view on the interrelationship between Jewish needs and world needs, Hillquit expressed his own position: "But it wasn't long before he [Lassalle] understood that Jewish oppression was only a part of a greater problem. The Jewish question is part of a general problem."[16]

It was indicative of Hillquit's assimilationist persuasion that he chose to write about non-Jewish subjects during 1890-1891, the years that he worked on the Yiddish *Arbeter zeitung*. His articles were about classical antiquity—Caesar's life or Tiberius and Gaius Gracchus. He also wrote a series on the history of Christianity which stressed Jewish-Christian relations in the Middle Ages. It was as if he wished to expose the Jewish readers (who perhaps were learned only in the Torah and the Talmud) to the secular and, in his mind, the more sophisticated world of Western history and ideas.[17]

Despite his lack of ease with most Jewish intellectuals of the SLP and with Jewish workers, Hillquit served his apprenticeship in the socialist movement as a Yiddish journalist and union organizer. This was the only period in his long career as a socialist leader when he directly and intimately dealt with workers in the context of forming special workers' organizations.

In the summer of 1888, he and Bernard Weinstein, an immigrant from Odessa who had worked at one time in a cigar factory in New York City with Samuel Gompers, were sent by the Jewish sections of the Party to make a survey of the existing Jewish unions in New York.[18] Weinstein recalled how he and Hillquit spent "every evening for weeks on end going to the meeting places of Jewish workers, trying to find unions to invite to a conference with the purpose of founding a federation of all Jewish workers."[19] Except for the small Hebrew Topographical Union and a few members of the Chorus Union, the two young socialists found only the remnants of bakers', garment cutters', and shirtwaistmakers' unions which had seen more active days in the early 1880s.

The paucity of trade unions shocked Hillquit. "The Jewish workers seemed to be unorganizable," he observed in his autobiography. "They had not been trained in any form of collective action in the countries of their birth. They were dull, apathetic and unintelligent." Furthermore, he thought that the Jewish workers of this period were "mercilessly exploited by their employers and despised by their fellow workers, they completely lacked self-assertiveness and the power of resistance. They were weak from overwork and malnutrition, tired, listless, meek and submissive."[20] As late as 1929 (and despite the vital radical militancy displayed by Jewish workers from 1909 through the 1920s), he remembered that Jewish workers of the 1880s and 1890s were "a race of timid, submissive, cheerless and hopeless drudges."[21]

Eleven delegates representing the two Jewish sections of the SLP, three small Jewish trade unions, and the United German Trades met in October 1888 at the Party's Fourth Street headquarters to create a United Hebrew Trades. The nineteen-year-old Hillquit and Weinstein had drafted a grandiose "Declaration of Principles" which the assembled delegates accepted. It sounded very much like the Erfurt program which the SPD in Germany published two years later in 1891. In its opening statement, the UHT declaration set forth a revolutionary socialist interpretation of history which included the key Marxist concepts of the labor theory of value, class struggle, and the need for working-class solidarity. Then the document proposed a reform platform: the eight-hour day, abolition of child labor, equal pay for equal work for men and women, and the repeal of the sedition laws under which fines were levied for strikes, boycotts, and picketing.[22] Hillquit was appointed corresponding secretary of this new union.[23]

As an official of the UHT, Hillquit helped develop a Jewish labor movement. Between 1889 and 1891 he spoke to workers at meetings on the East Side; he wrote union constitutions and he supported strikes. Publicly, at the time, he praised Jewish workers for their "heretofore unexpressed class consciousness."[24] Years later in his autobiography he criticized the Jewish workers for their behavior during strikes and for their "strike mentality."[25] He found the strikers incapable of conducting practical strike operations. He was disappointed by the disorder of the meetings, the lack of stated demands, the inability of the strikers to conduct picketing or provide relief, and by their ignorance of trade union principles and of socialist philosophy. These impressions were echoed by Weinstein, who also remembered that the leaders of the UHT became "everything for the Jewish unions."[26]

Hillquit claimed in his autobiography that "in the minds of the Jewish workers. . .unions were associated with strikes and were little more than instruments of strikes." Unions "were mostly born in strikes and died with the end of strikes."[27] While many Jewish unions did not last beyond the strike, Hillquit tended to place an inordinate amount of blame upon the immigrant worker's so-called strike mentality. However, there were several other reasons for the instability of Jewish unions. The constant influx of large numbers of new Jewish immigrants intensified competition and not cooperation between workers. Familial or religious pressures were often used by employers to dissuade unionists. Internally, unionization was weak because of the seasonal nature of the garment industry; the generally high unemployment tended to reduce the trade unions at certain times of the year. Thus it was difficult to keep up a consistent union membership.

In contrast to his derogatory estimation of Jewish workers, Hillquit held the Jewish leadership of the UHT in high esteem. He regarded them as stable and farsighted. Later, Hillquit brought this attitude with him into the International Ladies Garment Workers' Union.

Hillquit's lack of confidence in workers, especially immigrants, contributed to the passive role he assigned to trade unions in his evolving socialist ideology. In his earliest writings (1890) for the Yiddish *Arbeter zeitung,* Hillquit considered the didactic function of trade unions more significant than their function as a weapon of the class struggle. He was willing to admit that unions served to develop a sensitivity to working-class interests and that strikes helped to politicize workers. In a literary debate with New York Jewish anarchists, he even argued that "unions and above all strikes are the best schools for the workers to learn and understand the social questions. . . ." He went as far as saying that the militant trade union was the agent of revolution when it provided the daily environment which enabled the worker to become a thoughtful and sensitive person. In one 1890 article he wrote that trade unions were important because "each cent more wages, each hour less work brings the worker one step closer to the social revolution." But this social revolution did not require mass violent action.

Hillquit abhorred violence and he rejected concepts which favored the physical destruction of society. He was as repelled by the thought of revolutionary workers running through the streets as were any of his more conservative contemporaries. Perhaps, as a Jew living among recent victims of Russian pogroms, he imagined all revolutions were brutal and mindless. The following fantasy was written by Hillquit in Yiddish for the *Arbeter zeitung.* It was called "Vos iz revolutzie?" and was printed in April 1890. The article suggested Hillquit's fears:

> The revolutionaries contructed a gallow on every street. . . . The murderous revolutionaries killed one person after another. Jokes and laughter accompanies the last moments of the innocent victims' lives. The entire country overflows with lakes of blood. . . . Wherever one looks or touches, all nature has become wild, the whole world is being destroyed. . . .[28]

Along with his fear of what might happen if workers became violent revolutionaries, Hillquit also sensed the powerlessness of direct working-class action as a weapon in the class struggle. He was impressed with the formidable power of the State. In comparison the small unions seemed insignificant. Employers were reinforced by state laws and by the police while workers had no such support.

Laws were altered to suit employers' interests. Hillquit learned this latter fact when he helped develop a Jewish bakers' union in 1889. The union had successfully pressed the New York State legislature into enacting a law limiting work in bakeries to ten hours a day. To Hillquit's consternation, the Supreme Court of the United States reversed the state's decision. The case seemed to highlight the futility of trade union action.[29]

The young Hillquit was convinced that the real mechanism for social change lay outside the kinds of pressures ordinary labor unions could bring to bear upon the American government. He was not radicalized by this realization, that is, he did not become an advocate of more stringent methods such as revolution or the mass strike. On the contrary, he appeared to have concluded that a radical's work required changing the legal structure of the State (as well as the legal relationship between the working class and employers). He acted upon this conclusion in several ways. For instance, Hillquit decided to become a lawyer in 1891 and this decision might have been part of his perception that radical change, that is, socialism, required the assistance of socialists with power who could maneuver within the legal structure of the State. In later years he became a staunch advocate of labor arbitration and he approved of garment workers relinquishing their right to strike if they could exchange this right for a legitimate place within the collective bargaining-arbitration system which governed the industry.

Hillquit emerged from this period of unionizing Jewish workers with the firm conviction that socialists in America would have to rely upon piecemeal and gradual "boring from within" the established system. This could be done best by a political party.

Notes

1. Hillquit's account of the paper's purpose is in *Loose Leaves,* pp. 35-57.

2. For statistics, see *Eleventh Census of the United States, 1890,* "Population," part 2 (Washington, D.C., 1897), pp. 472-83.

3. Melech Epstein, *Jewish Labor,* 1: 108-31.

4. See Hillquit's impression of Jewish workers in *Loose Leaves,* pp. 16-17.

5. Ibid., pp. 7-8.

6. Ibid., p. 37.

7. Abraham Cahan, *Bleter fun mein leben,* 5 vols. (New York, 1926-1931), 3: 16-17.

8. New York *Times,* October 25, 1924.

9. J. P. Nettl, *Rosa Luxenburg* (Oxford, 1969). p. 517.

10. Quoted in Bernard Wolfe, *Three Who Made a Revolution* (New York, 1957), p. 169.

11. Mentioned in Emma Goldman, *Living My Life* (New York, 1931), p. 635.

12. Letter from Morris Hillquit and Sophie Levene to Phoebus A. Levene, ca. July 16, 1895, Correspondence, Hillquit Papers.

13. Morris Hillquit, "The Rise of Russian Jews," *American Hebrew,* November 22, 1929, Writings, ibid.

14. In this negative view of the Jews Hillquit appeared to be influenced by Marx's argument in *On the Jewish Question.*

15. Moishe Olgin, "Interview mit Morris Hillquit," New York *Jewish Daily Forward,* October 25, 1916.

16. Morris Hillquit, "Ferdinand Lassalle," *Der fraynd* May 1925, p. 12.

17. See, for example, Morris Hillquit, "Geshichte bilder: Cezar un Brutus," New York *Arbeter zeitung,* December 10, 1890; "Oys geshichte fun kristentum," ibid., August 28, 1891; "Di spanishe inkvezitzie," ibid., March 27, April 10, and April 17, 1891; "Geshichte bilder: di brider Tiberius un Gaius Gracchus," ibid., November 14, 1890.

18. *Loose Leaves,* p. 18.

19. Bernard Weinstein, *Di yidishe yunyons,* p. 144.

20. *Loose Leaves,* pp. 16-17.

21. Morris Hillquit, "The Rise of Russian Jews."

22. Aaron Antonovski, *The Early Jewish Labor Movement in the United States* (New York, 1961), p. 328.

23. *Loose Leaves,* p. 20.

24. Morris Hillquit, "Der strik fun di knee pants arbeter," New York *Arbeter zeitung,* April 25, 1890.

25. *Loose Leaves,* p. 23.

26. Bernard Weinstein, *Di yidishe yunyons,* p. 147.

27. *Loose Leaves,* p. 29.

28. Morris Hillquit, "Ver iz a revolutzionair," New York *Arbeter zeitung,* April 25, 1890, and "Vos iz revolutzie?" ibid., April 18, 1890.

29. *Loose Leaves,* p. 28.

Americanization and Hillquit versus De Leon, 1891-1899 Chapter 3

Hillquit's experiences in the Socialist Labor Party were not limited to his contacts with Jewish intellectuals and workers. The German immigrant leaders at national headquarters in lower Manhattan on Fourth Street adopted him as a protege. The German-speaking Hillquit had an easy rapport with the German party officials based upon his linguistic fluency and their shared admiration for German culture and especially for the Sozialdemokratische Partei Deutschlands (SPD). William L. Rosenberg was then the national secretary, although he was ousted from this office in 1899 for his Lassallean proclivities. Rosenberg hired the young man as a clerk at the national headquarters' book store and publishing company for a salary of four dollars a week. Rosenberg "had taken a liking to me the first time he noticed me at a party meeting. . . ," Hillquit recalled with pride in his autobiography.[1] Hillquit stopped working in a factory and contributed his salary to the Hillkowitz family household.

The clerkship gave the young man access to an extensive socialist library (which leaned heavily in the direction of German thinkers) and the job stimulated his already strong desire for systematic study of political theory. Also, as Hillquit candidly admitted, "Stability of employment and income came to me only with what I may term my first political job."[2] It was significant that the ex-Russian gymnasium student and ex-shirtwaistmaker never returned to manual labor. With this job he permanently joined the Party leadership and began to develop a feeling of propriety about his place in the Party bureaucracy—a sentiment which never left him. The Party became the center of his life. This fact (and perhaps his early contacts with his mentor Rosenberg and other Lassalleans) was reflected later in the theoretical emphasis he placed on the political organization of the socialist movement.

By the middle of 1891 Hillquit's career in the Party began to change. He entered New York University law school and supported himself by tutoring private students in Latin and by teaching English to immigrants in the evening public schools.[3] These tasks kept him from devoting as much time as before to the Party although he participated in its propaganda program. He lectured on a "circuit." Occasionally, he wrote an article in the SLP's English-language the *People:* "German Social Democracy" was published on December 29, 1895, and "Our War and Our Weapons" appeared on March 1, 1896.

At about this time Hillquit also seemed to lose interest in the United Hebrew Trades and he discontinued his journalistic work for the *Arbeter zeitung* as well. In fact, as early as October 1890 Hillquit declined to serve as secretary for a new, yet-to-be-formed federation of Yiddish-speaking labor organizations in the United States and Canada.[4] Shortly thereafter, he transferred his membership from the all-Jewish Russian-speaking branch of the SLP to the newly formed "American" section of the New York Party. As he noted in his autobiography, "As soon as I judged, rather leniently I believe, that my English could pass muster, I transferred my membership. . .to the 'American'. . ." section.[5]

Hillquit's rejection of the Jewish sections in 1891 reflected his growing disapproval of ethnically oriented socialism. This view was to be a significant aspect of his socialist ideology. In the future it would bring him into sharp conflict with many other Jewish socialists. The "ethnic" issue would become one of Hillquit's most poorly resolved dilemmas. Hillquit alone among all his earliest companions who created UHT and the *Arbeter zeitung* left the Jewish immigrant environment. The other Jewish Party leaders remained exclusively within the Jewish milieu for the rest of their careers. For example, Louis Miller eventually rejected socialism but he founded and edited Yiddish-language newspapers. Bernard Weinstein, Hillquit's former constant comrade in organizing unions and strikes, wrote books about the Jewish trade union movement in Yiddish. Abraham Cahan, who tried to interpret the processes of Jewish assimilation and acculturation to American readers in his English-language novel *The Rise of David Levinski* (1917), nevertheless was instrumental in founding the Yiddish *Jewish Daily Forward* in 1897. Joseph Magidoff, who had been the first member of the SLP to conceive the idea of the UHT, compared Hillquit with Cahan in this way:

> Outside of his activities as a socialist leader, Hillquit is a bourgeois. . . . Cahan while not intimate with his colleagues, spends time with them. He comes to the known rendezvous places of the East Side. He discusses the issues of the day. . . . Cahan is a *folksmentsh.* Hillquit is far from the *folk.*[6]

While Cahan, Miller, and Weinstein were to remain in the Jewish environment, Hillquit moved into the more comprehensive American scene. In an important sense, he transferred his allegiance from the Jewish *folk* to the American people.

In the early 1890s Hillquit was undergoing a personal process of Americanization by learning the language, separating himself from immigrant ties, and acquiring a profession. He was pursuing the American dream of success. In 1893, after studying law for two years, he passed the bar examination. Hillquit, then still called Hillkowitz, and his older brother Jacob, also an attorney, opened a legal office at 132 Nassau Street in Manhattan. Within a short time, the brothers achieved financial security. Morris, in particular, began to gain a reputation as an up-and-coming young lawyer. The firm, renamed Hillquit and Hillquit in 1897, moved to 320 Broadway in the late spring of 1898.[7] The legal office took on an air of bourgeois respectability—indistinguishable from any non-socialist's successful practice.[8]

Although Hillquit's desire to succeed as a lawyer took precedence over his SLP activities in the first years after his admission to the bar, he did maintain at least tangential relationships with the Jewish unions. In fact, John Spargo, the British-born socialist, recalled in his memoirs that he was hired by Hillquit to work as a legal assistant at a separate office Hillquit maintained on the lower East Side. This office handled cases related exclusively to the defense of Jewish workers disabled on the job (long before a Workman's Compensation Act was passed in New York).[9] Also in this period Hillquit acted as the lawyer for several unions of the UHT. Nina Hillquit, describing her father's account books for the first three years of his practice, noted that "the largest single entry was: Children's Jacket Makers Union $350."[10]

Some of Hillquit's financial transactions gave rise to accusations that he was a "corporation" lawyer and thus a hypocrite in the light of his socialist opposition to the capitalist system. Like other socialist lawyers, Hillquit justified his legal career on the grounds that it enabled him to defend working-class interests and to extend and to safeguard the legal rights of radicals and radical causes. As we shall see, he made good this claim. Yet, at the same time, by engaging in lucrative business practices, he offended the basic sense of socialism's criticism of capitalist society. Throughout his career, Hillquit tried to avoid dealing with this aspect of his behavior. "I can see nothing wrong . . . in principle," he once said, "for a socialist to practice law in a capitalist system or to engage in any other capitalist activities."[11] This attitude tended to weaken his credibility as a socialist leader.

Besides cultivating a legal career, Hillquit also began to set up a household. On December 31, 1893, the year he passed the bar, he married his first cousin Vera Levene, who was a fellow student at the law school. The Hillquit and Levene families were on close terms even in Riga and the Levenes lived with the Hillquits for a while when they first arrived in the United States. Vera did not follow a career in law. She became a traditional middle-class housewife who encouraged her husband in his up-and-coming career but stayed very much in the background. Eventually, the couple had three children: Nina, Leonard who was mentally retarded, and Walter who died shortly after his birth.[12]

Hillquit occupied an office in lower Manhattan with Jacob and his brother-in-law (and cousin) Dr. Phoebus A. Levene. The latter who was then a young physician later became an internationally known biochemist and the head of that division at the Rockefeller Institute for Medical Research.[13] Hillquit and his cousin shared many interests. Nina said her father and uncle "used to go bicycle riding mornings before going to the office. There was strong resemblance between them. They. . .were often mistaken for each other by their respective clients and patients."[14] A correspondence between the two men in the 1890s reveals their intense interest in European literature and, in particular, Russian literature, which they both read fluently. Levene, in fact, was planning to write a history of Russian literature in English.[15]

In general, Hillquit's family life appeared to have been close knit, stable, affectionate, and conventional. Perhaps the family's most outstanding characteristic was its rapid movement from poverty into the professional middle class within less than ten years' residence in the United States. Yet the family approved of Hillquit's socialist allegiances. In fact, he derived a good deal of special attention because of his participation in the Party. Both Jacob and Vera were socialists and, in later years, they and other relatives helped him campaign for public office.[16]

It is important to note that the Hillquit family regarded themselves as "cultured" people. They were not at all interested in the culture of either Jewish immigrants or American workers. In addition, Hillquit's interests and manner of life distinguished him from most of his colleagues in the SLP. Even his appearance—always well groomed and expensively tailored—offered a distinct contrast to the socialists around him. Morris Winchevski, one of the earliest founders of a Jewish socialist party in England who first met Hillquit in 1894, humorously commented that he could not find fault with Hillquit even though Morris was "a young man cleanly dressed who believed that washing oneself was not a monopoly of the Hasidim and the Franks; that a necktie can be tastefully tied and lying as it should, without breaking the principles of proletariat socialism, God forbid,"[17]

Hillquit, the young lawyer in his twenties, emulated the cultural habits and tastes of German socialists. He admired leaders of the German Social Democratic Party, such as Wilhelm Liebknecht and August Bebel, for their intellectual prowess, their elegant cultural life, and their ability to create a powerful party in Germany under seemingly insurmountable opposition. He also admired their central position of authority within the SPD. It is possible that in the 1890s Hillquit first formed the idea that he too might create a major socialist political party and become a socialist "statesman."[18]

Hillquit was not a leader of any faction within the SLP before 1898. However, he was particularly friendly with the group who controlled the Party's German-language *Volkszeitung* edited by Herman Schleuter.[19] But the *Volkszeitung* group was not the major authority in the Party. In August 1891 Daniel De Leon, a Curaçao-born lawyer who joined the SLP in 1890, took over the editorship of the *People*. As historian Howard Quint noted, "It was as editor of the *People* . . . that De Leon stamped his personality on the party . . . .Once ensconced in the editor's chair he remained there until death removed him in 1914."[20]

Reactions against De Leon's political and trade union policies as well as his control of the Party's press precipitated factional divisions. The first major split occurred in 1895 when an important group of Jewish socialists, including Morris Winchevski, Abraham Cahan, and Meyer London of the Jewish sections, left the Party.[21]

It was a measure of Hillquit's estrangement from the intraparty life of the Jewish sections that he did not leave the SLP along with the major Jewish leaders in 1895. Later, in 1899, his criticism of De Leon was ostensibly the same as theirs. To the consternation of Winchevski and other Jewish socialists, Hillquit continued to write for the De Leon-controlled *People* and to advertise his law firm in that paper until July 9, 1899.[22] However, in his autobiography he said, "When the Socialist Trade and Labor Alliance was organized and officially sanctioned by the party at its national convention in 1896, I could not accept it and for a time retired from active party work."[23]

In 1899 Hillquit decided to challenge De Leon and his supporters. Hillquit never explained why he and his companions, the Kangaroo Faction, specifically chose that year to split from the SLP although he once remarked that "the split was preceded by a long and bitter fight within the party."[24] Morris Winchevski offered his own version of Hillquit's decision. Winchevski conjectured that Hillquit did not leave the SLP in 1895 for two reasons. Privately, he was enmeshed in his own law career and had no time for politics. Tactically, Hillquit thought the methods used by the Jewish dissenters—verbal and literary attacks against the De Leonite position—were inadequate for a proper solution. However, when Winchevski met

Hillquit in the early part of 1898, the young lawyer was settled in his new office. Winchevski related their conversation at that time:

> "Well," he [Hillquit] said one day, "it looks like in May I will be free of several personal concerns. I'll get to work."
>
> He thought a moment and with a charming smile but with a serious tone in his voice he said: "The first of October I will become active in the Party against De Leon and his leadership."
>
> I thought to myself that this was extremely calculating. And I regarded Hillquit with the kind of scepticism one reserves for a deserter who because he is now ashamed of his past will say, "I will, I will . . . ."
>
> To make a long story short, he did become active on the first of October [1898]. Not a day earlier or a day later. In a few months, almost overnight, he became the leader of a new opposition movement composed of the German *Volkszeitung* and its followers.[25]

Winchevski's ambivalent attitude toward Hillquit was typical of many other Jewish socialists. While they admired what he could accomplish, they were disappointed by his "desertion" and a bit put off by his calculation.

What is clear from Winchevski's acount was that Hillquit emerged rather unexpectedly in 1898, at the age of twenty-nine, as one of the central figures in the controversy which split the SLP. This rupture was a crucial turning point in his political career. Throughout the rest of his long life in the socialist movement, he retained the aura of importance he originally acquired as the leader of the oppositional faction in the New York section of the SLP.

In July 1899 a decisive split took place. It originated in the New York section of the Party where a group of anti-De Leonite socialists, with the support of the German daily *Volkszeitung*, attempted to unseat the De Leon-dominated National Executive. This opposition group, the Kangaroo faction, elected their own national executive, of which Hillquit was a member. The Kangaroos seized the Party press and the national headquarters. Proclaiming themselves the authentic voice of the SLP, the insurgents continued this civil war among the SLP sections throughout the United States. By October 1899 their new National Executive Committee had won the allegiance of approximately 45 percent of the national party's seven thousand members.[26] The Party was now split in half. De Leon kept the SLP name and the *People* (after a battle in the capitalist courts). The Kangaroos searched for new allies.

Three basic issues entangled the SLP in this internecine quarrel: the trade unions, "Americanization" of the Party, and intraparty control. The trade union issue was the most important. Impatient with the anti-socialist and craft union orientation of organized labor, De Leon wanted to create a labor movement which included unskilled workers and which, in and of itself, would act as a politically revolutionary force.[27] He was critical of the way unions attempted to wrest minor improvements from employers. Instead De Leon envisioned industrially organized trade unions as enabling the "working class to assume and conduct production the moment the guns of the public powers fall into its hands. . . ." In De Leon's blueprint for the future, a socialist system would be achieved through a politically conscious working class voting socialist candidates into power. The unions, having previously politicized the workers, would become the basis for "the future constituencies of the parliaments of the Socialist Republic."[28] Thus in 1895 De Leon had founded the Socialist Trade and Labor Alliance which presented an alternative to the established unions.

Hillquit and other SLP labor leaders such as J. Mahlon Barnes of the Cigarmakers Union and Max Hayes of the Typographical Union opposed De Leon because they were confident that a "boring from within" the AFL was still a potentially promising tactic. While Hillquit was critical of the conservative nature of the AFL leadership and most of its members, he believed that the persuasive qualities of the socialist argument would eventually win over both the leaders and the workers.

Hillquit refused to support an anti-AFL, seemingly more militant, and industrially organized new trade union. "I considered his [De Leon's] trade union policy as suicidal to the party . . . ," he recalled in his autobiography.[29] Hillquit argued against the Socialist Trade and Labor Alliance from three standpoints: first, that the new union was not innovative in its tactics since it merely used strikes and boycotts; second, that it reduced the chances of creating a viable American labor movement by its disruptive techniques which split an already unsure American working class into two camps, and third, that the emphasis on the revolutionary nature of trade unions failed to take into account the necessity for political action. "One thing is sure," Hillquit told an audience in 1901, "that, if the social revolution will have to depend on the Socialist Trade and Labor Alliance to make its appearance, we will have to wait an eternity."[30]

A second area of contention in the SLP was over the question of "Americanizing" the Party. The anti-De Leon faction claimed that De Leon's leadership kept the Party an immigrant sect. In their own defense, the De Leonites contended that they wanted to broaden the Party and that the Alliance would, in fact, attract American-born workers. It is interesting to note that after the split in 1899, when the dust of the battle had settled, the actual composition of the two factions was similar; that is, both sides were composed of both immigrant and American-born members. When John Spargo was interviewed in 1950, he recalled that:

> Curiously, [on] De Leon's side there was rather more native American—second generation American-stock—English-speaking—than there was on the right, the Hillquit side where German predominated and they were either actual immigrants or the children of actual German and Russian immigrants. There were more American elements in De Leon's left wing and more foreign elements in the right wing when the party split.[31]

Since the desire to become an American party pervaded both camps, this issue appears to be mainly employed by the insurgents as a rhetorical device against the De Leonites. Possibly differences over trade union philosophy and "Americanization" would not have split the SLP if an intraparty power struggle had not been infused into the ideological issues. Generally, De Leon is blamed by historians and contemporary critics for his heavy-handed attempts to impose authoritarian rule over the party through personal invective, expulsion of opponents, dictation of a "party line" on the Alliance question, and control of the SLP press and executive offices. In fact, Hillquit's harsh autobiographical appraisal of De Leon's personality and tactics influenced historians of the socialist movement to regard De Leon as the singular cause of the split. Hillquit's often cited evaluation contained the following accusations:

> De Leon was a fanatic. A keen thinker and merciless logician, he was carried away beyond the realm of reality by the process of his own abstract and somewhat Talmudic logic. . . . He was strongly influenced by the Blanquist conception of the "capture of power" and placed organization ahead of education, politics above economic struggles, and leadership above the rank and file of the movement.[32]

Apparently, Hillquit was as adept as De Leon at invective. However, even if contentiousness was the "style" shared by most socialist intellectuals,[33] nevertheless De Leon certainly managed to antagonize—on a very personal basis—enough of an opposition to ultimately undermine the Party's cohesiveness.

The younger leaders felt thwarted in their personal ambitions for a political career within the SLP by De Leon's seemingly dictatorial behavior. Hillquit was seventeen years younger than De Leon. This motive for opposing De Leon need not have had sinister "opportunistic" implications. For example, historian Ira Kipnis, who consistently disagreed with Hillquit's views, applied a derogatory interpretation to Hillquit's motives when he claimed that "Hillquit's opposition to De Leon's policies was heightened, perhaps, by the fact that 'Pope' De Leon stood in the way of his ambition to be a power in the Socialist Labor Party."[34] It is common enough for generational antagonisms to exist within political parties without it necessarily meaning that either Hillquit or De Leon were reprehensibly calculating or self-serving. While it is true that under such circumstances ideological considerations were distorted by personal feelings, it was unfair to discredit Hillquit solely on the charge of ambition.

The July split brought Hillquit into prominence as the leader of the New York Kangaroo faction and as an important member of the insurgent National Executive Committee. His leadership was acknowledged by the De Leonites who devoted some opening moments of their 1900 national convention to attacking him as a lawyer who made "worthless contracts for Jewish unions in their settlement of the numerous strikes against sweatshop bosses" and who divided "the swag with the union, or perchance, only with the union leaders."[35] Later official historians of the SLP such as Henry Kuhn continued to portray Hillquit as "Moses Hillkowitz" who had been active in the Jewish movement but "subsequently vanished from the movement and now had come back, having undergone a metamorphosis from a button-hole maker to a lawyer of the contract-writing type."[36]

Notes

1. *Loose Leaves*, p. 33.
2. Ibid.
3. Ibid., pp. 38-40.
4. I.S. Hertz, *Di yidishe sotzialistishe bavegung in amerika* (New York, 1954), p. 32.
5. *Loose Leaves*, pp. 44-45.
6. Joseph Magidoff, *Der shpigel fun der East Side* (New York, 1923), p. 83.
7. Hillquit's change of name and legal office address can be located through his advertisement in the Socialist Labor Party's the *People*. The first advertisement was printed on May 10, 1897, under Morris Hillkowitz, 132 Nassau Street. On June 2, 1897, the advertisement read Hillkowitz and Hillquit (referring to Jacob, his brother) at 320 Broadway and on June 5, 1898, the advertisement was altered to read Morris Hillquit.
8. The description of Hillquit's office is found in James E. Morrow, "Interview," n.p., July 5, 1908, Clippings, Hillquit Papers.
9. John Spargo, Oral History Research Project, Columbia University, pp. 122-23.
10. Nina Hillquit, "Morris Hillquit," pp. 5-6.
11. Morris Hillquit, "Statement," Paris, June 11, 1931, p. 2, Morris Hillquit Papers, Tamiment Library.
12. Nina Hillquit, "Morris Hillquit," pp. 3-6.
13. *The Morris Hillquit Papers: Guide to a Microfilm Edition* (Wisconsin, 1969), p. 13.
14. Nina Hillquit, "Morris Hillquit," p. 7.
15. Letter from Phoebus A. Levene to Morris Hillquit, January 21, 1896, Correspondence, Hillquit Papers.
16. Jacob and Vera were frequently mentioned in the New York *Call*'s

reports of Hillquit's political campaign meetings in 1908 and 1917.

17. Morris Winchevski, "Morris Hillquit als mentch," *Zukunft* 22 (November 1917), pp. 615-16.

18. Morris Hillquit, "The Soldier of the Revolution," October 1901, Writings, Hillquit Papers.

19. *Loose Leaves*, p. 47.

20. Howard Quint, *The Forging of American Socialism* (Columbia, S.C., 1953), p. 145.

21. Harry Rogoff, *An East Side Epic: The Life and Work of Meyer London* (New York, 1930), p. 14.

22. Hillquit's split with the SLP is documented by the fact that his advertisement in the *People* terminated on July 9, 1899.

23. *Loose Leaves*, p. 47.

24. Ibid.

25. Winchevski, "Morris Hillquit als mentch," pp. 615-16.

26. Ira Kipnis, *The American Socialist Movement: 1897-1912* (New York, 1952), p. 36.

27. Daniel De Leon, "What Means This Strike?" (published speech delivered on February 11, 1898).

28. Cited in Nathan Fine, *Labor and Farmer Parties in the United States 1828-1928* (New York, 1928), p. 152.

29. *Loose Leaves*, p. 47.

30. "Berry-Hillquit Debate," New York *Weekly People*, December 7, 1901.

31. John Spargo, Oral History Research Project, p. 115.

32. *Loose Leaves*, pp. 46-47. Marc Karson in his *American Labor Unions and Politics, 1900-1918* (Carbondale, Ill., 1958), p. 46, uses Hillquit's estimation of De Leon as does Daniel Bell, *Marxian Socialism in the United States* (New York, 1967), p. 33.

33. Glen Seretan, "The Personal Style and Political Methods of Daniel De Leon: A Reconsideration," *Labor History* 14 (Spring 1973), pp. 163-201.

34. Kipnis, *American Socialist Movement*, pp. 27-28.

35. *Proceedings of the 1900 Socialist Labor Party Convention*, p. 20, microfilm in the University of California, Los Angeles, Research Library.

36. Henry Kuhn and Olive M. Johnson, *The SLP during Four Decades, 1890-1930* (New York, 1931), p. 40; see also Carl Reeves, *The Life and Times of Daniel De Leon* (New York, 1952), p. 60.

Unity, 1899-1901

Chapter 4

Hillquit and the Kangaroo faction did not plan to remain an isolated and independent New York socialist party. From 1899-1901, Hillquit acted as a spokesman for the Kangaroos in the open and secret meetings which traced the tortuous course of bringing about the unified Socialist Party of America.

Within a few months of their break with the SLP in July 1899, the New York Kangaroos made overtures to unite with a new national socialist party which had been founded in 1898—the Social Democratic Party. By 1900 the SDP had about 5,000 members and 226 branches in twenty-five states.[1] The National Executive Board of the SDP included Eugene V. Debs, founder of the American Railway Union, veteran of the Pullman strike, and recent convert to socialism; Victor Berger of Milwaukee who had left the SLP in 1893, and Frederick Heath, Jesse Cox, and Seymour Stedman, also midwestern socialists.

The SDP was still in the initial stage of forming its ideological program. Not all the members agreed with one particular brand of socialism. However, the SDP did reject "utopian" varieties of socialism. The Party declared itself "a class-conscious revolutionary social organization" and an advocate of "Pure Socialism and No Compromise."[2] This meant that the SDP membership wanted to build a strong political socialist party along with socialist trade unions. Political good sense and an understanding of the urban working class were considered as basic to a viable American socialism.

In 1899 the Kangaroo group had been joined by several other ex-Socialist Laborites, including the California SLP, in their formal offer to unite with the SDP. This combined group claimed to represent a national rank and file of more than 4,500 members.[3] However, the National Executive Board of the SDP was not enthusiastic about such a merger.

A few of the board members were opposed to unification because they feared losing control of the Party by introducing into it a potentially influential new leadership. Berger, in particular, disapproved of the ex-Socialist Laborites. Although he was a Jewish immigrant, a *Galitsyaner* born in Ruthenia, Berger claimed that the Kangaroos were "Easterners and foreigners." He singled Hillquit out for attack by calling him "Moses Hillkowitz from Warsaw," a "Polish apple Jew," and the "rabbinical candidate."[4] Berger and some of the other midwestern socialists also claimed that the Hillquit group was too intellectual and that the Socialist Laborites' taste for ideology smacked of European origins, of disputatious Marxism, and of a lack of feeling for the kind of practical politics they admired.

The Kangaroo group called their own convention in Rochester, New York, on January 27, 1900. The purpose of the conference was to work out a unification policy and a way to approach the SDP. Fifty-nine delegates from all parts of the United States attended the convention.

Hillquit acted aggressively and decisively at Rochester.[5] His importance to the conference lay in the fact that he urged the Kangaroos and their allies to take the offensive against the leaders of the SDP who appeared to oppose unification. The NEB had written the conference a condescending letter welcoming the Socialist Laborites into the Party on an individual basis and thus implying that the Kangaroos, as a group, were unimportant. Commenting on their letter at the conference, Hillquit declared that the SDP ought not to assume "our party is in a state of anarchy, without a name, organization or cohesion," and he advised the NEB to meet the Rochester Convention "half-way" since the Socialist Laborites would not come begging for admission. Both at the conference and later in the Kangaroo paper, the *People,* Hillquit threatened to take the unification question out of the hands of the NEB and bring it directly before the SDP's rank and file through a referendum.[6] This was never done. But the strength of his position as well as the visibility of championing a distinct faction firmly ensconced Hillquit as the leader of a group with which the SDP would have to reckon.

Between the Rochester Convention in January 1900 and the Unity Convention, which created the Socialist Party of America, Hillquit strengthened this coalition. By the time of the Unity Convention in July 1901, the coalition had been renamed the Springfield faction and it consisted of a nationally based group of socialists, heavily eastern but also including midwesterners and westerners. In part, this broad base of support explains Hillquit's rise to national prominence in the Socialist Party of America. The socialist thinking of the Springfield faction was characterized by its concept of class consciousness (and the class struggle), by an urban working-class orientation especially focused on the organization of trade unions, and by a belief in a broadly based political party. Its tone was decidedly reformist although individuals including Hillquit did not rule out revolutionary methods—in theory. Most of these socialists had working-class backgrounds, or at least their parents were workers. All of them had moved into white-collar status as journalists, lawyers, or permanent trade union officials. In a sense, like Hillquit, the others considered the socialist movement to be not only an ideological persuasion but also a profession.

The main figures in the Hillquit-Springfield Faction, in addition to Herman Schleuter of the *Volkszeitung*,[7] were Job Harriman and Max Hayes. Harriman became the SDP vice presidential candidate and Debs's running mate in 1900. He and Hillquit were close personal friends and the two men corresponded often. Hillquit thought Job a person of "rare eloquence, deep sincerity and irresistible personal charm."[8] For several years after Harriman contracted tuberculosis in 1900, Hillquit helped to support his family. Born in Indiana, Harriman had once been in the ministry of the Christian Church and, like Hillquit, he began to practice law in the mid-1890s. In 1898 he had run for governor of California on the SLP ticket and had polled 5,600 votes.[9] His opposition to De Leon pivoted on the trade union issue since Harriman thought socialists ought to fuse with non-socialist labor organizations in order to form a labor party and win elections.[10] While Hillquit did not favor such a right-wing position (and after 1903 it became a point of contention between them), Harriman's support of the Springfield Faction was welcome nonetheless.

Hillquit's ideas were probably more directly in tune with those of Max Hayes, the editor of the Cleveland Central Labor Union's weekly newspaper. This midwestern socialist had considerable power within the local Cleveland labor movement and he had successfully introduced a socialist platform into the CLU. Hayes defended "boring from within" the AFL as a socialist tactic.

A few other important Hillquit associates were also non-New Yorkers and non-foreign-born: Algernon Lee, J. Mahlon Barnes, and the Massachusetts Haverhill group (that is, John Chase and John Carey). Algernon Lee, the Iowa-born son of a carpenter, was educated at the University of Minnesota. He edited an SLP paper, the *Toscin,* in Minneapolis and left the Party to edit the Kangaroos' the *People* and later the New York *Worker* and the *Call* both of which consistently supported Hillquit's views. J. Mahlon Barnes, a Philadelphia trade union leader of the International Cigar Makers' Union, was prominent in AFL affairs. Some Massachusetts-Haverhill socialists held such offices as mayor and state representative. Their experience made them amenable to the reform tendencies inherent in "municipal" socialism.

Some important New York Jewish socialists, in particular Meyer London, did not support the Hillquit coalition. As has been pointed out, the Jewish ex-Socialist Laborites who left the SLP in 1895 and then joined the SDP in 1898 distrusted Hillquit. In 1899 Meyer London, for example, joined Berger in voting against unification with the Hillquit people.[11] Yet London and Hillquit had much in common. They were both New York lawyers and both worked with the Jewish trade unions. Ideologically, London took a position close to Harriman's fusion stand. In fact, in 1899 London and several of the Jewish socialists and labor leaders had tried to form an Independent Labor Party in collaboration with non-socialist trade unions. They hoped to run a fusion candidate in New York City but were censured at the 1900 Indianapolis SDP convention for doing this.[12]

The Unity Convention which transformed the Springfield (Kangaroo) faction and the Chicago SDP faction into a unified Socialist Party of America opened on July 29, 1901, in Indianapolis. Of the 125 delegates seventy came from the Springfield group with 4,789 votes, forty-seven represented the Chicago Berger-Debsites with 1,329 votes, and eight came from independent parties with 352 votes.[13] Most delegates were journalists, lawyers, and experienced socialist party leaders. With few exceptions, the delegates were in their twenties and thirties. Ideological differences crossed factional lines. The number of American-born delegates was especially remarked upon at the time. Morris Winchevski noted in the *Jewish Daily Forward* of July 31 that "fully four-fifths of the delegates were American-born, the Germans and the Jews for once—and I am afraid for all time now—taking a back seat."[14]

The thirty-two-year-old Hillquit, although foreign-born and the possessor of a distinct European accent which some people claimed sounded almost French, did not take a back seat. He not only entered the debates with his own point of view but also, at times, assumed the role of convention mediator—a part which became characteristic of his behavior at innumerable later Party conventions.

Early in the convention Hillquit (among others) set the tone for unity by insisting that the Chicago and Springfield factions be given equal representation on the various committees although the Springfield people far outnumbered their former opponents. Futhermore, Hillquit opposed both general voting on the basis of faction and the right of factions to submit minority reports if their position was defeated. "If this is a unity convention," he said, "the only thing to do is to act as one body, and adopt one set of resolutions, one constitution and one platform."[15]

As the convention proceeded, the fear that voting would merely reflect factions was dispelled. Instead there was significant crossing of factional lines. Looking just at Hillquit's voting record, we find that he voted with his adversary Berger in favor of keeping the name of the old party, the Social Democratic Party (a measure which lost by a vote of seventy-nine to nineteen).[16] However, in favoring the inclusion of immediate political and economic demands in the Socialist Party platform, Hillquit voted against his supporter Max Hayes.[17] Hillquit and Harriman voted on opposite sides of the farm issue.[18]

Of all the issues discussed at the convention, perhaps concern over "immediate demands" was the most central to the Party's subsequent development. Ought a socialist party, whose ultimate aim is revolutionary transformation of society, support gradual and reform goals? At their 1900 convention the De Leon SLP had rejected all immediate aims on the philosophic grounds that such demands compromise the revolutionary nature of a socialist party. Among the European parties of the Second International, this issue aroused intense controversy. The German Party, the SPD, which was the most prestigious and seemingly successful among the national parties of the International, had set an example in 1891 by accepting the Erfurt program. The program contained a set of revolutionary goals for a future socialist society alongside an enumeration of immediate demands. But since 1899 and the publication of Eduard Bernstein's *Evolutionary Socialism*, the European socialists had been in the throes of debate over a profound reform issue. Bernstein's ideas of "revisionism" implied, among other things, that if the reform demanded by socialists was adopted, then socialism might come to fruition gradually and without revolution.

Few American socialists had read Bernstein in 1901. The group which spoke out in favor of immediate demands, men like McCartney who had recently been elected to the Massachusetts legislature, or Morgan, a lawyer and veteran of the Chicago labor movement, or the Christian Socialist George Herron, emphasized the need to create a stable political party through a specific program. Those opposed to the measure, such as A.M. Simons who was later the editor of the *International Socialist Review* and labeled an "impossibilist" for this position, claimed that special conditions in America made immediate demands unnecessary. "Nowhere else on the face of the earth have the interests that we propose to sever through immediate demands grown of so little importance as here. Nowhere else in the world has the struggle between capital and labor narrowed down as clear a point and as clear an issue as it has in America."[19]

Hillquit took a position during the convention similar to the German Erfurt program. He stated that the party platform ought "to express the cardinal principles of socialism, not only our ultimate aims and views, but also our present action, our activities." He concluded with this statement which revealed both a tactical shrewdness and a clear conception of practical politics:

> If we ever attempt to go before the working class and promise them the cooperative commonwealth in three or four years and if they wait six and ten and see no chance of its realization, then we will be much worse off, for they will lose faith in our propaganda. On the contrary, if you show to the working man what we know perfectly well and understand, that we are dealing with the complex problem of social evolution, and that we do not know whether or not the ultimate end in which we believe and for which we are working will be reached today, tomorrow, or in ten years or half a century—if you show them. . . that all we know is the general tendency and all we can do is work along these lines and that all we call upon them to do is to cooperate with us along these lines, then real progress is begun.[20]

The vote was 5,358 in favor of including immediate demands as part of the program and 1,325 against.[21]

Despite his support for immediate demands, Hillquit insisted that the convention recognize the revolutionary nature of the socialist movement. In this sense he took a radical position. At the July 31 evening session of the convention, he asked that the term *revolutionary* socialism be employed to describe the international movement. "I am for revolutionary socialism all the time. . . ," he said, and "International Socialism is revolutionary, and for this reason I think it should be put in the platform."[22]

Hillquit also took a mediator's stand on whether the Socialist Party program ought to include special demands for the American farmer. The Social Democratic Party had eliminated all proposals which dealt with farmers' demands in 1899. Now, at the Unity Convention, this issue elicited sharp controversy. James Carey and Job Harriman, both within the Hillquit faction, rejected socialist cooperation with farmers. Harriman, for example, argued that "we are building in the convention a wage working class platform; the farmers do not belong to the working class, because the farmers own the farms. . . . I know that the harder the work of the farmer is, the more intensely will be the struggle to reduce the wages of his help." Chicago lawyer Seymour Stedman argued to the contrary that "the farmer is forced by present conditions to throw his commodities upon the market, just as much as the laborer is forced to do it."

Hillquit sided with Stedman but he did not discount the class-conscious arguments of Harriman. "The interests of the farmers are not identical with those of the wage workers," he admitted. However, he thought "the condition of the farmer as it is today is practically that of a hired laborer of the capitalist class." Ultimately, he hoped the farmer would realize he was a victim of the capitalist system; only the modes of exploitation were different.[23] The convention did not come to a definite stand on this issue.

The period of disunity and the unification process (1899-1901) brought Hillquit to the fore as a major figure in the socialist movement. He had a talent for directing the inner circles of a political party and he had a sensitivity for mediation. At this point in his career, Hillquit's theoretical socialist concepts placed him in what might be termed the "center wing" of the new party—between the revolutionary left and the reformist right. In 1901, despite tensions within the Party, there seemed little reason why he ought not become the focal person around whom a powerful party might form.

Notes

1. *History of Socialism*, p. 304.

2. Bell, *Marxian Socialism*, p. 53.

3. Kipnis, *American Socialist Movement*, p. 36.

4. Quoted in a circular written by Morris Hillquit and Job Harriman, Chicago *Social Democratic Herald*, April 2, 1900.

5. Letter from Morris Hillquit to Vera Hillquit, January 27, 1899, Correspondence, Hillquit Papers. The date of this letter ought to read January 27, 1900, but both Hillquit and the editor of his letters made an error.

6. See *Proceedings of the 1900 Socialist Labor Party Convention*, Rochester, N.Y. Transcripts are also in the Tamiment Library. See New York *People* (anti-De Leon), February 4, 1900.

7. According to John Spargo's Oral History Research Project, Hillquit was less important in the "Hillquit faction" than Henry Slobodin, who be-

came the first national secretary for the insurgent Kangaroo group. Spargo felt that Slobodin, a law student, was an underestimated figure of the 1899-1901 period.

8. *Loose Leaves*, p. 48.

9. Quint, *Forging*, p. 48.

10. See Knox Mellon, "Job Harriman: The Early Years and Middle Years, 1861-1912" (Ph.D. dissertation, Claremont College, 1971).

11. New York *People* (anti-De Leon), March 18, 1900.

12. Quint, *Forging*, p. 345.

13. *Proceedings of the Socialist Unity Convention*, Indianapolis, Ind., 1901, pp. 2-3. Copy in the Tamiment Library.

14. New York *Jewish Daily Forward*, July 31, 1901.

15. *Proceedings of the Socialist Unity Convention*, p. 39.

16. Ibid., p. 294.

17. Ibid., p. 275.

18. Ibid., p. 539.

19. Cited in Fine, *Labor and Farmer Parties*, p. 205.

20. Ibid.

21. Ibid.

22. *Proceedings of the Socialist Unity Convention*, pp. 219-20.

23. Cited in Fine, *Labor and Farmer Parties*, pp. 209-11.

Ideology Chapter 5

Before discussing Hillquit's career in the pre-World War I Socialist Party of America, it is important to pause and consider, in some detail, his views on socialism. Hillquit thought of himself as an intellectual on a par possibly with one of the most reknowned German socialist theorists, Karl Kautsky, whom he admired. Hillquit's vanity led him to collect reviews of his own books, even banal ones, and he saved the most superficial letters of appreciation from people to whom he sent his works.[1] In the United States his *History of Socialism*, for example, was welcomed by the socialist press as a milestone in the development of an American socialist literature.[2] Perhaps the only sour note among his contemporary American critics was sounded by Louis Boudin, also a New York lawyer and a more radical socialist than Hillquit. Boudin and Hillquit competed for the honor of being *the* theorist for the Socialist Party. When Boudin in his 1907 *The Theoretical System of Karl Marx* criticized the failure of American Marxists to understand Marxism as a complex system, he also included Hillquit's efforts.[3]

The books Hillquit wrote before the war did not elicit especially favorable comment from European intellectuals. While he was called a distinguished "theorist" by the popular socialist press, for example, in the French daily *L'Humanité*[4] edited by Jean Jaurès, his ideas were not taken seriously among scholars. European radicals tended to regard his work (as did two German Communist writers in the 1930s) as an example of the "superficial popularization of socialism which spread throughout the working class movement at the beginning of the twentieth century and which despite Marxist phraseology, retained none of the real content of Marxian socialism."[5] This did not mean that his books were without effect in Europe. For instance, his *History of Socialism* was translated and sent abroad. The book's widespread influence was attested to by Tzivion, an important Yiddish journalist, who recalled reading the *History* in Russia on the eve of his emigration to the United States—his first awareness of the existence of an American socialist movement.[6]

Those critics who claimed Hillquit's works were unsophisticated and lacking in profundity or in scope may be correct. Those who condemned his work as mechanical vulgar popularization meant to be accepted as a "credo" were misunderstanding his original intentions. Such critics were also missing the value of his work as a significant expression of American Marxist thought.

As for his intentions, Hillquit was first and foremost an educator and his concept of education focused primarily upon information. Perhaps naïvely, like many idealists of the pre-Freudian and pre-World War I era, he held an "enlightened" view which imagined that rational knowledge in and of itself altered a person's perspective. In 1903 Hillquit contended that "in its present phase, socialism in this country is primarily an educational movement."[17] Thus he wrote his books, articles, and lectures especially to familiarize a working-class audience with what he believed was the comprehensive range of socialist thought. Max Eastman, who disagreed with many of Hillquit's views, nonetheless sympathetically understood this didactic sense. In his autobiography *Love and Revolution,* Eastman admiringly noted that Hillquit could even turn a trial into a "postgraduate course at college."[8]

Hillquit never meant his work to serve as dogma. While his brand of Marxism might have encompassed elements of philosophic determinism, he was flexible on political and economic issues. He was capable of acting and reacting in response to specific circumstances without the aid of a catechism. In 1908 he wrote, "Of course, socialists do not consider Marx infallible. Marxism is the philosophy of a live, growing and changing social movement, not an ossified dogma or a final revelation."[9]

Hillquit valued Marxism for those very characteristics his critics accused it of lacking: its flexible analytic nature, its logical, rational conclusions, and its profound practicality as a guide to understanding the past and to formulating future programs.

What kind of a Marxist theorist was Hillquit and what, if any, contributions did he make to American Marxist thought? First it is necessary to say that Hillquit was not the only socialist theorist before the war. His work represented a small portion of a genre of books written by such party ideologues as John Spargo, W.H. Ghent, William E. Walling, Charles Vail, A.M. Simons, and Louis Boudin which defined, described, and proselytized the socialist movement. Hillquit was neither the most prolific (that dubious honor probably goes to Spargo) nor the most profound. Stylistically, his prose was simple, if not at times simplistic; his material was arranged with textbook clarity. He was often careful to cite sources, particularly the French, British, German, and Russian writers with whom he was familiar: Marx, Darwin, Spencer, Huxley, Stirner, Kropotkin, Veblen, MacDonald, E.B. Bax, Kautsky, and Bebel. Perhaps the most original aspect of his work was the interest he showed in the international socialist movement and its thinkers—a characteristic which set him apart from most other American socialist writers.

Hillquit was an eclectic thinker. He borrowed and syncretized ideas about socioeconomic and historical processes from the major figures of nineteenth-century thought—particularly Hegel, Darwin, Marx-Engels, and their various interpreters. It might be more exact to say that he created a socialist paradigm from elements he extracted from the general "orthodox Marxist" view which was popular with a majority of socialists in the pre-World War I period. Orthodox Marxism was a particular interpretation of Marx's philosophy developed by Engels and a few of Marx's other followers after the master's death. Essentially, the orthodox Marxist regarded himself as a social scientist capable of proposing a set of concepts which explained the course of history, described the present society, and predicted the tendencies of future development.

Simply put, the orthodox Marxist held that economic systems and political-social institutions were the result of historical processes—the products of gradual growth and subject to constant change. The determining factor which shaped the institutions of a given historical society was its basic economic structure. The way in which the means of production and distribution were organized reflected directly upon the society's class structure, law, government, family relationships, and so forth. The Marxist appreciated capitalism as an advanced form of civilization and yet predicted that the contradictions inherent in capitalism would eventually lead to its demise.

The proletariat, viewed as the crucial agent of the destruction of capitalism, would assume power and bring a classless society to fruition. In the new society, the means of production and distribution and the political agencies of the State would be cooperatively owned and democratically administered. While the orthodox Marxist concept of the assumption of power by the proletariat was revolutionary in nature, it also had evolutionary aspects. Before revolution was possible, the proletariat had to attain the proper conditions of immiseration and self-consciousness and the forms of production ought to have reached a specific stage of development. Furthermore, the Marxist also suggested that socialism came to fruition within the framework of the national State and only after the State passed through certain specific political phases.

While Hillquit reiterated all these concepts in his theoretical work, he actually stressed two factors: the evolutionary process of societal change and the conscious understanding of this change by both the working and middle classes. This emphasis imbued his theory with its special flavor.

The evolutionary concept was the more important of the two and can be traced back to one of his earliest articles, "The End Is as the Beginning," in the Yiddish *Arbeter zeitung* published on December 5, 1890. Here Hillquit explained Hegel's concept that "world-history is a science and like every other science it has specific laws." The one Hegelian law Hillquit singled out for comment was that "the end is as the beginning." As he put it, "In the most important developmental aspects of society, human beings return to the same point from which they began *but on a higher and more refined level.*" World history, for example, moved in stages from primitive communities where social organization was based upon common needs but lacked social equality, through capitalism where neither equality nor commonality existed, full circle back to socialism where both commonality and equality both will be realized.[10]

By the first decade of the twentieth century, Hillquit had come to rely more upon Darwin's evolutionary ideas and less upon Hegel. Through Darwin Hillquit tried to explain the basic forces which impelled societal change. Using Darwin's ethical interpretations, Hillquit attempted to prove the moral superiority of socialism. For instance, Hillquit contended that the process of adaptation bred "more highly and efficiently organized individuals." Whereas the struggle for existence was purely an individual struggle in the lowest forms of life, Hillquit thought "in the ascending scale of organic existence the struggle between individuals of the same species gradually abated and was superseded by the collective struggle of such individuals against hostile kinds and adverse forces of nature around them." He expressed optimism for this Darwinesque bio-historical process by prophesying that "henceforward the process of evolution is one of growing solidarity and cohesion among individuals of the same group or species as against their common enemies, and this instinct of solidarity and cohesion is the first germ of the sense of social duty or moral consciousness."[11] Essentially, Hillquit argued—through Darwin—that there was a natural and instinctual course of human development which led in the direction of social solidarity and moral perfectibility.

The Social Darwinists of Hillquit's time employed the theory of struggle and instinct to rationalize the so-called moral superiority of the capitalist system which relegated communality to the "dark ages." Hillquit attempted to turn the arguments of the Social Darwinists around 180 degrees to bolster the case for socialism. He argued that the very same elements—instinct, struggle, selection—would be instrumental in achieving a new kind of "natural" world—a socialist one.

By 1903 Hillquit wrote that socialism already existed (albeit in embryonic form) within capitalism. Describing modern production, he said, "The individual laborer is practically obliterated; what is before us is a world-wide community of socially organized labor of all gradations, from the highest and most skillful to the lowest and most common—working together collectively for the needs of our race."[12] In 1913 he went so far as to say, "We are already living at least in the outskirts of the 'Socialist State'."[13]

Part of Hillquit's faith in the ongoing evolutionary process rested upon the confidence he placed in the productivity of the capitalist system. He thought productivity would have two consequences. Sophisticated economic institutions would dispense with the need for the individual capitalist and the abundant availability of goods would encourage economic equality. He optimistically felt that "society will with comparative ease produce enought to afford all its members without distinction all necessaries and even luxuries. . . ."[14]

In keeping with his evolutionary views, Hillquit doubted that the sort of revolution which disrupted the continuity of societal institutions would ever really become necessary. But he was not a Bernsteinian Revisionist. His concept of change was in the mode of his mentor Kautsky. In 1903 the German theorist wrote in *The Social Revolution* that socialism would be born naturally, like an infant, at the moment of its proper maturity.[15] Hillquit was even more cautious. He denied that socialism would "be established by a rabble made desperate by misery and starvation." He speculated that "the socialists will realize their ideals probably through a series of industrial and political reforms. . . brought about directly or indirectly by the struggles of an intelligent, well-trained and well-organized working class, supported by numerous men and women from all classes."[16]

As part of his gradualist perspective, Hillquit reasoned that the State already was taking on new significance as an instrument of social and economic reform, "a most potent instrument for the modification and ultimate abolition of capitalist rule."[17] The State would not be abolished under socialism. Rather the State would represent *society as a whole* and would function democratically as the central administrative unit of the community. As a safeguard against a "monolithic" State, and to insure democratic processes, Hillquit suggested a program of autonomy for municipalities and a limitation of the powers and functions of the central government.[18] "The city," he wrote, "with or without political or industrial subdivisions, will absorb the most important government activities under socialism, and the central government will as a result be limited to the management of the 'national' industries and to the enactment of general laws and regulations."[19]

Hillquit analyzed the possibilities for a socialist future in the United States. Unlike many other pre-World War I American socialists (and some Europeans as well) he did not think socialism would develop first in America. He contended that "America has long held an exceptional position among the nations of the earth." In the *History of Socialism in United States* he discussed why this "exceptionalism" worked both for and against the eventual success of a socialist movement in America. On the positive side, he noted that the abundance of natural resources, the "astounding" rapid industrialization of America, and early political enfranchisement provided the potential environment for a socialist transformation. However, on the negative side, he pointed "to a variety of circumstances rooted in the economic and political conditions and historical causes peculiar to this country," which "operated to retard the progress of the movement."[20] Basically, these circumstances were psychological in nature and pertained to the "state of consciousness" of the American working class. Class consciousness arose among European workers out of the slow and gradual process of industrialization over two centuries. "The European wage workers are several generations old," Hillquit wrote. "They had their class traditions and sentiments; they were 'class conscious'."[21] This was not true of American workers. Americans did not acquire this consciousness for three reasons:

> Their existence as a class was of too recent date to have developed decided class feelings in them; they had yet before them the example of too many men who before their very eyes rose from the ranks of labor to the highest pinnacles of wealth and power; they were still inclined to consider wage labor as a mere transitory condition.

Two other major factors contributed to make the progress of socialism in America slower and more laborious than in most countries of Europe. In the United States, Hillquit said, "the working men enjoyed full political equality at all times, and thus had one less motive to organize politically on a class basis." Second, "the periodical appearance of radical reform parties on the political arena of the country often had the effect of side-tracking the incipient socialist movement into different channels."[22]

Hillquit's particular theoretical stress upon the evolutionary nature of capitalist-socialist development, his belief that socialism existed within society, and his interpretation of American working-class consciousness contributed to the reformist attitude he held in regard to the functions of a socialist party in America. Because he took a long-range view of the developing economy, he did not think the Party needed to play a revolutionary role within American society—that is, to threaten economic and political expropriation. He thought time and history would make the appropriate radical changes. The Party needed to explain those changes, guide the present course of events, and anticipate, perhaps predict, the coming course of societal development. In addition, the Party's "educational" function was to make, as Hillquit put it, "the adjustment of the socialist movement to the conditions of the country, the acclimatization of socialism on American soil."[23] For Hillquit acclimatization meant assisting in the formation of social and labor legislation. It meant supporting working-class movements, trade unions, or political groups, which accepted the structure of capitalism while attempting to transform it.

Hillquit and those socialists in the Party who regarded him as their spokesman were a significant force in the Party—but not the only force. There were serious disagreements on theoretical and tactical issues to the right and to the left of the Hillquitians.

Notes

1. See letter from George Herron to Morris Hillquit, October 23, 1903, Correspondence, Hillquit Papers; Job Harriman to Morris Hillquit, October 25, 1903, ibid., and Eugene V. Debs to Morris Hillquit, October 29, 1903, ibid.

2. "Kritik," *Zukunft* 15 (June 1910), p. 396.

3. Louis Boudin, *The Theoretical System of Karl Marx* (New York, 1907).

4. Letter from William Mailly to Morris Hillquit, November 17, 1903, Correspondence, Hillquit Papers.

5. Carl Grunberg and Henryk Grossman, "Sozialismus und Kommunism," in Ludwig Elster, ed., *Worterbuch der Volksmortschaft* 3 (Jena 1931, 4th ed.), p. 326. This was cited by Paul M. Sweezy, "The Influence of Marxian Economics," in Egbert and Parsons, eds., *Socialism and American Life* (Princeton, N.J., 1952), p. 463.

6. Ben Zion Hoffman (pseud. Tzivion), "Der alter bakanter Morris Hillquit," New York *Jewish Daily Forward*, September 23, 1929, Clippings, Hillquit Papers.

7. *History of Socialism*, p. 364.

8. Max Eastman, *Love and Revolution* (NewYork, 1964), p. 87.

9. Morris Hillquit, "Socialist Plan of Wealth Distribution," *Putnam's Monthly*, April 1908, Writings, Hillquit Papers.

10. Morris Hillquit, "Dem onhayb iz der sof," New York *Arbeter zeitung*, December 5, 1890.

11. Morris Hillquit, *Socialism in Theory and Practice* (New York, 1912), p. 47.

12. Ibid., p. 26.

13. John Ryan and Morris Hillquit, *Socialism: Promise or Menace?* (New York, 1920), p. 240.

14. Morris Hillquit, "The Socialist Plan of Wealth Distribution," Writings, Hillquit Papers.

15. Karl Kautsky, *The Social Revolution*, trans, A.M. and Mary Simons (Chicago, 1916), pp. 12-20.

16. Morris Hillquit, "Socialism and Its Growth in the United States," Writings, Hillquit Papers.

17. *Socialism*, p. 98.

18. Ibid., p. 102.

19. Ibid., p. 136.

20. *History of Socialism*, p. 139.

21. Ibid., p. 135.

22. Ibid., pp. 139-40.

23. Ibid., p. 141.

The Socialist Party: The First Years

Chapter 6

From the beginning Hillquit was a controversial figure in the Socialist Party. Considered a "centrist," he shared positions with both its left and right wings. Both sides praised and blamed him. By stressing one or another aspect of his actions or by viewing the Party in a particular perspective, it was possible to make a case for him as a hero or as a villain.

He was admired by some socialists for acting as a lightning rod, the target for oppositional sentiment in the Party. George Herron, a Christian Socialist and one of the founders of the Rand School, offered high praise when in 1913 he explained that the hostility and misunderstanding toward Hillquit was due to "his effort to be wholly fair to everyone, to do the uttermost right by everyman and measure, to try to give each voice a sympathetic hearing. . . . He is but seeking a synthesis—a coordination of all the motives and modes of action within the movement."[1] Hillquit was typed by friends as " the Party's Henry Clay, its Great Pacificator."[2]

Some critics, mainly left-wing fellow socialists, vilified him as an unconscious adulator of capitalism, a tacit creator of business unionism, and a cultural bourgeois whose thinly veiled intellectual elitism and contempt for working-class intelligence and ways made him an inappropriate leader for the proletariat. Many left-wing critics classified his choice of Socialist tactics for American society as "reformistic," or even worse, as "opportunistic." Moreover, within the Party, Hillquit often was held responsible not only for setting the tenor of factionalism through his so-called dogmatic inflexibility, but also for outmanuevering his opponents with his guileful lawyer's logic. In 1903 western socialists characterized him as a "smooth" and slippery "manipulator" who always had a "job" or a "trick" to spring on the meeting.[3] The development of power groups, the domination of East Coast provincialism, bureaucratization, and antidemocratic procedures within the Party were also attributed to Hillquit's influence. Perhaps most seriously, of all, his detractors claimed that Hillquit's version of Marxism, which cast socialists as responsible members of the body politic, "sacrificed revolutionary integrity for the sake of shoddy respectibility."[4]

Between 1901 and 1905, the first few years of the Party's life, Hillquit held a decidedly centrist role or mediating position in Party councils. He then became the New York representative to the Party's national committee (1901-1906);[5] intraparty political quarrels abounded and threatened to split the new organization.

Hillquit's earliest battles were fought with right-wing socialists whose policies tended toward "fusion," or the merging of non-socialist reformistic or labor groups with the Socialist Party. While Hillquit favored a reform platform (that is, the 1901 immediate demands), he opposed the tactic of combining with other parties. Socialists, he thought, ought to practice "political isolation" if they wanted to build an ideologically pure and inviolate party. As he told Isaac Hourwich: "Experience teaches us that whenever a young revolutionary movement permits itself into alliances with other and more conservative movements it is doomed to perdition. . . ."[6]

The question of "fusion" first arose in relation to whether the Socialists ought to support independent non-socialist trade union parties. In the first decade of the twentieth century the Socialist Party had several opportunities to support state or city trade union parties. For instance, Job Harriman in California was particularly active in organizing a fusion coalition between the California Socialist Party and a set of trade unions called the Union Labor Party. The ULP was an organization of non-socialist California trade unionists who hoped to launch a political party which would advocate labor legislation. The National Committee of the Socialist Party censured such a coalition. In fact, Hillquit voted along with Victor Berger, on January 29, 1903, in favor of removing the national secretary, Leon Greenbaum, from office for defending California socialists who endorsed a California Socialist-ULP ticket in their state.[7] At that time the National Committee unanimously passed a resolution declaring that the Party would under no circumstances "fuse, combine or compromise" with any other political party and that the Socialists would not take sides in "purely trade union disputes."[8]

In 1903 Hillquit's strong anti-fusionist sentiments were criticized by his friend Harriman. "The trouble with Socialists like yourself," Harriman complained, "is that they do not see the difference between fusion with capitalists and reform parties, as against cooperation with the organized working class, and the safety afforded to our movement by that organization dominating the Socialist Party."[9]

Very few socialists, including Hillquit, agreed with Harriman or pressed for the formation of a labor party in the prewar years. Along with the theoretical anti-fusion concept, there were other reasons why a labor party did not interest socialists. First, the organized labor movement, as represented by the leaders of the AFL, were not enthusiastic about a socialist-trade union fusion. Except for a brief interlude in 1906, Gompers did not even ask the AFL membership to support political candidates, let alone socialists. Second, the conservative as well as the more radical wings of the Party, in their own way, were convinced that a labor party was unnecessary. For example, Berger, the right-winger, and Hillquit, the centrist, both believed in the "double arm" theory of separation of party and union. Both wanted to see a strong socialist party and an equally strong but separate socialist trade union system—on the German socialist model. That is why when William E. Walling, a left-winger who had not yet become a Party member, accused Hillquit, Berger, Spargo, and several other Party leaders of conspiring to form an AFL-dominated labor party and thus destroy the autonomy of the SP in November 1909, he could not have been further from the truth.[10] Simultaneously, left-wing leaders of the SP such as Debs and Bill Haywood did not want a labor party with conservative trade unionists. They hoped to turn the trade unions into revolutionary organizations.

Another intraparty controversy, one with even more serious divisive potential than the fusion issue, threatened Party harmony in the first years. This issue focused upon a power struggle between so-called western and eastern socialists for control of the Party's headquarters and executive. This seeming East-West split was complicated by the fact that the supposedly "agrarian" western socialists supported the newly emerging American Labor Union, a militant industrially organized union of western miners in open revolt against the AFL.

In this controversy Hillquit came to side with the "Eastern," urban-oriented socialists and especially with the anti-American Labor Union position. Harriman, himself a westerner, as well as a group of middlewestern National Committeemen like Berger and easterners like Carey joined to compose the "Eastern faction."

The western socialists, in 1903, wanted to move the new seat of the national headquarters to Omaha, Nebraska—the heart of the proletariat movement. The westerners wanted the Socialist Party to support the efforts of the ALU. Harriman, who thought the small-town western socialists harbored populist aspirations and that the ALU was just another version of De Leon's ST and LA, advised Hillquit to oppose them. "Arguments will not work in their camp. They must be whiped [*sic*]," he wrote Morris on March 6, 1903.[11] Hillquit tended to agree with this position. In 1903 he worked hard to have the national headquarters moved to Chicago and he did not support the ALU.[12]

Hillquit, however, was displeased with the East-West antagonism generated by these quarrels. Writing home from a meeting of the National Committee in St. Louis in February 1903, he expressed apprehension at what he termed "this unreasoning prejudice so utterly out of place in our movement" which pitted East against West. Revealing his own desire to appear impartial he explained to the New York readers of the *Worker:*

> During the last year or two our movement has made rapid progress in the West, new locals have sprung up by the scores and new state organizations have been effected. From all I could learn and observe the movement is clean and healthy and full of promise. But it is as yet very young and the men in it somewhat inexperienced. . . . Some men in our party who should have known better, have made it their business to con-

> jure up an antagonism between the West and the East. An appeal to our sectional prejudices. . .is the cheapest way to gain popularity. . . .[13]

Actually, Hillquit never warmed up to the western socialists. Despite his emphasis on building an "American" party, he did not realize their importance. He could not identify with their agrarian rhetoric[14] nor could he sense the significant contribution that the radical Western proletariat of the mining towns was making to American socialism. His discomfort with western socialists drove him to seek allies among "urban" socialists—even those much further to the right than himself—in the conviction that the future of American socialism resided in the cities.

Between 1905 and World War I Victor Berger became Hillquit's most significant ally in the Party. Berger's career seemed at that time to illustrate the success of socialist urban politics. Berger built an effective socialist organization in Milwaukee by offering the city's voters an extensive platform of reform including municipally owned utilities, public work projects for the unemployed, free medical services, urban renewal, a graduated income tax, universal suffrage, direct legislation, state farm insurance, and the prohibition of labor for those under the age of sixteen. Consequently, the Milwaukee Social Democrats attracted a wide range of supporters: organized labor (the socialists were allied with the Federated Trades Council and the Wisconsin State Federation of Labor), radical German immigrants, and an urban middle class who were weary of the corruption and incompetence of the local Democratic and Republican parties. Berger was also an exceptionally forceful leader. By playing a leading role in the Milwaukee FTC and by controlling the *Social-Democratic Herald* (the major voice of organized labor in Milwaukee), he came closest of any socialist to being a "city boss."[15] In 1910 Berger was elected to the federal House of Representatives as the first Socialist member of that body.[16]

Personally, Hillquit had ambivalent feelings toward Berger who had attacked him in the pre-unification days. "He was not an orator. . .but he had a thorough mastery of the Socialist theory and an abundant fund of knowledge in the spheres of social science and history," Hillquit wrote. "He was sublimely egotistic, but somehow his egotism did not smack of conceit and was not offensive," he added.[17] Whereas Hillquit saw Berger's weaknesses, he still admired the electoral growth of the Milwaukee party. Actually, from 1903 onward Hillquit and Berger began to form a tentative alliance —on the national level. By November 1903 William Mailly, the national secretary, could write Hillquit that "Berger spoke very warmly of you and Slobodin and the New York boys. . . ."[18]

Hillquit wanted to build a socialist organization in New York on the Berger model. This goal was particularly difficult in New York where a vocal leftwing resisted reformist policies. Other problems thwarted Hillquit's attempts to emulate Berger. Hillquit had no control of the local labor unions or of the press. The Jewish labor movement—that is, the International Ladies Garment Workers' Union and even the Yiddish socialist press like the *Jewish Daily Forward*[19]—only first began to gain momentum in 1909-1910. Before his appointment as attorney for the ILGWU in 1914, Hillquit's liaison with city labor was tangential at best. Furthermore, Hillquit did not have a strong electoral appeal for Jewish workers or the confidence of many Jewish socialist leaders. Consequently, he failed to be elected to Congress from Jewish districts in 1906 and 1908 (and to a judgeship in 1910).[20]

There was still another important factor which weighed against Hillquit's building a socialist "machine." While he and the New York Socialist Party culled middle-class support in the form of votes and even members, New York-based reform parties such as Hearst's Independent Party were competitors.[21] The reformers, through their advocacy of labor legislation and urban improvement programs, attracted workers and reform-minded business and professional people away from the socialists. Obviously, Hillquit's problems in New York were legion. Thus Berger's success in Milwaukee loomed large and the example he set was important for Hillquit.

Notes

1. George Herron in the *National Socialist*, November 23, 1913, Clippings, Hillquit Papers.

2. Albert Fried, "Introduction to Dover Edition," in Morris Hillquit,

The History of Socialism in the United States (New York, 1971, 5th rev. ed.), p. viii.

3. Clarence Smith, "Impressions at St. Louis," *American Labor Union Journal*, February 12, 1903.

4. Crystal Eastman, "The Socialist Party Convention," *Liberator* 3 (July 1920), p. 28.

5. See, for example, New York *Worker*, August 31, 1902, which announced Hillquit's nomination by the New York State Party.

6. Morris Hillquit, "The Class Struggle," February 20, 1908, Writings, Hillquit Papers. Hillquit's opening address and reply in a debate with Isaac A. Hourwich. Also see *Loose Leaves*, p. 170.

7. For Hillquit's personal reaction to Greenbaum see letter from Morris Hillquit to Vera Hillquit, January 20, 1903, Correspondence, Hillquit Papers. In describing the St. Louis Convention, Hillquit noted, "The fun of the situation is that Berger and Barnes and Carey and myself are always fighting together and always find ourselves linked with Greenbaum and the quorum whose stand we approve of just as little as the rest." For the reason for Greenbaum's removal see Job Harriman to Morris Hillquit, January 11, 1903, ibid.

8. "National Committee, Report of Proceedings at St. Louis," New York *Worker*, February 8, 1903.

9. Letter from Job Harriman to Morris Hillquit, May 2, 1903, Correspondence, Hillquit Papers.

10. See David Shannon, *The Socialist Party of America* (New York, 1955), pp. 63-68.

11. Letter from Job Harriman to Morris Hillquit, March 6, 1903, Correspondence, Hillquit Papers.

12. Some issues of the 1903 controversy are dealt with in a letter from Charles Dobbs to Morris Hillquit, March 9, 1903, Correspondence, Hillquit Papers. Other letters include Morris Hillquit to Russell C. Massey, February 13, 1903, ibid.; Charles Dobbs to Morris Hillquit, March 6, 1903, ibid.; Job Harriman to Morris Hillquit, March 6, March 14, and March 31, 1903, ibid.; William Mailly to Morris Hillquit, April 26, May 8, and June 22, 1903, ibid.

13. "Hillquit's Observations: New York National Committeeman Writes of St. Louis Meeting," New York *Worker*, February 8, 1903.

14. See Edward J. Muzik, "Victor Berger, a Biography," (Ph.D. dissertation, Northwestern University, 1960).

15. Ibid.

16. He was elected again in 1918, but was denied a seat because of his antiwar stand. Twice reelected he was kept out of Congress until 1922

when he was finally seated. He was elected again in 1924 and 1926.

17. *Loose Leaves*, p. 53.

18. Letter from William Mailly to Morris Hillquit, November 17, 1903, Correspondence, Hillquit Papers.

19. The *Jewish Daily Forward* was on shaky ground in the first decade of the twentieth century. See, for example, a letter from Joseph Barondess (and thirty others) to Morris Hillquit, November 3, 1902, Correspondence, Hillquit Papers, about the possible demise of the *Forward*.

20. In 1910 Hillquit was the Socialist candidate for Associate Justice of the Court of Appeals in New York and received 1,581 votes for that office. See *Official Canvass of the Vote Cast, City of New York*, December 31, 1910, p. 41.

21. Irwin Yellowitz, *Labor and the Progressive Movement in New York State, 1897-1916* (Ithaca, N.Y., 1965), pp. 195-96.

Fighting the Reformers

Chapter 7

In the pre-World War I years it was not fusion or the possible formation of a labor party which threatened the independent growth of the Socialist Party in New York. The challenge to socialism came from outside, from the middle-class urban reformers known as "Progressives." The Progressive movement was not always organized. Most often it consisted of lower and upper middle-class business people, professionals (doctors, lawyers, journalists, professors, and social workers), corporation white-collar workers as well as the traditional working class. Although these people were not organized into a political party, they were receptive to ideas of achieving meaningful political, economic, and social adjustments within the complex newly emerging industrial system.[1] However, when Progressives formed political parties, they competed with socialists in two signficant ways—in their view of reform and in their ability to attract middle and working-class support.

Hillquit combatted the organized urban reform movement in New York on both a theoretical and a political level. In the area of theory he developed a cogent argument which differentiated the aims of the socialist movement from middle-class goals. In politics he ran as a candidate against reformers and he electioneered in New York against Theodore Roosevelt, who in 1912 ran for a third presidential term on a "Progressive Party" ticket.

There were some reformers such as Charles Sprague Smith who suggested that the socialist movement was merely a form of left-wing Progressivism. Smith wrote Hillquit in 1908 that "what I feel about Socialism is that it is a very important element in the whole Progressive movement."[2] Hillquit denied this. For example, on February 20, 1908, as part of his debate with Isaac Hourwich, he launched a full-scale theoretical attack against middle-class reformism. He argued that while the Socialist Party and some reform parties advocated the same measures, "the true character and social effects of the measure and the manner of execution are entirley different in each case." As an illustration he cited the issue of state and municipal ownership of certain utilities. The Socialist Party advanced this demand to improve the facilities, decrease the charges, and create a democratic administration. In contrast, capitalist or middle-class reform parties believe "public or municipal ownership is primarily a means of reducing the taxes of the possessing classes without decreasing the exploitation of the employers in these industries." In the last anaylsis, "state and municipal ownership in the hands of the present capitalist or middle class government, only strengthens the political superiority of those classes over the working class."

Hillquit told reformers that he had little faith in just piecemeal changes, that is, child labor laws, factory acts, or extensions of suffrage. He derided socialists "who would chop up our program into fifty separate parts to be realized separately and independently, and who would make our movement a tail to the kite of various freak reform parties. . . ."[3] For him the socialist program operated as an organically integrated entity. The middle-class reformers regard "each social abuse and evil as an isolated and casual phenomenon," Hillquit wrote. "They fail to see their common source and insist on treating the symptoms rather than attacking the disease."

Moreover, Hillquit was skeptical of the efficacy of those reforms which were brought about by middle-class efforts. "The reforms which the workers conquer in battle are substantial and lasting," he wrote. "The reforms bestowed on them as a gift or sop are ineffective and short-lived."[4] He went so far as to claim that reforms inaugurated by small farmers, manufacturers, or traders cause an "arrest of development or even a return to conditions of past ages, while the reforms of the more educated classes if less reactionary are not of a more efficient type."[5]

Hillquit's special Progressive adversary was the New York newspaper publisher and self-styled reformer William Randolph Hearst. He had a very receptive audience. The workers and the lower middle class of New York City bought Hearst's morning and evening dailies. In those papers Hearst attacked the trusts, political corruption, and illegal ties between business and politicians. His paper appeared to protect the interests of the lower middle class and laborers. He supported strikes and labor legislation. At the same time Hearst often backed the Democratic Party and Tammany Hall.

Hillquit thought Hearst personified all that was misleading, self-seeking, and hypocritical in middle-class reform politics. He also realized that Hearst and Hearst-supported candidates appealed to the same group of working-class and reform-minded middle-class voters as did the socialists. In fact, Hearst's political behavior directly affected Hillquit's own aspirations. In 1906 Hillquit ran for Congress in the Ninth Congressional District, the lower East Side. As an immigrant, a Jew, and a socialist he hoped to receive votes from citizens of similar background. Hearst, however, endorsed the Democratic candidate Goldfogle, who was also a Jew and who also claimed to be seeking reform legislation for the district's population. Goldfogle won the election on a fusion ticket, combining the backing of Tammany and Hearst's Independent League.

Hillquit was dismayed by Hearst's growing influence among working-class voters in New York.[6] He even planned to explain the "Hearst threat" to the International Socialist Congress at Stuttgart (1907) where he had been invited to address the gathering on the state of American socialism. Curiously, in the original draft version of his Stuttgart speech, he drew a line through the section about Hearst. However, the deletions are legible. One can still read Hillquit's harsh accusations against Hearst's "pseudo-socialistic daily press" and against Hearst's "trading upon the popular feeling of discontent and building up enormous circulation by feigning an ultra radical attitude on all questions agitating the public mind."

Nevertheless, Hillquit's disapproval included admiration. When he mentioned Hearst in his Stuttgart speech, Hillquit also expressed wonder at the journalist's ability to rally more than 200,000 votes for his gubernatorial candidacy in New York without the support of a well-established political machine. He suggested Hearst had touched "the spirit of revolt against existing conditions" which had previously remained latent in voters' hearts. Drawing upon the Hearst experience, Hillquit explained to the Stuttgart Congress that the immediate effect of these radical developments upon the organized socialist movement were not favorable.

> The powerful reform movements holding out to the impatient masses the phantom hope of instantaneous relief, distracted their attention from the more radical but slower remedies offered by the Socialist Party and while the socialist vote during the last few years. . .shows a marked increase, it does not by any means keep pace with the growth of socialist sentiment in the United States.[7]

On the level of national politics, Hillquit's primary "Progressive" target was Theodore Roosevelt, the 1912 presidential candidate of the Progressive or Bull Moose Party. In 1912 Roosevelt aspired to a third term as President on a reformist platform. It was believed, at least by the conservative press in New York, that the Progressive Party's "Declaration of Principles" duplicated the Socialist Party's platform. Hillquit conceded, in his article " 'Comrade' Bull Moose," that Roosevelt's set of principles, his New Nationalism, included socialist-sounding phrases. He observed that the declaration was "interspersed with headlines which seem to have been bodily lifted from the composing room of the New York Call. . .'The Rule of the People,' 'Social and Industrial Justice,' 'Equal Suffrage' and many more hoary headed gents of the same family." Hillquit imagined that a superficial perusal of Roosevelt's ideas might give the impression that "the Bull Moose is an animal of the Socialist species, and is either to be condemned by us as a thievish rival or to be welcomed as a comrade. . . ."

Hillquit denounced Roosevelt and dispelled the illusion that the Progressive and Socialist Parties shared common socioeconomic philosophies. As he said, the Socialists advocated the end of capitalism, whereas "the new party stands for the continuance of the system of capitalist domination, private industry, wage work and exploitation of labor in the same way as the much abused old parties." The Progressives had no conception of the class war. The

Progressive Party platform failed to include such important reforms as child labor laws, minimum wage, social insurance, and the initiative, referendum, and recall amendments. Hillquit summed up his comparison between Roosevelt's progressivism and socialism with this analogy:

> . . . the great Progressive Party . . . imitated the Socialist tone, phraseology and form in its platform, but it was powerless to breathe into it the breath of the class struggle and social revolution;—it created not a virile, intelligent and militant being, but an impotent ape.[8]

While Hillquit made strenuous efforts to clearly differentiate progressivism from socialism, he and other New York socialists such as John Spargo and William Ghent tried to attract individual Progressives into the Socialist Party and tried to make socialism appeal to middle-class voters. Hillquit did not seem to perceive a contradiction in the concept of a working-class party built on a solid base of middle-class supporters. Although he disclaimed the German revisionist Eduard Bernstein, he, Spargo, and others were influenced by the new theories of Marxism.[9]

Bernstein advanced the concept—in direct opposition to the orthodox Marxists—that the middle class was growing in numbers and complexity rather than disappearing into an elite and immiserated proletariat. Thus a semipermanent middle class was to be a long-term phenomenon of industrial society. According to the revisionists, in the future the economically and intellectually dissatisfied members of the middle class would be attracted to socialism through its message of a better world which spoke to the middle-class sense of enlightened self-interest.[10]

Essentially, this was the argument Hillquit adopted in what he observed was a gradual transformation of the middle class toward socialism. He built his sociology around the concept that the bourgeois structure was not monolithic but complex, not in a state of disintegration but in a state of relative stability.

Hillquit thought the Party ought to welcome the disaffected bourgeoisie into its ranks. He noted with satisfaction that since the days of Marx's First International workingmen were by no means the sole supporters of socialism. Socialist ranks, even in the United

States, were continually being swelled by members of the middle classes because the ideology appealed "to large numbers of ideologists from all classes of society including those of the capitalists." He conjectured that "bourgeois ideologists" joined the socialist movement either because "they perceive in its lofty social ideal the realization of justice and freedom, or because they have become convinced, through scientific analysis of modern tendencies of social and economic development of the inevitability of socialism."[11] Once in a debate with Father Ryan, a Catholic priest, Hillquit maintined that the "Socialist working-class is the instrument of an impending superior civilization. . . ." From this he concluded that "while a class as such can never act in opposition to its direct and immediate economic interests, the individual often is guided in his sympathies and actions by the broader considerations of ultimate public benefit."[12] Hillquit hoped that the middle class would recognize that "the working-class will free not only their own class but so all other classes of modern society."[13]

Armed with this view, Hillquit devoted an enormous amount of time and energy to creating a general environment whereby socialists and middle-class intellectuals and voters might discover common interests. His most extensive activities were those involved directly with the dissemination of propaganda among professionals and middle-class intellectuals. Hillquit virtually immersed himself in propaganda work which included contributing articles to such recently published reformistic papers as *Survey*, *Metropolitan Magazine*, and *Putnam's Monthly*; writing popular books explaining the socialist movement; debating in public, mainly with reformers; meeting in private with sympathetic and influential reformers, and organizing special conferences and discussion groups such as the Intercollegiate Socialist Society, the "X" Club, and the Collectivist Society.[14]

Propaganda did not bring great numbers of middle-class intellectuals into the Party. But in these prewar years there appeared to be enough success to warrant Hillquit's enormous expenditure of energy. He contended it was his "mellowest and suavest manner" which convinced the educated and the rich to join the SP. Once, comparing his rhetoric to that of the bombastic Victor Berger, he characterized his own careful style with the succinct aphorism, "C'est le ton quit fait la musique."[15]

Hillquit was proud of the intellectuals his gentle tone had brought into the Party. He particularly boasted of his conversion to socialism of millionaire-reformer J. G. Phelps Stokes and also Helen Stokes, Rose Pastor Stokes, Robert Hunter, and Charles Edward Russell. According to Hillquit, the final conversion of this group immediately followed a three-day conference in March 1906 at Stokes's Noroton, Connecticut, estate.[16]

Hillquit claimed that at Noroton he excelled in the art of subtle oratory. Stokes, who originally planned the conference to introduce socialists to social critics, was already favorably disposed toward the Party as well as in agreement with its educational aims among middle-class intellectuals. In fact, as early as September 12, 1905, he had joined Hillquit, Clarence Darrow, Charlotte Perkins Gilman, and Jack London in the organizational meeting for an Intercollegiate Socialist Society.[17] Although this organization was not an official organ of the Party, it was designed to promote "an intelligent interest in Socialism among college men and women," on the grounds that socialism is "the most important question before the citizenship of this country today."[18]

After Stokes and Hunter joined the Party, they served with Hillquit (and others) on the ISS's Executive Board and Stokes was elected president of the society in 1907.[19] Both Stokes and Hunter also joined the New York political campaign in 1908 by running for the Assembly in districts which were adjacent to Hillquit's East Side congressional race. Hillquit experienced a sense of satisfaction in having drawn these like-minded reformers into the active ranks of the Socialist Party.

Victor Berger, who also attended the Noroton Conference, had reservations about bringing raw recruits into the Party. He cautioned Hillquit, in a letter marked "Personal," that the "New York comrades [ought] not to urge Brisbane to join the organization."[20] Arthur Brisbane, who Hillquit thought both brillant and cynical, was the son of Albert Brisbane, a Fourierist and one of the founders of the famous utopian Brooks Farm colony.[21] Berger did not think Brisbane was ready to enter the Party. On March 9, 1905, he wrote Hillquit that "the best thing will be to leave him alone and give him *time* to work out his own salvation." He added, "No man can become a Socialist in a day, and sometimes when the process is forced too rapidly, it results in a failure."[22]

Hillquit also used his persuasive techniques to enlist the aid of powerful individuals who were in a position to press for immediate reform measures advocated by the Party. In his autobiography, Hillquit recalled how he and socialists Algernon Lee, Ghent, and Walling dined and debated at the New York "X" Club, a discussion group founded in 1903 which lasted until America's entrance into World War I in 1917.

It is difficult to assess either the exact effect Hillquit's socialist concepts had upon influential reformers, or to estimate to what extent exposure to his ideas altered anyone's specific judgment. Yet the testimony of several men who belonged to the "X" Club revealed that they acquired a favorable impression of socialist ideas there. For example, George Algers, a New York City administrator who acted as an arbiter in the labor disputes of the New York cloak and suit industry at a time when Hillquit represented the union in the 1920s, recalled that he met "quite a number of cut-and-dried Socialists like Morris Hillquit, Algernon Lee and W.J. Ghent" at the "X" Club in the prewar years. He noted that "the range of topics which we discussed included most of the Socialist criticism of existing society. I could see the merits of the criticism; I couldn't see the merits of socialism as a cure, but the club was very helpful in my social education which was rather backward at best."[23]

In addition to courting reformers, Hillquit also pursued particular issues—those which might attract middle-class votes at the polls. Women's suffrage was just such an issue and Hillquit became an ardent champion of a cause that had the approval of many reform-minded voters in New York as well as the women workers of the ILGWU, a union which he represented as an attorney.

Although Hillquit spoke to audiences about working-class women and their plight, his most direct work was with Progressive women suffragists. His singular goal was to have suffrage legislation pass in New York State. In 1908 he spoke before the New York State Judiciary Committee for Amendments demanding the franchise for all as a social right.[24] Harriet Stanton Blatch, the suffragist president of the Women's Political Union, commented that Hillquit's speech in Albany "was one of the finest, most convincing I have ever heard. With apt historical references, he eloquently urged the need of democratic evolution. . . . In no small measure the women of the Empire State owe their enfranchisement to Comrade Morris Hillquit."[25]

In 1912 Hillquit gave lectures to the National League for the Civic Education of Women at the Waldorf Hotel in New York City. The New York *Times* reported that the Green Room was not big enough to hold the audience. "They stood at the rear, they stood at the doors, they stood in the aisles and they huddled around the platform," wrote the reporter as a testament to Hillquit's popularity.[26] Again in 1917, during his mayoralty campaign, Hillquit aggressively electioneered in favor of woman's suffrage. In fact, he sent a letter to the other three candidates urging them to declare themselves in favor of suffrage and thus elevate the issue above partisan politics. Furthermore, he told them that the suffrage issue transcended the class issue. He wrote, "The suffrage is not a mere privilege, but lies at the most vital foundation of self-government or democracy. . . . The working woman needs the vote as badly as the working man. The professional or business woman is entitled to it as much as her male colleague. The idle woman will make no worse use of the vote than the idle man."[27]

City planning and municipal reform also came under Hillquit's purview in the pre-World War I years. In 1911 when socialist George R. Lunn was elected mayor of Schenectady, New York, Hillquit was appointed legal consultant to the municipality. He humorously termed himself "a sort of special counsel and foreign advisor to the administration."[28] Hillquit's unique contribution to this experiment in socialist city administration was the ordinance he composed to create a Board of Public Welfare. (For a period Helen Keller served as a member of this board). According to Charles Mullen, city commissioner of Schenectady, the major achievement of the board was its purchase of an automobile which was driven by a socialist chauffeur on Sundays and holidays to take fifty children out into the "real country."[29]

Notes

1. For a historical-sociological overview of the question of socialism and reform see Roberta Ash, *Social Movements in America* (Chicago, 1973), pp. 152-92. Daniel Bell in *Marxian Socialism* held the position that

socialists were impractical dreamers and operated outside the real framework of politics. Kenneth McNaught, "Socialism and the Progressives: Was Failure Inevitable?," in Alfred F. Young, ed., *Dissent: Exploration in the History of American Radicalism* (De Kalb, Ill., 1969), pp. 253-71, refuted Bell's thesis and regarded socialists as working within a constructive ideal of politics along with other reformers of the Progressive era. Richard Fox, "The Paradox of 'Progressive' Socialism: The Case of Morris Hillquit," *American Quarterly* 26 (May 1974), pp. 127-40, was in the Bellian mode and tried to prove that Hillquit's attempts at reform and his Marxist ideology were incompatible and thus offered a clue to the failure of socialism in America. For an extensive discussion of Progressive support in New York, especially working-class support, see J. Joseph Huthmacher, "Urban Liberalism and the Age of Reform," *Mississippi Valley Historical Review* 44 (September 1962), pp. 321-41.

2. Letter from Charles Sprague Smith to Morris Hillquit, May 18, 1906, Correspondence, Hillquit Papers.

3. Morris Hillquit, "The Class Struggle," February 20, 1908, Writings, ibid.

4. Morris Hillquit, "Socialism and Social Reformers," New York *Call*, June 2, 1908.

5. Cited in William English Walling, *Socialism as It Is* (New York, 1912), p. 210.

6. Discussion of Hearst and labor in Irwin Yellowitz, *Labor and the Progressive Movement*, mentions the SP vote on pp. 195-98.

7. Morris Hillquit, "A Socialist View of the Progress and Prospects of the Socialist Movement in the United States," August 1907, Writings, Hillquit Papers.

8. Morris Hillquit, " 'Comrade' Bull Moose," Morris Hillquit Papers, Tamiment Library.

9. Hillquit denied a personal adherence to revisionism in his 1913 debate with Father Ryan published as *Socialism: Promise or Menace?* (New York, 1920), pp. 131-33. Karl Kautsky, however, criticized Hillquit for not taking a clear enough oppositional stance to Bernstein in his letter to Hillquit, June 16, 1914, Correspondence, Hillquit Papers.

10. See Peter Gay, *The Dilemma of Democratic Socialism* (New York, 1952), passim.

11. *Socialism*, pp. 155-61

12. Debate with Father Ryan, *Socialism*, p. 100.

13. Morris Hillquit, "Declaration of the Principles of the Socialist Party," (1908), Writings, Hillquit Papers.

14. Examples of Hillquit's articles in Progressive papers include "The Court of Appeals," *Survey* 26 (April 29, 1911), pp. 185-96, ibid.; "The

Socialist Plan of Wealth Distribution," *Putnam's Monthly* 4 (April, 1908), pp. 54-57, ibid. For Hillquit's lengthy description of the "X" Club see his *Loose Leaves*, pp. 67-70 and 74-78.

15. Ibid., p. 59.

16. Ibid. For the invitation to the Noroton Conference see letter from Robert Hunter to Morris Hillquit, February 11, 1905, Correspondence, Hillquit Papers.

17. Shannon, *The Socialist Party*, p. 55.

18. Letter from J.G. Phelps Stokes (president) and Morris Hillquit (treasurer) of the Intercollegiate Socialist Society to C.D. Thompson, February 6, 1913, Socialist Party Papers, Duke University.

19. Referendum to the members of the Intercollegiate Socialist Society from the Executive Committee of the ISS, June 14, 1907, box 25, "ISS and Forerunners, 1905-1916," J.G. Phelps Stokes Papers, Columbia University.

20. Letter from Victor Berger to Morris Hillquit, March 9, 1905, Correspondence, Hillquit Papers.

21. *Loose Leaves*, p. 57.

22. Letter from Victor Berger to Morris Hillquit, March 9, 1905, Correspondence, Hillquit Papers.

23. Interview with George Algers, Oral History Research Project, Columbia University.

24. New York *Worker*, January 22, 1908, Clippings, Hillquit Papers.

25. Harriet Stanton Blatch, "Hillquit and the Woman Suffrage Cause," New York *New Leader*, October 1934. A letter to the New York *Times*, February 10, 1909, signed "Anti-Socialist," Clippings, Hillquit Papers, took a different position on Hillquit's suffrage speech. The author said, "The question whether woman suffrage is a good or bad thing can be answered by answering the question whether Socialism is a good or bad thing. . . . In spite of denials from some of the fashionable recruits to the equal suffrage movement, a study of its history and demands of its leaders both in this country and abroad, show the essential socialistic nature of the suffragists' program."

26. New York *Times*, February 28, 1912.

27. Letter from Morris Hillquit to John P. Mitchell, John F. Hylan, and W.H. Bennett, 1917, Correspondence, Hillquit Papers.

28. *Loose Leaves*, p. 72.

29. Letter from Charles A. Mullen, commissioner, Schenectady, N.Y., to Carl D. Thompson, June 30, 1912, Socialist Party Papers, Duke University. For a lengthy treatment of the Lunn administration see Kenneth E. Henrickson, Jr., "George Lunn and the Socialist Era in Schenectady, New York, 1909-1916," *New York History* 47 (January 1966), pp. 22-40.

Hillquit's Critics

Chapter 8

Hillquit relished his contacts with middle-class reformers; in fact, he titled the chapter of his autobiography which dealt with his pre-World War I work among the middle class "The Golden Age." Many of his contemporaries in the Party criticized him for this interest. He also was criticized for his lifestyle—his expensive and meticulous dress, his $2,000-a-year Riverside Drive apartment overlooking the Hudson River, his art collection, and his enthusiasm for the theater and classical music. It appeared he cultivated the manners and tastes of the educated bourgeoisie.

Hillquit's attitudes toward American socialist criticism of his personal living habits have not been recorded. However, John Spargo, the English-born socialist and Hillquit's constant companion in the early 1900s, described their social relationships with wealthy, influential reform-minded people and the response of some of their comrades in the Party. Spargo noted:

> If Mrs. Rand wanted somebody to fill out a whist game and if I was free I would go over and play whist. If she wanted an extra man for dinner I would come over. And the fact that some of our righteous more-Marxist-than-Marx brethren got on to the fact and went over and established a watch and reported that of all things in the world some of us were coming up there in evening clothes made us suspect. Hillquit and I and a few others were suspect of all kinds of treason because we wore evening clothes on occasion at things like that —certainly the proletariat was being betrayed.[1]

Hillquit's interest in intellectuals and in the middle class particularly was criticized severely by socialists in the New York Party. He was accused of failing to take serious note of the working class. Generally, his critics observed that while he made attempts to distinguish socialist ideology from reformist middle-class goals, he nevertheless absorbed certain bourgeois concepts which were not appropriate for one who espoused a working-class cause. For example, his critics thought that his use of reformistic vocabulary obfuscated the socialist content of his ideas. He was admonished for unconsciously joining his opponents and thus undermining the logic of his supposedly dissenting position.

Nowhere was Hillquit's rhetoric called into question more than in his debates with reformers. Often the content of his debates with liberal opposition, college professors, religious leaders, or trade unionists, revealed his repeated emphasis upon the idea that the socialist system and socialist aims incorporated, fulfilled, and ultimately surpassed some of the basic criteria of a liberal ethos. Individualism, civil liberties, freedom of cultural expression, and even a brand of American patriotism were the vital elements in Hillquit's description of socialism.

One of his earliest debates, "Socialism and Individualism" (1907), was with Jacob G. Schurman, president of Cornell University and later ambassador to Germany. Hillquit playfully recalled in his autobiography how he put his opponent off balance by not following the line of argument Schurman expected. "Instead of belittling the merits of individualism, I cheerfully admitted them, but maintained that the system of capitalism tends to throttle true individual development, which could flourish only under an equitable Socialist economic order."[2] Hillquit further argued that socialism was not just a collectivist theory. On the contrary, it supported the "claims of individualism in modern society."[3] Socialists were "consistent individualists," he told Schurman and the large audience, many of whom had traveled by train and trolley from New York City to New Rochelle to hear Hillquit speak.[4] Socialists desired "full and free opportunity of every individual to develop his special abilities and gifts, and the right to follow his individual tastes and inclinations." Hillquit also reassured his opponent that Socialists honored nonconformism. "The struggles of Socialism," he said, "are very largely directed against those conditions in modern society which operated to suppress individual genius and tend to reduce the. . .population to one homogeneous, uniform and indistinguishable mass."[5]

In later debates Hillquit reiterated these themes. For example, when arguing with Dr. Isaac Franklin Russell over "Socialism versus the Present Order," on January 23, 1910, he told an audience at the Brooklyn Labor Lyceum that Socialists had no intention of denigrating individuality. "The only equality which Socialism advocates is the equality of economic opportunity," he said. "It admits the greatest possible diversity in intellect, talents, temperament and tastes." Hillquit took obvious pleasure in pointing out to Dr. Russell the ironic truth that capitalism, with its so-called love of free enterprise, had in fact brought about conformity never dreamed of in a socialist future system. Inveighing against capitalist culture he noted:

> It is not Socialism that would bring about an unnatural state of equality, it is Capitalism which tends to reduce mankind to a dead level of unattractive and uninteresting equality. . .crushes all native genius of the working population by the monstrous, exhausting and stupid work in the mills. . .debauches the minds of superior men by diverting them in the service of mammon. . .tends to create an equally ignorant, limited, and spiritless working class and a leisure class equally and uniformly hideous in its mad methods of pursuit of wealth; its narrow views and its insipid prescribed sports and pleasures.[6]

In a 1912 debate with Attorney General Carmody, "Socialism Against Individuality," he restated this theme. "After all," he asserted, "our tremendous growth under the system of individualism has been an abnormal one-sided growth of one organ of the body social and politic, leaving the other organs dwarfed and crippled."[7]

During several debates with Progressives in the prewar period, Hillquit argued that socialism would not only rectify society's diseases but it would do so as a fulfillment of American ideals. For example, he told Dr. Russell in 1910 that "we are better and truer patriots than those who would surround law and justice with a cloak of divinity and shield it from all criticism and discussion."[8] Again in 1910 as part of the debate, "Is Socialism a Menace to American Institutions?," he informed his opponent Cleveland Moffet that socialism is not a menace to American institutions because "it is their only hope and salvation." He said democracy was part of the American revolutionary tradition but "under the present industrial regime it has become a hollow meaningless phrase. . . ." Hillquit drew this conclusion:

> If our democratic institutions are menaced, they are menaced solely by the capitalist system. Socialism alone will restore to the people of this country a true and lasting democracy, and will truly guarantee to them the right of life, liberty and the pursuit of human happiness.[9]

Some of Hillquit's New York critics, who disapproved of his rhetoric, were also dismayed by his open courting of reformers and middle-class intellectuals. They did not want the Party to become predominantly middle class. Rather, they insisted it become as exclusively working class as possible. And these critics felt that the Party leaders ought to be making greater efforts at enlisting workers. Hillquit's critics argued cogently that his concepts of propaganda and public education not only attracted middle-class support, but actually tended to discourage workers' support.

In 1908, for example, a group of New York Party members began to wage open war against what they considered the middle-class tendencies within the Party. Several New York radicals initiated a plan for a special workers' school within the Party. It was to be called the Proletarian Society and although it never published a statement of specific goals, the society laid claim to Robert Rives La Monte's slogan, "Workers, trust your brains"—that is, your own brains and not those of middle-class intellectuals. Frances M. Gill, a prospective society member, defended the organization's worker-oriented position by offering Kautsky's admonition from the closing chapter of his *Social Revolution* (1903): "The proletariat will require high intelligence, strong discipline, perfect organization. . . . We may expect it will only succeed when it will develop these qualities in the highest degree." Therefore the mission of the Proletarian Society, as expressed in Gill's letter, "Vive le Proletariat," in the New York *Worker* of February 15, 1908, was to develop within its own ranks "such a high degree of collective intelligence. . .as will enable it [the proletariat] to attain the requisite psychological conditions of a Socialist society. . . ." It was evident from another portion of Gill's letter that the intention of the Proletarian Society was not only worker education. The society was also formed in response to the New York Socialist Party's intellectuals and political leaders, or as Gill said, "The party standard bearers, sometimes misnamed 'leaders'." In rather dramatic terms Gill stated "The LEADERS are foreign to the spirit and teachings of Socialism; that the power temporarily delegated to any officeholder or party representative in any capacity whatever is forever resident in the collective body, which is the LEADER of its own forces, the MASTER of its own destinies."[10]

Hillquit tried to prevent the formation of the Proletarian Society. A workers' school, perhaps run by workers, seemed too radical. But when he wrote his critical analysis of the organization's prospective goals, he said he opposed the school because it was too exclusive and because he detected an anti-intellectual tone on the part of the school's founders. One would-be founder, the left-wing socialist Moses Oppenheimer, sarcastically commented that Hillquit employed "an ancient legal practice formula" against the society: "When you have no case, abuse your opponents."[11]

Hillquit's major argument against the Proletarian Society was printed in the February 9, 1908, issue of the New York *Worker.* "I have always believed," he wrote, "that all dues-paying party members constitute the rank-and-file of our party, whether they work with the pick or the pen, whether they write or distribute leaflets. . .whether they hold no offices in the party or, as in the case of Comrade Oppenheimer. . .they are members of our executive committees. . . ." He believed that this new proletarian organization intended to "teach the proletarians to cuss the intellectuals," and he suggested that the term *proletariat* "has been sorely abused, distorted and maltreated" in certain Party circles in recent times. He contended that there were even advertisements for "proletariat villas, automobiles and gold mines" in socialist newspapers. The concept of the proletariat had taken on "the same suspicious past in some spheres of our movement, as the word patriotism plays among the bourgeois jingoes."

Hillquit wanted to call a halt to "the battle cry of 'Proletarians against Intellectuals'." Like Gill he also realized that the fight between the two included the element of an intraparty struggle for power. Thus he remarked that manual workers rarely criticized Party intellectuals. Negative criticism 'emanates from certain intellectuals or semi-intellectuals who find an excellent weapon in their petty and ambitious struggle against the more successful intellectuals in the party." Hillquit maintained the socialist movement would remain proletarian in its aims, character, and methods as long as it was based on Marxian philosophy, "even if forty per cent of its adherents should belong to non-proletariat classes." He added:

> Our movement does not recognize an inherent antagonism between the proletariat and intellect or intellectuals. The Socialist theory is a profound scientific and intellectual philosophy; the Socialist movement contains and always contained some of the most accomplished thinkers and scientists of our times; and the Socialist workingmen are the most intelligent and instructed of their class.

Hillquit further emphasized that "the hostility to intellect, the senseless cry against the 'students and Jews' are characteristic of the 'Black Hundreds' in Russia, but are entirely foreign to the Socialist movement."[12]

What Hillquit failed to mention in his 1908 polemic against the yet-to-be-founded Proletariat Society was that a school designed to educate workers already existed in New York since 1905. It was the Rand School for Social Science which was founded and directed by the very middle-class intellectual group within the New York Socialist Party who were so severly criticized by the "proletarians."

The Rand School clearly was modeled on contemporary institutions of higher learning. Hillquit's correspondence in late 1905 and 1906 revealed that there were diverse opinions among Party intellectuals over the specific aims of a socialist school. On October 6, 1905, for example, Hillquit received a letter from A.M. Simons whose own school for workers in Chicago had been in operation for over a year. On the basis of his experience, Simon advised Hillquit to keep the Rand School plant small, to use the public library rather than to develop a special socialist library, and to offer correspondence courses since "there is no other method comparable to this . . . [for] an institution reaching the working class." Mentioning his own work, Simons bragged that he and his wife had created a school "on an equality of scholarship with any university in the country." Furthermore, he wrote Hillquit, "We have elaborated three courses which I do not hesitate to say will stand comparison with those offered by any university in the country."[13]

Karl Kautsky advised Hillquit to dispense with rudimentary courses for workers and instead to follow the example of the Belgian socialists. In his letter to Hillquit on January 12, 1906, he seriously suggested that the Rand School be turned into an institute for advanced theoretical research.[14]

Hillquit relayed this letter to George Herron, then living in Florence, Italy. As he wrote Kautsky later, "You spoke so enthusiastically about the Rand's foundation that I thought it was best, before I wrote to you, to find out the opinion of my fellow trustees the Herrons.[15] George Herron certainly had his own opinion on how "to create a trained, thoughtful and spirited Socialist body." Chiding Kautsky, he wrote to Hillquit on February 27, 1906, that "I am aware that it is rather hazardous to put up an opinion contradictory to that of so wise and authoritative a Socialist, but I shall. . . ." Herron thought Kautsky missed "the whole motif of the school and what I take to be the fundamental educational need in the Socialist movement." He advised Hillquit that

> Kautsky's point of view is academic and not humanistic, nor is it in accord with what ought to be the real spirit or impulse of Socialist development. Our present and urgent need is not merely that of trained specialists, pensioned for skilled research, but of diffusing both accurate and inkindling [*sic*] knowledge among those who constitute the Socialist body.[16]

On March 20, 1906, Hillquit wrote a diplomatic reply to the German socialist's suggestion that the character of the Rand School be radically altered in favor of theoretical research. In his letter, Hillquit tried to strike a balance between Kautsky's academic aspirations and Herron's concept of a daily diffusion of education through the working class. The key to Hillquit's reply was the distinction he drew between the German and the American working class:

> You must consider that we are concerned here not with the socialist movement of Germany but with the movement in America. It is highly possible that the German comrades have reached a point in their development of theoretical socialism and are capable of appraising and applying their knowledge to the concrete problems of modern society. The American workers are still far from reaching this point.

Hillquit told Kautsky that he thought socialist literature in English sufficient for the educational needs of American workers. Here workers required only an "elementary *Weltanschauug*" since they did not have the background nor the time for a thorough study of theoretical socialism. According to Hillquit, the "present needs of our movement" include

> . . .an evening school in which the principles of socialist theory can be taught orally in an easily understandable way. But you understand it is not our intention to be content with these lectures. Together with the lectures we will recommend that the best socialist works be studied. We also intend to found a complete socialist library and an archive in connection with the school.[17]

The Rand School operated without a "proletarian" rival in the New York Socialist Party. Its programs and goals continued to reflect the tastes and the educational philosophies of the Party's acknowledged intellectuals. Its courses, although meant to attract workers, were not intended as store-front, grass-roots experiments in working-class culture.

Notes

1. Interview with John Spargo, Oral History Research Project, Columbia University, pp. 156-57.
2. *Loose Leaves*, p. 85.
3. Morris Hillquit, "Socialism against Individualism," January 20, 1907, Writings, Hillquit Papers.
4. *Loose Leaves*, p. 84.
5. Morris Hillquit, "Socialism against Individualism."
6. Morris Hillquit, "Socialism versus the Present Order," January 23, 1910, Writings, Hillquit Papers.
7. Morris Hillquit, "Socialism against Individualism," January 28, 1912, ibid.
8. Morris Hillquit, "Socialism versus the Present Order," January 23, 1910, Writings, ibid.
9. Morris Hillquit, "Is Socialism a Menace to American Institutions?," January 24, 1910, Writings, ibid.
10. Frances M. Gill, "Vive le Proletariat," New York *Worker*, February 15, 1908.
11. Moses Oppenheimer, "Intellectuals and Others," ibid., February 22, 1909.
12. Ibid., February 8, 1908.
13. Letter from A. M. Simons to Morris Hillquit, October 6, 1906, Correspondence, Hillquit Papers.
14. Letter from Karl Kautsky to Morris Hillquit, January 12, 1906, ibid.
15. Letter from Morris Hillquit to Karl Kautsky, March 20, 1906, ibid.
16. Letter from George Herron to Morris Hillquit, February 27, 1906, ibid.
17. Letter from Morris Hillquit to Karl Kautsky, March 20, 1906, ibid. In 1909 the curriculum of the Rand School included an introductory and advanced course in socialism, economics, public speaking, composition, American civil history, biology, American labor history, and American history. The list of instructors included Charles A. Beard, John Spargo, Algernon Lee, W.J. Ghent, and Hillquit. See Minutes of the Meeting of the Board of Directors, June 9, 1909, American Socialist Society Papers, Tamiment Library.

Hillquit and the Jews, 1901-1908

Chapter 9

In the pre-World War I years, tensions existed between Hillquit and many New York Jewish socialists and between Hillquit and Jewish voters. Within the Party Hillquit showed a marked disinterest in perpetuating an exclusively Jewish socialism among immigrant workers or among intellectuals. If nationalism was at all a concern to him, it took the form of Americanism. He wanted to build an American Socialist Party along the lines of the French or German parties of Europe. He hoped to recruit American-born members to whom religion was a private matter and to whom the English language as well as other less obvious American cultural forms were a totally natural expression. Despite the ethnic variety already present in the American socialist movement, he imagined that the Party could and would eventually transform heterogeneity into homogeneity by emphasizing American working-class solidarity. He believed that differences such as the formation of foreign-language federations within the Party ought to be discouraged.

Many Jewish socialists who also joined the Socialist Party in 1901 did not share Hillquit's indifference to the question of a special Jewish identity within the Party. Meyer London, Isaac Hourwich, and Morris Winchevski, for example, assumed that the Jewish immigrant environment in New York and other major American cities was becoming an increasingly receptive field for socialist propaganda. They could point to the dramatically increased Jewish population attributable to the accelerated emigration from Russia at the turn of the century. The immigrant economy also expanded to absorb this new work force. The New York garment industry burgeoned. For example, in the ladies garment industry, the decade between 1890 and 1900 witnessed the growth of shops from 1,224 to 2,701 or 120 percent. The number of workers in the industry, proportionately about 85 percent Jewish to 15 percent Italian, rose 85 percent from 39,149 to 83,739.[1]

Furthermore, Jewish socialists could claim that the immigrant society of those years had undergone a marked Jewish political-cultural flowering which was experienced by all classes and which directly enhanced the possibilities of successful socialist propaganda in Jewish neighborhoods.[2] Still more directly pertinent to the issue of a special Jewish socialism in America was the fact that at the end of the nineteenth-century Jews who came to the United States had an intensified feeling of national consciousness. After 1897, increasing numbers of immigrants from Russia were either influenced by or were members of the newly formed Marxist Jewish Labor Bund or the Poale Zion. In 1906 Hillquit commented that socialism on the East Side was greatly enhanced by "ready made Socialists who came from Russia."[3] However, he did not wish to recreate the Bund in America and he was even more wary of the zionist Poale Zion.

But socialists such as London, Winchevski, and others wanted to form a special Jewish group within the Party, a Jewish Agitation Bureau which would provide Jewish workers with socialist information in their own language and with a social and intellectual milieu to which they could readily relate. Hillquit, who was then an important member of the National Executive of the Party, actively opposed the creation of separate Jewish sections. At the May 1904 Cleveland Convention of the Socialist Party, Hillquit rejected a proposal for the formation of foreign-language federations. He based his argument on the fact that the Jewish branches of the SLP "caused a lot of trouble and introduced division into the ranks of the party" in the 1890s. He said that during the last decade of the nineteenth century Jewish unions, especially the United Hebrew Trades, were torn by rivalries between supporters of the Knights of Labor, the AFL, and the SLP De Leon Socialist Labor and Trade Alliance. He noted that Jewish socialists in the SLP quarreled with De Leon and the national organization over questions of press autonomy and trade union militancy while within the Jewish branches themselves the members—in particular the old leadership and the would-be leadership—vied for control of the Yiddish press. Hillquit did not want this to happen in the Party; thus at Cleveland he opposed the formation of special foreign-language locals. If foreign-language groups did form, he urged that they be denied the right to have a national executive composed exclusively of their groups. He suggested instead that loosely organized propaganda groups were more than sufficient for the purpose of agitating and organizing the foreign-born.[4] Hillquit's policy did not win him friends among the majority of Jewish socialists.

In fact, Hillquit's lack of rapport with other Jewish socialists was one of the contributing factors in his failure to win election to Congress in 1906. He decided to run for Congress in New York's Ninth Congressional District, an area which was predominantly Jewish. It is possible that he chose this district because he thought his Jewish origins would stand him in good stead. Perhaps he thought that as a successful lawyer and a prominent figure in the international, national, and state socialist movements who had risen from the poverty of the East Side, he would be perceived as a rare Horatio Alger-like figure—attaining and retaining worldly success and yet persisting in dedication to a selfless cause.

Hillquit had some positive qualities as a candidate in a Jewish neighborhood. He was a good, clear, and coherent speaker with years of experience in street-corner oratory. He spoke German, Russian, and Yiddish while his accent in English attested to humble origins. Hillquit's campaigners hoped that the Jewish immigrant voter would respect his cosmopolitan polish which implied that he possessed a degree of social acceptability that enabled him to move easily between the ethnic environment of Jewish immigrant New York to the *haute* culture of the European intelligentsia and the eclectic American society of academics, lawyers, and American socialists.[5]

But Hillquit and his campaign assistants were wrong. He did not appeal to the majority of Jewish voters in the Ninth District for a number of reasons. First, his political style tended to be cool and levelheaded. He gave an impression of remoteness. Hillquit may have wanted to present himself in this way since he disapproved of a special cult of leadership. By rejecting the use of personal attractiveness or other charismatic ploys as a tool for winning supporters, he hoped to appear as a rational representative of the socialist ideology. In his opening campaign speech before a mass audience on September 25, 1906, Hillquit proclaimed, "I understand, of course, that your cheers are but in very small degrees a personal tribute to me: that they are meant principally and primarily for the great cause which has brought us together tonight, and which on this occasion I happen to represent in a more prominent way."[6]

Moreover, many of the issues Hillquit chose to highlight in this 1906 campaign, although relevant to immigrants, tended to be expressed by him in abstract, often rhetorical terms which lacked concrete applicability. Although within the Party Hillquit was an advocate of "immediate demands" or reforms, the type of socialism he urged on his listeners seemed to be a general panacea for every ill without the clarity of specifics. In a sense Hillquit tried to compete with his Democratic opponent, incumbent Henry M. Goldfogle, who was Jewish and reformistic, and endorsed by the Hearst-led Independent Party which itself claimed to hold socialistic ideals. To counteract Goldfogle, Hillquit characterized the Socialist Party in such sweepingly general terms as "the only party that has the honest desire and the full ability to remove the evils of our society . . .because it stands for the complete abolition of the cause of all evils. . . ."[7]

Furthermore, Hillquit tried to steal Goldfogle's reformistic thunder by adopting a reformer's attitude toward conditions on the East Side and by enlisting the support of non-Jewish, non-socialist liberals. Both tactics misfired. In the instance of the liberals, it is difficult to tell exactly what effect these individuals had upon the Jewish voters of the district. Hillquit thought they were important. As early as August 1906, the Brooklyn *Citizen* described Hillquit as the counsel "for over fifty unions" and enthusiastically listed the prospective socialist congressman's admirers. A "Juvenile Workers' League, composed of several hundred boys between 13 and 17 years of age is among the most industrious supporters," the article said. "A young woman's league has also been formed. So has a professional league of 300 members, comprising lawyers, doctors, pharmacists, journalists, chemists. . . ."[8] As Hillquit related in his autobiography, the Professional League held a special dinner for him where Edwin Markham, Professor Franklin H. Giddings, Hamilton Holt, Eugene Wood, and Charlotte Perkins Gilman, all well-known men and women from outside the district (and Jewish life) spoke in support of his candidacy.[9]

But the lurid way in which Hillquit characterized the problems of the Ninth District, the lower East Side, did not win him many votes. The manner in which he expressed his disapprobation offended East Siders who while not blind to the faults of the district felt that such blatant criticism was in line with similar accusations leveled at Jews and Jewish neighborhoods by anti-Semites.[10] His description of the East Side published in the Party paper the *Worker* specifically illustrated what Louis Miller of the *Warheit* and others found offensive. "There are several reasons why this district in particular should be represented in Congress by a Socialist," he wrote:

> *In no other part of the United States are the social conditions of the inhabitants so pitiable, in no other spot on the globe is the need of radical change so crying. . . .*
>
> Our district covers a territory of barely one square mile, and it contains a population of over 200,000. It is a cold, cheerless existence that these people lead. . . . [the East Side is] the Home of the Tenements, Pushcarts, Paupers, and Consumption.[11]

Although Hillquit might have offended some people by his portrait of East Side life, he was particularly sensitive to the intense feelings of the district's population toward events in their former Russian homeland. He had shared the elation of most Jews over the January 1905 Russian Revolution. As early as February 4, 1905, Hillquit was involved in raising funds to aid the revolutionaries.[12] He was horrified when the revolution was repressed. The rise of anti-Semitic groups known as the Black Hundreds and the outbreak of pogroms aroused Hillquit's anxiety and ire.

Hillquit employed the 1906 campaign to express his indignation over the Russian situation before irate Jewish audiences. His speeches urged the American government to protest the Russian system and its brutal behavior. His arguments linked the plight of the Jews in Russia, the desirability of liberal government everywhere, and the moral commitment of the American revolutionary tradition. In fact, the very article which condemned East Side conditions explained his views regarding the Jew, the Russian Revolution, and America's responsibilities. "The majority of the citizens and inhabitants of our district are of Russian birth," he wrote. The Jews are loyal to their former country and "have a vital interest in the sublime struggle of the Russian people against their tyrannical government." Jewish sympathies are with the revolutionaries in prison and the victims of the pogroms. The civilized countries of the world, he insisted, "*owe it to humanity, to themselves, to intervene. . . and to call a halt to the atrocities of Russian absolutism.*" Above all, Hillquit thought "*this moral duty devolves on our republic*, itself the creature of a comparatively recent political revolution, itself a protest against gross political injustice." Hillquit promised, if elected, to "raise my voice in congress. . .in favor of the unfortunate people of Russia and against their brutal oppressors."[13]

In a personal sense, the Russian Revolution directly affected Hillquit's life. He befriended the noted radical novelist Maxim Gorki. The New York *Times* reported how on October 10, 1906, Gorki spoke at the lower East Side's Grand Theatre in behalf of Hillquit's candidacy. Describing the scene, the *Times* reporter wrote:

> Accompanied by Hillquit, Gorki appeared on the stage. . . . Immediately every person in the theatre stood up and cheered, while the orchestra played the "Marseillaise". . . . Gorki said: "I am a poor orator, and you can find out what I feel and think better by reading what I write. I am going to the other side, where I can continue the work of freedom. I urge you to elect Morris Hillquit, that we may have an apostle of freedom in the United States Congress."[14]

Hillquit's friendship with Gorki endured beyond the 1906 election. He became the author's legal advisor and literary representative in the United States. A Gorki-Hillquit correspondence persisted into the 1920s.

As has been mentioned earlier, Jewish socialists, within and outside the Party, were not wholeheartedly in support of Hillquit's candidacy. The Yiddish-language socialist press reflected the ambivalent attitudes present at the time. The *Jewish Daily Forward*, which more or less represented the Party's point of view, supported Hillquit and predicted victory. But the Socialist Labor Party's Yiddish organ *Der arbeter*, edited by Joseph Schlossberg, continued the old SLP hatred of Hillquit. The SLP did not endorse any candidate in the Ninth District yet it excoriated the Socialist Party's campaign methods on the East Side. Wrote *Der arbeter's* editor:

> Principles, socialism, the class struggle are absolutely ignored.... [The SP took a] simple-minded lawyer to whom the working class movement is a business, they gave him command of the party and the party's principles and they ask the public to admire him....Can a party which permits particular individuals to use it and use the working class for their own purposes, can such a party serve the interest of the worker? *Es iz beemes imeglich* [It is truly impossible].[15]

Other Jewish socialist papers were undecided. Louis Miller's *Warheit* criticized Hearst (and thus indirectly Goldfogle) as being unfriendly to the Jews. And the paper carried an enthusiastic description of Gorki's pro-Hillquit speech at the Grand Theatre.[16] But the *Warheit* did not come out directly for Hillquit. Miller admitted "that of all the possible candidates for the ninth district Hillquit is the best." But he qualified this endorsement by suggesting that outside of the Party "environment" Hillquit is not known in the Jewish quarter. Furthermore, Miller commented, "In his best and most active years Hillquit did not have a strong popularity among the Jews. Now that he is gone from the Jewish movement, from Jewish interests and the Jewish people for more than ten years, he is still less of a vote getter." The *Warheit* would have preferred the more popular labor figure Joseph Barondess as SP candidate.[17]

The *Yidisher kaempher*, the official paper of the socialist-zionist Poale Zion, also did not endorse Hillquit but instead ran a set of lively letters arguing the pros and cons of his qualifications as a

Jewish representative to Congress. A letter signed "H. Cahan" noted "Hillquit is not one of the Jewish working class and should not be their representative." Another letter signed "Abraham Pearl" praised Hillquit for his devotion to the Jewish labor movement and claimed not to know Hillquit's views about "Jewish questions." Pearl contended, "We've heard Barondess, Miller and Cahan but Hillquit hasn't spoken yet. Nevertheless we do not have the right to label Hillquit an assimilationist."[18]

Hillquit indirectly retaliated against the Poale Zion not long after the 1906 election. As a member of the International Bureau of the Second Socialist International, he was asked to intervene in behalf of Zionists who sought entrance into the Socialist International. Hillquit informed the Bureau, by letter, that "the 'Zionist Socialists' do not represent a separate group or part of the international socialist movement." He described them as a group scattered all over the world who are social democrats "except that they happen to hold some additional nationalistic views on the Jewish question." Hillquit concluded his comments by advising:

> Those of them who really are socialists, are also members of the regular socialist parties in the countries in which they reside and are represented in our congresses through such parties; those of them who are only 'Zionist' socialists are not entitled to special representation in our congresses. The representation at the International Congresses is by nations, not by creeds or special views, and if 'Zionist Socialists' as such are admitted, the 'Christian Socialists,' the 'Revisionist Socialists' and the 'Spiritualist Socialists' may claim special representation. . . .[19]

On November 3, 1906, the Socialist paper the *Worker* predicted, on the basis of a house-to-house canvass, that Hillquit's vote would almost double that of Goldfogle. Charles Adler, the Republican candidate, was not considered a threat. In the same issue, a front-page article in Hillquit's behalf, written by the New York Socialist gubernatorial candidate Ben Hanford appealed overdramatically to Jewish sympathies and Jewish fears."A vote for Adler or Goldfogle," wrote Hanford, "is a vote for the Tsar of Russia. It is worse. It is a vote for a Russianized America." Hanford predicted "Kishneff's yet to come to America" and he portrayed Hillquit as a future congressman who "will represent the starving and striving . . . just as truly as though he were in Russia making bombs and earning his glorious way to Siberia or to a hero's grave. . . ."[20]

Hillquit lost the election to Goldfogle. The New York *Times* published results showing Goldfogle with 7,265, Adler with 2,733, and Hillquit with 3,616 votes.[21] Hillquit did not attribute his defeat to the lack of appeal of his socialist position or to his failure to touch the "ethnic" nerve of the Jewish voters. He explained his loss by the fact that Goldfogle ran on two tickets, the Democratic Party and Hearst's Independent League. "That meant," Hillquit wrote, "that under the form of ballot in use every straight vote marked for the Independent League, headed by William R. Hearst for Governor, would also count for Goldfogle."[22] The New York Socialist Party claimed that this was illegal but the New York Court of Appeals authorized the fusionist tactic. The SLP's *Der arbeter* gloated that "Hillquit was defeated, badly defeated. If the present count is correct Hillquit received many less votes than De Leon's 4,300 ten years ago and even less than Barondess' 3,100 votes two years ago."[23]

Two years later Hillquit ran for Congress again from the Ninth District. The New York Party expressed confidence that he would win.[24] Early predictions not only in the socialist papers but also in the general New York press indicated that his success was highly probable. In late May 1908, the Socialists, with a good deal of help from Hillquit, launched a new daily paper, the New York *Call*. The paper was to become the Party's major voice (in English) in the coming 1908 election.[25] At the inaugural celebration of the paper's birth Hillquit and the Socialist presidential candidate Eugene V. Debs spoke of the importance of the *Call* in the coming election. Hillquit's speech stressed that the paper would express the needs of the workers. "There were many capitalist papers published in English for the capitalist class," he was quoted as saying, "and now there was one speaking for and conducted by the working class."

Through the *Call* the Party prepared to campaign on issues particularly relevant to New York voters. Thus, as early as June 1908, the *Call* covered news about the East Side and specific Jewish concerns. On June 22, the paper, in a front-page article, described the increasing economic misery in the Jewish working-class neighborhoods. Conditions were harder than during the depression of 1893, the paper contended. In the next issue on June 23, the *Call* reported the trial of several Russians convicted of killing 166 Jews during a pogrom. The trial was a farce, the paper said, and the article praised the Jewish self-defense groups in Russia which had resisted the pogromists. Jewish acts of resistance closer to home were also covered by the paper. The lead article on June 1 read: "Meat Strike on East Side: Kosher Butchers Revolt Against Trust's Order of Hoisting Prices." By June 24 the paper informed its readers that "Higher Meat Prices Cause Serious Riots," and on June 25 the headline read: "Meat Riot in Ghetto: Police Use Clubs."[26]

Originally, Hillquit intended the tactical thrust of his 1908 campaign to focus upon exposing the superiority of the socialist position vis-à-vis the Progressive or "reformistic" view. He planned to fight the reformers on their own terms or, rather, in their own style. For this purpose he especially selected J. Phelps Stokes, a millionaire (married to a Jewish, former needle-trades worker) and recent convert to socialism, and Robert Hunter, Stokes's relative and former writer of exposés on municipal corruption. Both men were former Progressives and both were to run as Socialist candidates for East Side Assembly districts included in Hillquit's own congressional territory.[27]

Hillquit was incorrect in anticipating that reform versus socialism would be the central issue of the coming campaign. Instead, by attacking Hillquit's stand on immigration, his opponents made the question of free versus restricted immigration the vortex of a heated controversy which significantly weakened Hillquit's chances of being elected on the lower East Side. Hillquit defended himself against an aggressive opposition through articles in the *Jewish Daily Forward* and the *Call* and by calling special public meetings to explain his stand on immigration. But the complexity of the matter entangled him in sophistry and hairsplitting. What seemed to remain in the minds of many Jewish voters was a general impression that Hillquit was unsympathetic to free immigration.

Hillquit's leading antagonist was Louis Miller of the *Warheit* who had maintained a hostile neutrality toward him in 1906 but now set the tone of the attack. Miller supported the candidacy of the SLP's Daniel De Leon against Hillquit. Although in previous years Miller had tagged De Leon an out-and-out anti-Semite, the *Warheit* editor now claimed he was mistaken. A comparison between De Leon's immigration views and Hillquit's decisively altered Miller's opinion. He concluded that De Leon championed the Jewish proletariat immigrant while "Hillquit as a friend of immigration quota is not an appropriate candidate for a district in which the majority are Jewish immigrants."[28]

The views which Miller and others publicized during the 1908 campaign were the positions on immigration taken by De Leon and Hillquit in their capacity as delegates to the International Socialist Congresses at Amsterdam (1904) and Stuttgart (1907). At the 1904 Amsterdam Congress De Leon, representing the SLP, opposed any resolution on the part of the socialist parties encouraging their governments to restrict immigration. In contrast, Hillquit, representing the SP, joined Verdorat and van Kol of Holland and Thompson of Australia in submitting a resolution broadly implying that they would support their governments' exclusion of "backward races."[29] The congress shelved the issue.

At Stuttgart, three years later, the vast majority of international socialist delegates rejected immigration restriction. The SLP's representative Julius Hammer concurred with the majority. Hillquit represented a minority opinion by proposing a resolution that had been passed by the American Socialist Party's National Executive and adopted by its National Committee. The resolution called on all Socialist parties to educate immigrants in the principles of socialism and trade unionism but at the same time required Socialist parties "to combat with all means at their command the willful importation of cheap foreign labor calculated to destroy labor organizations, to lower the standard of living of the working class, and to retard the ultimate realization of Socialism."[30]

Hillquit, who might well have authored this resolution originally, believed that restrictive legislation expressed the practical needs of organized labor in the United States. He tried to stay clear of racial implications but he did not succeed. In fact, his speech to the International Congress exposed him and the American Party to public censure for their prejudices against Asians. Nina Hillquit recorded (perhaps with less than perfect accuracy) her father's words at Stuttgart. Hillquit informed the congress that "the problem of emigration and immigration is complex and serious" and that the American resolution attempted to be "realistic" and not prejudicial. He drew distinctions between several kinds of emigration. "Natural emigration," he said, "claims our full support." But another kind of immigration "is only an importation by the capitalist of foreign workers. The capitalists import workers, who work cheaper, and who thus involuntarily become strike breakers to make disastrous competition to the native worker." Hillquit opposed such immigration and especially attacked the Chinese and Japanese workers. "None of us are prejudiced against the Chinese," he said, "but we must declare with sorrow that they are altogether unorganizable." Kato, the delegate from the Japanese Socialist Party, attacked Hillquit's statement by stating, "It seems to me that race plays an important part here and that the Americans let themselves be guided by the famous phantom of the yellow peril."[31]

Although at Stuttgart Hillquit made a special speech conceding to the non-restriction resolution adopted by the majority of the International, he later wrote the International Socialist Bureau that the National Executive of the American Socialist Party was "unprepared to dispose definitely of the problem of the exclusion of Asiatics, and postpones its decision. . . ." Furthermore, "we must bear in mind that the resolutions of the international congresses are only theoretical guides and that they were never intended to be binding on the tactical and practical work of the affiliated parties."[32]

In the American Socialist press Hillquit presented himself as the mediator between two so-called extremes within the Party: the right, represented by Victor Berger and the AFL-influenced trade unionists who wanted restriction of all labor immigration, and an amorphous left who wanted absolutely free immigration as defined by the majority Stuttgart resolution. Hillquit criticized what he believed were the shortcomings of these "extremes." He attacked Berger's racism. "Comrade Berger," he noted sarcastically, "takes a stand which the most conservative pure and simple unionists reject as too conservative. His objects are. . .not solely for economic reasons, but frankly on grounds of race antagonism."[33] He criticized the leftist opponents of any immigration restrictions because he thought free immigration was not practical in light of both American economic "realities" and the expressed demands of organized labor.

Many East Side Jewish socialists were unimpressed with Hillquit's self-defined "moderate" position on immigration. They did not view any form of restriction as being a compromise between extremes. Rather like Louis Boudin, one of Hillquit's most adamant opponents within the Party, most Jews objected to Hillquit's resolution because it attempted "to establish the principle of dividing immigrants along racial lines into 'organizable and unorganizable' and to lay down as a rule of socialist policy, based on such a principle of division, the demand for the exclusion of the so-called 'unorganizable races.'"[34]

The Bundist Gornberg expressed the Jewish opposition even more strongly. In his pamphlet *Emigratzia un immigratzia*, Gornberg wrote that Hillquit's division between workers with pure consciousness and those without consciousness "cut him like a knife." It revealed that Hillquit was truly unacquainted with the actual plight of immigrant workers. Astutely, Gornberg suggested that Hillquit's resolution at Stuttgart placed the blame for economic competition on the worker. "Instead of seeking ways to combat those who import immigrants, the resolution unleashes anger at those who are oppressed," noted Gornberg. Hillquit might believe he is acting in a practical way but, according to the Bundist, "this dry practicality. . .which does not think ahead to the future is characteristic of small-hearted trade unionism."[35]

During the congressional election of 1908, the non-socialist Jewish press also attacked Hillquit for his stand at Stuttgart. The *Tageblatt* which supported the Republican slate wrote that "Hillquit is an opponent of immigration; knowing that immigration is the only solution for hundreds and thousands of Russian, Rumanian and Galician Jews, it is therefore positive that every Jewish vote for Hillquit is a direct vote against Jewish interests." Furthermore, in a tone which was to become more shrill in 1917, the *Tageblatt* warned the Jewish voters of the East Side that a Socialist in Congress represented a threat to the security of the Jews in America.[36]

In his general campaign speeches Hillquit tended to minimize the immigrant issue. On September 12, 1908, speaking at the opening rally of the campaign, Hillquit suggested that the question of Asiatic exclusion was only of remote interest to the workers of the Ninth District. The ethnic interests Hillquit wanted to stress in the campaign were those which the Jewish working class shared with other American workers. He wanted the Jewish worker to shed a sense of nonbelonging and of peculiar separatism. He urged their identification with and participation in American politics. The Jewish immigrant, he told his audience, had no reason to feel inferior to other citizens or to ask less of society than other oppresed workers. He reassured his audience that

> the interests of the workingmen of the Ninth Congressional District are, therefore, entirely identical with those of the workingmen of the rest of the country, and if elected to Congress I will not consider myself the special representative of the alleged special interests of this district, but the representative of the Socialist Party and the interests of the working class of the country as understood and interpreted by my party.[37]

Although by mid-October Stokes wrote to a friend in Chicago that "we are having a splended campaign in New York and the outlook is exceedingly encouraging,"[38] and although Debs, the Party's presidential candidate, made a special visit to the East Side just before the election, Hillquit lost again to the incumbent Democrat Goldfogle. But Hillquit's 21.23 percent of the vote was considerably higher than other Socialist candidates of the district. For example, in the Ninth district De Leon polled only a meager 1.29 percent and Debs's vote in the district was only 13.56 percent. Hillquit's vote also compared favorably with the Socialist candidates for the Assembly since William Mailly in the Second Assembly District received 9.09 percent of the vote, Max Pine in the Fourth received 11.56 percent, Robert Hunter in the Sixth received 12.93, and J. Phelps Stokes in the Eighth received 19.78.[39] Hillquit never again ran for Congress in the Ninth District.

Notes

1. Epstein, *Jewish Labor* 1, p. 233.

2. Arthur Goren, "A Portrait of Ethnic Politics: The Socialists and the 1908 and 1910 Congressional Elections on the East Side," *Publication of the American Jewish Historical Society* 50 (March 1961), pp. 202-38, discusses the particular Jewish political climate that affected Hillquit's campaign.

3. New York *Times*, October 19, 1906.

4. Hertz, *Geshichte*, p. 92. See Hillquit's speech in *Proceedings of the National Convention of the Socialist Party* (Chicago, 1904), p. 282.

5. Three articles in Yiddish that praise Hillquit's cultural scope are A. Liessin, "Oif frishen kayver fun Morris Hillquit," *Zukunft* 38 (November 1933), p. 622; L. Fogelman, "Morris Hillquit," *Veker*, October 13, 1934, and N. Chanin, "Morris Hillquit," ibid., October 15, 1943.

6. Congressional campaign speech, September 25, 1906, Writings, Hillquit Papers.

7. Ibid.

8. Brooklyn, New York *Citizen*, August 1906, Clippings, ibid.

9. *Loose Leaves*, p. 109.

10. For a Progressive's view of the East Side see, for example, Burton J. Hendrich, "The Jewish Invasion of America," *McClure's Magazine* 40 (March 1913), pp. 125-65.

11. Morris Hillquit, "Letter of Acceptance by Morris Hillquit of the Socialist Party Nomination for Congress, 9th District, New York," October 1906, Writings, Hillquit Papers. Also published in the New York *Worker*, October 13, 1906.

12. Letter from Max Hayes to Morris Hillquit, February 4, 1905, Correspondence, Hillquit Papers.

13. Morris Hillquit, "Letter of Acceptance," Writings, ibid.

14. New York *Times*, October 10, 1906, Clippings, ibid.

15. New York *Der arbeter*, "Di sotzialist partey," November 3, 1906.

16. New York *Warheit*, October 10, 1906.

17. Ibid., September 18, 1906.

18. New York *Yidisher kaempher*, October 26 and November 2, 1906.

19. Morris Hillquit, "To the members of the International Socialist Bureau," ca. October 1908, Correspondence, Hillquit Papers.

20. New York *Worker*, November 3, 1906.

21. New York *Times*, November 8, 1906, and New York *Worker*, November 10, 1906. Also see Moses Rischin, *The Promised City*. Table 7 from *City Record Official Canvass of the County of New York* cites Hillquit (3,586), Goldfogle (7,276), and Adler (2,734).

22. *Loose Leaves*, pp. 114-15.

23. New York, *Der arbeter*, November 10, 1906.

24. New York *Call*, August 27, 1908.

25. New York *Sun*, May 29, 1908, Clippings, Hillquit Papers.

26. New York *Call*, June 1, June 22, June 23, June 1, June 24, and June 25, 1908.

27. Letter from J. Phelps Stokes to Samuel Kramer, July 24, 1908, box 25, Socialist Party 1904-1916, J. Phelps Stokes Papers, Columbia University.

28. New York *Warheit*, October 24, 1908.

29. Kipnis, *American Socialist Movement*, p. 277.

30. Ibid.

31. Nina Hillquit, "Research Notes: Stuttgart, 1907," n.d., Writings, Hillquit Papers.

32. Morris Hillquit, "To members of the International Socialist Bureau," ca. October 1908, Correspondence, ibid.

33. New York *Worker*, November 9, 1908.

34. Louis Boudin, "Immigration at Stuttgart," *International Socialist Review* 8 (February 1908), p. 491.

35. Boris Frumkin (B. Gornberg, pseud.), *Emigratzia un imigratzia: a bericht dem internatzionalen sotzialistishen congres* (Vilna, 1907), pp. 54-55. Pamphlet is in the Bund Archives, New York City.

36. New York *Tageblatt*, October 23, 1908. Also see New York *Warheit* for Hillquit's so-called un-American actions.

37. New York *Call*, September 12, 1908.

38. Letter from J. G. Stokes to Ellen Gates Starr, October 17, 1908, Stokes Papers, Columbia University.

39. *Official Canvass of the Vote Cast in the County of New York, The City Record, Board of the City Record, City of New York*, December 31, 1908, p. 158.

Chapter 10
Conflicts with the Left Wing

After his unsuccessful try for Congress in 1908, Hillquit turned his attention to national Socialist Party affairs, and to the issue of trade union development in particular. This brought him into conflict with the Party's growing left wing. Hillquit rose to national notoriety within the Party as the polemicist against the left. The factional quarrel did not bring out his best qualities; rather, it brought into play his didacticism and manipulative nature. His leadership fanned the fires of Party disagreement and although he was not alone in causing the break in 1913 with an important segment of its left wing, he certainly made a major contribution toward this unfortunate rupture.

When the Socialist Party was originally founded, its left wing was still undefined. From 1901 until 1905 a left-wing position was mainly a matter of holding a more or less militant view of trade unionism, perhaps doubting the efficacy of strictly political socialism or even just being skeptical of the need for immediate demands as part of the Party's platform. After 1905, with the formation of the IWW, being left wing in the Party came to include support for the Wobblies and, generally, the left took a clearer form. The left wing, in fact, became the critic of national Party leadership and its strong political orientation.

Hillquit's attitudes seriously clashed with the IWW's and hence the left on at least four major points. First, the Wobblies wanted to organize industrywide unions for skilled and unskilled workers and in this way challenge the trade union leadership of the AFL. Hillquit, whose experience with New York unions before the rise of a strong International Ladies Garment Workers' Union in 1909 taught him that unionization even among the skilled in America was unstable, thought the industrial union issue was bogus. He feared it would further alienate the AFL, which he was anxious to please. Second, the IWW encouraged strikes and discouraged arbitration. After 1909 Hillquit, in contrast, became the apostle of collective bargaining in the garment industry (see Chapter 16). Third, the IWW advocated a syndicalist philosophy in which the trade union was to play a central role in the organization of socialism. Hillquit had no faith in trade union-political synthesis. He believed in the separation of union and party. He envisioned the future of socialism through an active political party. Fourth, the IWW's "tone" was militant and its rhetoric included concepts of violence which antagonized Hillquit who hoped to convince Americans that radical ideas were "respectable."

After 1909 Hillquit's personal position in the New York Party was challenged by a growing left wing. This contributed to his hostility to the IWW and left-wing causes. For example, within the New York State Party Henry Slobodin, an essential member of the Hillquit faction who in 1899 had left the SLP, now supported the IWW and publically criticized the national leadership. Louis Boudin, who had always been Hillquit's adversary, became more outspoken in his opposition. Left-wing sections of the Socialist Party began to form in New York.

Furthermore, the trade union situation in New York tended to give rise to left-wing discontent. In 1910 at the conclusion of the great cloakmakers' strike, the leaders of the ILGWU signed the Protocol of Peace which created a collective-bargaining system in the garment industry but also prohibited the workers from striking. There was a considerable reaction against the Protocol by militant leaders of particular unions, many of whom were also socialists. Thus Hillquit, who was the lawyer for the ILGWU and liaison between the Party and the garment unions, found himself in the untenable position of being a socialist leader defending nonmilitant tactics, that is, the Protocol, against an increasingly dissatisfied, radicalized, and militant labor force. Perhaps he defended himself by attacking the IWW and thus the left in general.

Between 1905 and 1909 Hillquit was not openly critical of the IWW. He wanted to remain on good terms with Eugene Debs, the Party's charismatic leader and presidential candidate, who stood ideologically to the left of Hillquit and who was one of the founders of the IWW. Hillquit wanted Debs's support for his own political campaigns in New York and thus he aggressively courted Debs's good will. Debs appeared to have been a bit wary of Hillquit but nonetheless tried to reciprocate offers of friendship. For example, in December 1904 Hillquit sent Debs an article from a Dutch socialist paper which linked the two men ideologically. Debs's response revealed something of their relationship at the time:

> There was time, I confess, when I did not like Morris Hillquit. I did not know him. I know him now and am trying to make up for past remises. So it is with joy and pride as well that I find myself touching shoulders with you in the booklet as we are in fact on the field of battle to remain so until we fall in the fight or the field is won.[1]

Debs openly supported Hillquit's candidacy in 1906 and in 1908. After 1908 Debs also opposed the IWW on the grounds that its tactics involved "stealth, intrigue and necessitate individual acts of violence for their execution."[2] Debs's rejection of the IWW in 1908 seemed to have given Hillquit more freedom to criticize the organization.

Moreover, before 1908 Hillquit still defended the IWW when "radicalism" was attacked from the right, that is, the government and the press. In fact he vigorously protested the unlawful treatment meted out to three left-wing Western Federation of Miners (IWW-affiliated) officials Moyer, Haywood, and Pettibone. These men were accused of setting a booby trap for Frank Steunenberg, former governor of Idaho who had been elected with the support of the WFM but had supported the mine operators when in office. Early in 1906 the three men, who had been jailed on a murder charge in Denver, were "kidnapped" and moved to Idaho. It was a clear case of illegal action on the part of the government. Eventually Moyer, Haywood, and Pettibone were acquitted through the efforts of their lawyer, Clarence Darrow.[3]

Although Hillquit did not approve of the WFM or the general

tone of violence which surrounded the entire case, he actively supported the defendants. At a lecture delivered at the Rand School on March 22, 1908, Hillquit speculated that the Haywood case would "shake the American workingman in his unperturbable complacency and . . . make him think." He optimistically predicted that this illegal action "connived at and approved by all the capitalist powers of the country, including the press, the courts and chief magistrates of the nation" would "for the first time in history arouse . . . the conservative American trade unions to an acute realization of the class struggle . . . .[4]

The trial in Idaho took place in May of 1907. Many important politicians including President Theodore Roosevelt commented on the proceedings. In fact, Roosevelt charged that the men on trial and Debs were unwelcome citizens whose violent provocations resulted in bloodshed. Hillquit attacked Roosevelt. At a speech he delivered at the Grand Central Palace on May 4, 1907, Hillquit, the chairman of the meeting, told a large and excited audience that "to us, Mr. Roosevelt, it is not Moyer, Haywood and Debs, who are the unwelcome citizens, but it is those who extorted the enormous fortune for themselves from the toil of millions of persons. Those who in the course of business, annually silently witness an army of 500,000 workers wounded, maimed and murdered."[5]

Hillquit's militant tone surprised some of his New York followers. John Spargo, who shared the platform with Hillquit that May evening at the Palace, expressed shock and dismay at this old friend's impassioned attack on the President and the system. Spargo claimed the AFL unionists attended the meeting in order to hear Hillquit mildly denounce the government's illegal actions. Instead they were subjected to Hillquit's "calculated diatribe." Spargo remembered that Hillquit spoke on the program just after him. "He began," said Spargo, "by turning on me like a wild cat. 'I profess we're not here to demand a fair trial for these men, we're here to protest that they are innocent victims of a blood-thirsty oppressive regime' . . . .[6] It is interesting to note that in July 1907, soon after the Idaho trial, Hermon F. Titus, leader of the Party's left wing in the state of Washington, thought Hillquit was the one revolutionary member of the National Executive Committee.[7]

After Haywood was acquitted, he became a popular figure in the

Party, traveling to various cities expounding the IWW cause. He was invited to speak at mass meetings in New York. Spargo hated him. "I doubt," Spargo told an interviewer in the 1950s, "if I ever took such an instinctive dislike to a man as I took to Haywood. I would have staked my life, almost, on my judgement that he was a sinister, ugly, anti-social brute.....I said as much to Hillquit...."[8]

Hillquit began to criticize Haywood and the IWW openly in 1909. His active rejection of the IWW coincided directly with the rising militancy of the New York garment workers who between 1909 and 1910 carried through a set of successful strikes which brought the labor movement to life. Hillquit became one of the negotiators in the arbitration process which established the Protocol of Peace, the collective-bargaining mechanism designed to provide a so-called equal voice for labor and management although it deprived the workers of their right to strike. His interest in keeping industrial peace played an important part in his opposition to the IWW.

Thus in his new 1909 edition of the *History of Socialism in the United States,* he included a special negative evaluation of the IWW and stressed its violent and anarchical ideology.[9] In May 1910 at the Socialist Party National Congress Hillquit voiced his criticism of the IWW to the entire party. Referring to the IWW he said, "It is a grave mistake for our party or party members as such to attempt to direct the internal affairs of the economic organizations of labor from outside." And he thought that "the formation of new economic organizations of labor will not reform the existing labor movement, and the participation of Socialists in such enterprises will only serve to injure our cause in the eyes of organized labor. The histories of the Socialist Trade and Labor Alliance and the IWW are equal proof of the truth of this assertion."[10] After making these statements, Hillquit confidently wrote his wife that "there have been no wild outbreaks of any kind, although Mother Jones and Haywood are very busy lobbying for something and the rumor is that Debs will appear at the psychological moment and save the revolutionists."[11]

After the 1910 congress two new factors contributed to an intensification of Hillquit's opposition to the left wing within the

Party. First, the left seem to be gaining certain advantages in intraparty politics; second, the Party had several electoral successes which reopened the issue of socialist involvement in establishment politics. Within the Party, Haywood was one of the eight candidates elected to serve on the American delegation to the Socialist International Congress. Hillquit, who was also elected to the delegation, received fewer votes than Haywood.[12] And even more significant victory for the Party's left wing was the ouster of J. Mahlon Barnes as national executive secretary. Barnes, a definitely right-wing socialist, was a staunch defender of the AFL and one of Hillquit's closest friends. He was charged with inefficiency, misuse of party funds, drunkenness, and sexual promiscuity. Barnes resigned in August 1911.[13]

Pressure to attack Haywood and the Party's left wing came from right-wing "municipal"-oriented socialists who feared that the IWW leader's aggressive speeches and the militant strikes and free speech demonstrations of the IWW endangered the respectable and lawful image of the Party. After all, in the spring of 1910 the Milwaukee organization won the municipal elections and Berger was elected to Congress. In 1911 George Lunn won the mayoralty election in Schenectady, New York, and he appointed Hillquit as special advisor to the administration. The right-wingers did not want to be associated in the public mind with the IWW. Writing to Hillquit on December 21, 1910, Robert Hunter said, "I recognize that Haywood has a perfect right as a union man to speak exactly as he feels on the question of industrial organization, but apparently there is a considerable confusion in the public mind as to whether he was speaking the view of the Socialist Party."[14]

In 1911 Hillquit fully emerged as the Party's champion of the gradualist, lawful socialist position and as the adversary of "IWWism." In September 1911 he defended "political action" against the accusations of Charles Edward Russell. The former New York Socialist gubernatorial candidate assumed an IWW, left-wing stance in the *International Socialist Review* by attacking office hunting and by claiming that socialists were compromising revolutionary idealism by metamorphosizing the radical movement into a "Political Party." "I do believe in political action," he wrote, "but I don't believe in compromise, truckling, trading, thimblerigging, dealing, ducking and dodging." Hillquit replied to Russell and to the supporters of the left wing in the Chicago *Socialist* on September 26, 1911, by saying that there had "sprung up of late . . . a tendency to deprecate political action, trade union propaganda and every kind of constructive work, and to preach instead syndicalism, sabotage and 'direct action' whatever these phrases mean. . . ." He thought that this policy was "the greatest menace to the Socialist movement in America today." But he felt assured that "our movement has at least reached a stage that no power on earth can check its progress except our own wild folly."[15]

Following the debate with Russell, Hillquit launched his battle against this "wild folly." When Haywood accepted the nomination to the NEC in November 1911, Hillquit attacked Haywood's candidacy. Writing to the New York *Call* November 20, 1911, Hillquit charged that Haywood's pamphlet *Industrial Socialism* (1911) favored "illegal" acts to combat the capitalist class. Hillquit argued that "to preach to the workers lawbreaking and violence is ethically unjustifiable and basically suicidal." He said that since America was a political democracy, the minority would have to convert the majority. Furthermore, Hillquit maintained that Socialists ought to expect obedience to working-class laws when the proletariat came to power. If capitalists refuse to obey Socialist laws, then and only then should socialists "fight like tigers" from the barricades. But now, Hillquit warned, the capitalist would misunderstand working-class illegality. "Any indiscreet remark or expression is sure to be quoted against us forever."[16]

Hillquit's admonitions were well received by the right-wing camp, some of whom wrote him personal letters expressing their fears of Haywood.[17] Algernon Lee, the editor of the *Call*, wrote Hillquit on December 12, 1911, that he thought the election to the NEC of "Haywood alone would do so much to encourage the Anarchist elements that I could almost prefer seven plain incompetents to six good men plus Haywood."[18]

Hillquit's arguments against Haywood and for "legal" socialism were parodied by the left wing in the party press. Robert Rivers La Monte, for example, who was a Party-organizer, wrote a lengthy letter to the Chicago *Socialist* on December 11, 1911, satirizing Hillquit's "exhortation to passive law-abiding obedience and submission to 'our betters'." La Monte labeled Hillquit the "Apostle of Passive Obedience" and said that at one time he believed Hillquit to be "a sort of Moses whose mission it was to lead American workers out of the land of bondage." Now La Monte saw Hillquit in another light—as a Father Gapon, the Russian priest who naïvely led the peasants to their death on Bloody Sunday in 1905. La Monte thought it was comical that Hillquit claimed he would advocate force if in the final stage of socialism the ruling class tried to frustrate the workers by preventing socialists from taking office. Hillquit had said, "We will fight like tigers and mount the barricades if need be." Sarcastically, La Monte replied, "I fear the horrid picture of Comrade Morris fighting like a tiger perched up on the top of a barricade will disturb my slumber for many months to come. Let us hope he will not go to such dreadful extremes even to retain control of the national executive committee."[19]

Hillquit could not prevent Haywood's election to the NEC and the left-wing leader joined the committee late in 1911. However, within a few weeks of his election, Hillquit met Haywood in a lively debate held in New York's Cooper Union. Haywood rose to the occasion by advising Hillquit that socialists ought to try "a little sabotage in the right place at the proper time." The IWW leader then attacked Hillquit personally by charging him with abandoning the class struggle when he helped negotiate the garment workers' agreement that eliminated the right to strike. Haywood summarized his position by saying, "Industrial unionism comprehends all that Socialism comprehends, and the industrial union is Socialism with its working clothes on."[20]

In his rebuttal Hillquit confessed that he had no new message but merely took the stand of the Party in the national convention. He advocated the two-arm theory of socialism—politics and trade unionism, separate but equal. "A mere change of structual forms would not revolutionize the American labor movement as claimed by our extreme industrialists,"[21] he said.

The Haywood-Hillquit debate seemed to stimulate intense intraparty discussion on violence, sabotage, anarchy, and political action versus direct action. Louis Boudin, Hillquit's rival as party theoretician, attacked him for condemning "illegal" actions. In a letter to the Chicago *Socialist* on January 10, 1912, Boudin implied that Hillquit was an opportunist "always ready to compromise . . . whenever it was popular or seemed to be popular with the masses of people." Boudin accused Hillquit of misunderstanding Marxism. The Hillquit doctrine, he wrote, equated "law breaking" with ethical immorality. Neither Marx nor any other Marxist accepted such a definition, such a "bourgeois notion of legality." Boudin explained that while Marxism rejected anarchism, a Marxist did not dismiss the possibility of direct action nor did a Marxist oppose violence on principle—on so-called ethical grounds.[22]

Karl Kautsky, perhaps the most eminent German Marxist of this period, came to Hillquit's defense. "Kautsky," said the Chicago *Socialist* headline, "Says Hillquit Takes Right Position." The Chicago paper reprinted a letter Kautsky had sent to the New York *Volkszeitung* dated December 15, 1911. Kautsky argued first that the proletarian masses ought not to jeopardize the legal rights won in combat with the capitalists. Illegal and lawless practices were suitable only when legal rights did not exist. Second, the German theorist contended that "to preach the individual struggle against property means to turn the interest of the workers from mass action to individual action . . . to turn the interest from effective to the ineffective form of action." Kautsky relegated individual acts of violence to the domain of the *lumpenproletariat*, the slum proletariat, whose aim, he said, "is not the changing of the property laws, but the possession of the property of others." He warned that the capitalists have every reason to encourage individual action against property and life "because through this, they can hurt the cause of the working masses." Kautsky's paternalistic advice to the American comrades was to reject misguided socialists "no matter how worthy and unselfish the comrades may be who, through their love for the proletariat and their impatience, let themselves be carried away . . . ."[23]

Through the first half of 1912 the factional quarrel gained momentum and bitterness. By spring the ideological differences between the left and the right, which might have been resolved through discussion and compromise, were now complicated by the fact that both sides believed they had "real interests" to protect. The left wing and the IWW wanted to stand solidly behind the 1912 militant Lawrence, Massachusetts, texile strikes and the California

Free Speech demonstrations where workers and demonstrators were the recipients and not the cause of police and court violence. Although the IWW did not advocate violence and although their definition of sabotage was essentially one of passive resistance, nonetheless, on principle, the left refused to temper its use of violent rhetoric. They might have felt that even a verbal retreat meant a compromise or an abandonment of IWW support for the Lawrence and San Diego workers.

However the right wing considered the militant tone of the left as a threat to its interest in creating a political party and in "getting along" with the AFL unions. Hillquit's singular history as well as his present position in the Party made him especially adamant in wishing to curtail the left's influence in the Party and its visibility in general. Furthermore, he had expended a great deal of energy and risked his ego within the Party in his vigorous opposition to the IWW.

Hillquit's aggressive attack against the left wing continued in May 1912 at the Party's National Convention in Indianapolis. As chairman of the Committee on Constitution he more than likely authored the amendment to the Party's Article II, Section 6, which provided for the expulsion from the Party of "any member of the party who opposes political action or advocates crime, sabotage, or other methods of violence as a weapon of the working class to aid in its emancipation. . . ."[24] He voiced his justification for this anti-sabotage amendment by reassuring the convention that "if there is one thing in this country that can now check or disrupt the Socialist movement, it is not the capitalist class; it is not the Catholic Church; it is our own injudicious friends from within."[25] The amendment passed 191 to 90. The New York delegates voted 20 to 3 in favor of the amendment. Hillquit, it appeared, had outmaneuvered the left.

The anti-sabotage amendment was a pyhrric victory. In fact, it was a destructive force which set into motion a series of future negative and retaliatory acts which resulted in the first major split in the Socialist Party. Hillquit played a decisive role in initiating and then sustaining this rupture. He remained righteously defensive about his part in the affair but his body expressed his tensions. In

September 1912 he had his first tuberculosis breakdown and spent from March 1913 to May 1914 on the island of Bermuda recuperating.

After the May 1912 convention the left wing of the Party was well aware that they had been outmaneuvered on the "sabotage" amendment. Consequently, the left sought an issue by which to discredit the national leadership. This issue that was discovered was the appointment of J. Mahlon Barnes (the previously deposed national secretary) as national campaign manager for the coming 1912 campaign which was to run Debs as a presidential candidate and Emil Seidel, a midwestern socialist, as vice president.

Early in July the *International Socialist Review* published an article, "Shall Bossism Prevail in the Socialist Party," which charged Hillquit with falsely crediting the nomination of Barnes at the convention to the NEC and the Committee on Constitution while, in truth, the nomination came solely from him. "The issue," the left-wing paper asserted, "is Hillquitism."[26] At the same time a statement, "To the Reds," was circulated within the party. It read:

> The question is: Are we going to stand for bossism and paternalism in the Socialist Party?. . .Remember, the issue is not Barnes' personality or character or conduct. The issue is HILLQUITISM, which has already gone far enough. No true socialist can stand for the METHODS by which Barnes was elected.[27]

A special meeting of the executive and campaign committees took place on June 16, 1912, to discuss Barnes's appointment.[28] Debs, usually absent at inner-party conventions and meetings, attended this one and asked for Barnes's resignation. In the heated quarrel which ensued Hillquit and Spargo declared "that all those who protested against Barnes were not Socialists at all and the quicker the party was rid of them the better for the party."[29] Debs responded by telling the committee of the number of protest he had received against Barnes's selection and concluded his argument by saying, "And these are all good comrades, as good Socialists as Comrade Spargo." Hillquit retorted, "No, they are not, Comrade Debs."[30] Following this meeting, Debs published a "Statement of

Presidential Candidate to the Members of the Socialist Party" in the *Appeal to Reason* in which he clearly stated his opposition to Barnes and Hillquit.[31]

Hillquit vigorously tried to exonerate himself of the charges leveled at him. In a lengthy article, "In Self Defense," he claimed that he had acted legitimately and not on his own. He reaffirmed his confidence in Barnes by stating that "the convention elected Barnes because it had a well-founded faith in his ability . . . and because it had a healthy contempt for the unholy combination of preachers, soreheads and impossibilitists which hounded him out of office." He defended himself against the accusation of "Bossism." "I have no powerful financial backing behind me," he wrote. "Whatever little influence I may have gained in the Socialist movement, I have gained through service."[32]

The Barnes case continued to be a bone of contention. Throughout August the Party papers raged with factional strife.[33] Many socialists felt that the case disrupted the election campaign. Finally in October the Party membership voted 19,000 to 11,500 to continue Barnes's appointment through the campaign.[34]

Somehow Barnes's "vindication" did not satisfy Hillquit. He had become personally embroiled in this struggle beyond his usual mediational role. His quarrel with Debs was especially bitter and he felt misunderstood by the western socialists in particular.[35] One can sense this frustration in a letter he wrote to the *Appeal's* editor Fred Warren who had refused to print his rebuttal to Debs's charges and who accused him of fraud and treachery. Hillquit wrote:

> But I want to remind you Comrade Warren, that you and the *Appeal to Reason* have no monopoly of sincere devotion to the cause. I too have been working for the spread of socialism in an humble way but with sincere devotion . . . . The high ground which you take in your letter and in your recent articles . . . are pure cant. Our devotion to Socialism does not free us from the obligations of common decency.[36]

In September 1912 Hillquit became ill. Job Harriman, a fellow sufferer, invited him to recuperate in California. "I certainly am surprised to know that the physicians think your lungs are affected," wrote Harriman, "and inasmuch as you have six months' vacation, I want you to arrange to come out here. . . . Now do not say no. I know what it is to be sick. I know what you did for me when I was sick. . . ."[37]

Hillquit did not accept his friend's invitation. Instead he remained in New York, took a trip to Atlantic City, New Jersey,[38] and seemed to wait, moment to moment, for improvement. However, he continued to be weak and with the coming of winter he traveled to Bermuda. Poignantly, he wrote to his wife: "Somehow I have the impression that this year marks the dividing line in our lives. Within the first score of years of our married lives we have managed to crowd in an incredible multitude of suffering and misfortune." The letter was dated "Christmas 1912" and it ended with the following wish: "Let us see how much happiness and sunshine we can enjoy during the remaining span of life. Let us try hard, Verish."[39]

His illness forced Hillquit to leave the limelight in the intraparty quarrels. But he did this reluctantly. When he was elected to the National Committee in 1913 he accepted and planned to return to active party work by the next convention in May.[40] He wrote a series of articles about socialism in debate with the Catholic priest Father John Ryan which appeared in *Everybody's Magazine*.[41] Letters from Algernon Lee to Hillquit in Bermuda reveal that the *Call* editor tried to keep him in touch with party issues.[42] These letters indicate that Hillquit could not have masterminded the next and the last right-wing attack against the IWW left wing of the Party, the expulsion of William Haywood from the NEC.

On December 3, 1912, a left-wing branch of the New York Socialist Party sponsored a victory rally for two IWW leaders, Ettor and Giovannitti, both of whom had been acquitted of charges of provoking violence in the Lawrence strike. Haywood spoke at the meeting and remarked, "Well, direct action is the shortest way home. It is the surest way, particularly for the women and children, the black man and especially for the disenfranchised American workingman. . . . And I believe in sabotage, that much misunderstood word."[43] Two days after this Harlem Casino speech the Executive Committee of Local New York decided to prefer charges against Haywood for his advocacy of "sabotage."[44] Within two weeks the New York State Committee had voted, 31 to 4, to inaugurate a national referendum to recall Haywood from the NEC.[45] On January 22, 1913, Algernon Lee wrote Hillquit in Bermuda that "from all I can hear, the vote on the Haywood recall referendum is going very well in this city; and if one may judge by the tone of the State Committee, it will be the same all over the state. . . . Well I hope we shall have done with him."[46] Lee's hopes became reality when in February 1913 Haywood was recalled from the NEC by a national referendum vote of 22,000 to 11,000.[47]

Haywood's expulsion was followed by the exodus from the Party of many IWW-oriented left-wing socialists. Hillquit made no effort to "integrate" those of the left who remained in the Party with the right-wingers. Attending the May 1913 convention, he wrote home to Vera, in a rather smug tone, that "the Reds are in the minority and are quite tame." With some sarcasm he noted that "they are particularly nice to me. They all admire my ponderous physique and ruddy complexion and claim to be glad to see me alive and kicking. I never knew I had so many friends."[48]

Hillquit was not demoralized by the events of 1912-1913. He overcame his bout with tuberculosis. He seemed to have vanquished or silenced his opponents in the Party and he was prepared to continue building a strong American Socialist Party. His optimism for the future fortified him for the next event which shook the Party—World War I.

Notes

1. Letter from Eugene V. Debs to Morris Hillquit, December 31, 1904, Correspondence, Hillquit Papers.

2. Eugene V. Debs, "Sound Socialist Tactics," *International Socialist Review* 12, (February 1912), 8:483.

3. Shannon, *The Socialist Party*, p. 31.

4. Morris Hillquit, "Socialism and Labor Unions," March 1908, Writings, Hillquit Papers.

5. Morris Hillquit, "Speech at the Grand Central Palace for Moyer-Haywood," May 4, 1907, ibid.

6. John Spargo, Oral History Research Project, pp. 132-34.

7. Hermon F. Titus, "Executive Partisanship," Seattle *Socialist*, July 25, 1908.

8. John Spargo, Oral History Research Project, p. 136.

9. *History of Socialism*, pp. 329-32.

10. *Proceedings of the National Congress of the Socialist Party of America of 1910* includes Hillquit's "Propaganda of Socialism" statement, pp. 61-71.

11. Letter from Morris Hillquit to Vera Hillquit, May 16, 1910, Correspondence, Hillquit Papers.

12. *International Socialist Review* 10 (March 1910), p. 855.

13. Shannon, *The Socialist Party*, p. 69.

14. Letter from Robert Hunter to Morris Hillquit, December 21, 1910, Correspondence, Hillquit Papers.

15. "Hillquit and Russell on Political Action," Chicago *Socialist*, September 26, 1911, in Euguene V. Debs Scrapbook, SB 2, vol. 5, p. 31, Tamiment Library.

16. New York *Call*, November 20, 1911.

17. Letter from Robert Hunter to Morris Hillquit, December 10, 1911, Correspondence, Hillquit Papers.

18. Letter from Algernon Lee to Morris Hillquit, December 12, 1911, ibid.

19. "La Monte Replies to Hillquit," Chicago *Socialist*, December 11, 1911, in Eugene V. Debs Scrapbook, SB 2, vol. 6, pp. 20-21, Tamiment Library.

20. Cited in Shannon, *The Socialist Party*, p. 71.

21. Morris Hillquit, "What Shall the Attitude of the SP Be Toward the Economic Organization of the Workers?" Hillquit-Haywood debate, January 11, 1912, Writings, Hillquit Papers.

22. "Boudin Replies to Hillquit," Chicago *Socialist*, January 10, 1912, in Eugene V. Debs Scrapbook, SB 2, vol 6, pp. 42-43, Tamiment Library. This article was written in response to Hillquit's "Karl Marx, Frederick Engels and Wilhelm Liebknecht against Louis Boudin," December 27, 1911, Writings, Hillquit Papers. Throughout November and December 1911 the letters-to-the-editor column of the New York *Call* carried the debate.

23. Letter from Karl Kautsky to the New York *Volkszeitung*, December 13, 1911. Reprinted in the Chicago *Socialist*, January 4, 1912.

24. *Proceedings of the National Convention of the Socialist Party of 1912*, p. 122.

25. Ibid., p. 132.

26. "Shall Bossism Prevail in the Socialist Party?," *International Socialist Review* 13 (July 1912), pp. 77-78.

27. Algernon Lee et al., to New York *Call*, July 2, 1912, Correspondence, Hillquit Papers.

28. "Minutes of the Joint Session of the NEC and Campaign Committee,"

June 16, 1912, *Socialist Party Monthly Bulletin*, July 1912.

29. "Spargo Replies to Debs," Chicago *World*, July 26, 1912, in Eugene V. Debs Scrapbook, SB 2, vol. 8, pp. 1-2, Tamiment Library.

30. Ibid.

31. Eugene V. Debs, "Statement of Presidential Candidates to the Members of the Socialist Party," *Appeal to Reason*, July 20, 1912.

32. Morris Hillquit, "In Self Defense," Morris Hillquit Papers, Tamiment Library.

33. For example, see "John Spargo on the Barnes Case," *National Socialist*, August 10, 1912, in Eugene V. Debs Scrapbook, SB 2, vol. 8, p. 3, Tamiment Library; *Miner's Magazine*, August 15, 1912, p. 7, ibid. Also see letters from Mahlon Barnes to Morris Hillquit, June 27, 1912, and from John Spargo to Morris Hillquit, July 17, 1912, Correspondence, Hillquit Papers.

34. *Socialist Party Monthly Bulletin*, October 1912.

35. Letters from Fred D. Warren to Morris Hillquit, August 1 and August 9, 1912, Correspondence, Hillquit Papers.

36. Letter from Morris Hillquit to Fred D. Warren, August 12, 1912, ibid.

37. Letter from Job Harriman to Morris Hillquit, September 30, 1912, ibid.

38. Letter from Morris Hillquit to Vera Hillquit, October 10, 1912, ibid.

39. Ibid., December 23, 1912.

40. Letter from Algernon Lee to Morris Hillquit, January 22, 1913, ibid.

41. Hillquit corresponded with Father Ryan from Bermuda. See their correspondence in 1913, ibid.

42. Letter from Algernon Lee to Morris Hillquit, April 4, 1913, ibid.

43. "Haywood Causes Surprise," New York *Call*, December 3, 1912.

44. "Minutes of the Executive Committee of Local New York, December 3, 1912," New York *Call*, December, 6, 1912.

45. New York *Call*, December 10, 18, 1912.

46. Letter from Algernon Lee to Morris Hillquit, January 22, 1913, Correspondence, Hillquit Papers.

47. *Socialist Party Monthly Bulletin*, March-April 1913.

48. Letter from Morris Hillquit to Vera Hillquit, May 10, 1913, Correspondence, Hillquit Papers.

Hillquit and the War, 1914-1917

Chapter 11

Like most American socialists, Hillquit was surprised when war broke out in Europe in August 1914. He was shaken especially by the support which the socialist parties of Europe—Germany and France in particular—gave to their countries' war efforts. This support had not been anticipated and it was a reversal of the official international socialist attitude which, at international congresses, rejected capitalist imperialist wars that were precipitated by arms races, military cliques, and the stimulation of nationalism and national prejudice. Although wars of liberation and of national unification were approved by the Second International, the socialists planned to appeal to workers in all countries to use all means at their disposal to prevent war. If capitalist wars were beyond the control of the workers, the socialists urged either that efforts be made to bring them to a quick conclusion or, as the left wing of the International suggested, that the workers use the economic and political crisis to incite public opinion against the capitalist system.[1] However, in 1914, under the pressure of declared war, the majority of European socialists disregarded their own policy.

American socialists were stunned and, at least temporarily, confused by the European defection from a stance of international solidarity. Hillquit was one of the first Party leaders to recover. He was one of the first to make sense of the situation and subsequently to try, perhaps not always with success, to give direction to the Party in relation to the Europeans and to the war itself. The next three years, from the fall of 1914 to the fall of 1917, were to be the most vigorous and creative of his career. He mobilized and utilized his varied and diverse strengths: his knowledge of Marxism, his liaisons with socialists in Europe and middle-class reformers in America, his legal acumen, his trade union connections, and his strong political position in the New York Socialist Party. He used these talents to help hold the American Party together. Perhaps what is even more significant, he used his energies to keep the Party's integrity intact as well as to launch an aggressive antiwar crusade into the midst of American political life. Politically, the war drove Hillquit leftward, although he continued to be a major target for the Party's left wing.

In the first week of August, after war was declared, the German socialists in the Reichstag and the French socialists in the Chamber of Deputies voted in favor of war credits. Emil Vandervelde, the Belgian socialist through whose country the Germans marched, joined a capitalist cabinet and issued an address to the Socialists of Belgium in favor of supporting a war against Germany.[2] As one historian of the Second International aptly put it, "These acts struck a mortal blow to the International. It fell, the first victim of the world war."[3]

Hillquit's almost immediate response to the European socialists' support of their national governments was to try and shield the socialists from negative criticism. Instead of blaming the Europeans for deserting the international cause of solidarity, he portrayed the socialists as victims of those circumstances which were the logical consequences of a developing capitalist system. On September 6, 1914, his article "Socialist View of the War and Why They Failed to Stop It," was likely the first Marxist rationale, stated so definitely, published anywhere in the world. Hillquit wrote that the entire industrial and political development of Europe within the last generation inexorably determined Europe's fate. "The murderous war in Europe is but the inevitable culmination of murderous European capitalism." European capitalists wanted the war to solve their unemployment problem and to pursue their uncontrollable imperialist expansion. The socialist was "powerless to prevent the appalling catastrophe." Socialist and organized workers of Europe were blameless since "they could no more resist the brutal logic of capitalist warfare than they could escape the class war and horrors of the capitalist regime. . . .Reluctantly but irresistibly they were drawn into the insane vortex of mutual slaughter."[4] At a socialist street demonstration on September 21, Hillquit asked his audience to be tolerant of European socialists. "The Socialists are not responsible for this war," he said, and he reminded the audience that socialists had been in the vanguard of the prewar peace movements. Hillquit concluded his speech with the comment, "For the spirit of international Socialist solidarity has not been killed by the war. The International is not dead."[5]

On September 22, 1914, Hillquit was responsible for composing the NEC's appeal, "To the Socialist Workingmen of Warring Countries in Europe." The appeal exonerated "the conduct of our brother-parties in Europe—the victims of a criminally vicious industrial and political system which drives nations into fratricidal war." Although socialists could not prevent the war, Hillquit now called upon them to end it.[6]

Like the majority of American socialists, Hillquit was not quite sure how the Europeans ought to go about settling the war. By September 1914 he no longer thought—as he did in July—that a mass strike would be a practical measure. In fact the only American socialist to suggest that Europeans use the general strike was Hillquit's arch-opponent William Haywood.[7]

Nor did Hillquit think the time was opportune for the American Party to step in as mediator between the European socialist parties. When Walter Landferseik, the Party's national secretary, sent a cable to the socialist parties of ten European countries over the signature of Hillquit, Berger, and himself, asking them to persuade their governments to accept mediation by the United States at a conference in Washington, D.C., Hillquit was irate. On September 21 he wrote Landferseik that "when the time will be ripe for such a gathering, it will certainly have to take place in Europe. . . ."[8]

Even when Camille Huysmans, head of the International Bureau, called a conference for mid-January 1915 in Copenhagen, Hillquit was skeptical of the possibilities of a fruitful socialist conference which included belligerents in the war. Hillquit was not alone. John Spargo wrote to him on November 13 saying that he hoped the proposed "Peace Conference" would not be held. "It would be unrepresentative for certain, and would give a splendid chance for the freaks."[9]

None of the countries at war accepted the invitation to the socialist conference in Copenhagen. Although he was designated as the American Party's sole delegate, Hillquit also declined the invitation on the grounds that even the so-called neutral countries "are somewhat biased in favor of one or the other belligerent countries."[10]

Hillquit suggested in a December letter to the NEC that the American party had a new and special role to play in keeping the International alive. With a strong sense of American patriotism, he wrote that American socialist had no interest in this war. Therefore, when the war ended "somebody will have to initiate the work of resurrecting the shattered International of the workers." Hillquit believed "this great task will logically fall to the Socialists of America, the Socialists of the most important and least concerned nation.[11] In January Hillquit wrote Carl D. Thompson that "our policy...should be watchful waiting." Furthermore, "The best service we can render at this time to our movement and to the international movement is by fostering and encouraging a sane and neutral sentiment among our own members and to remain on the alert for the first opening for mediation among our comrades in Europe."[12]

Early in January 1915 Hillquit affirmed a neutral position by asserting in the *American Socialist* that he was neither pro-Ally nor pro-German. Although the Allies claimed to be fighting for democracy and the Germans for "culture," both sides were hypocritical. "The ghastly carnage in Europe has no redeeming features. It is not a war for democracy, culture or progress. It is not a fight for sentiments or ideals. It is a cold-blooded butchery for advantages or power...." Hillquit hoped neither side would win a decisive victory. Such a victory, he wrote, would "foster a spirit of military overbearing and pseudopatriotic exaltation on the part of the victorious countries, lasting resentment and increased military activity on the part of the defeated nations and a general condition of pan-European irritation with a tendency to another, perhaps even more pernicious war." He hoped for "cessation of hostilities from sheer exhaustion" which would reveal the bankruptcy of capitalism.[13]

Although the vast majority of American socialists agreed with Hillquit on the American Party's neutral stand as well as on his explanation of the general causes of the war, there were individual socialists who were considerably more harsh in their condemnation of their European socialist colleagues than Hillquit. The German party received the greatest amount of opprobrium. "I am sick with utter disappointment over the socialist movement," George Herron, the Christian Socialist, wrote Hillquit from Florence, Italy. "I have had a chance to see the seamy side of German social democracy. . . ."[14]

Hillquit carefully avoided criticizing the German socialists. As a result he was labeled pro-German by "neutral" American socialists who were decidely pro-Ally or by those socialists who now completely disavowed the European socialist movement. For example, in October 1914 the *New Review*, a magazine which expressed the viewpoint of left-wing socialists who had remained in the Party after the Haywood split, condemned Hillquit for what the paper claimed was his defense of the SPD. He was derided for saying that German socialists fought along with German capitalists rather than risk a Russian invasion of their country. He was quoted in the *New Review* as maintaining that German socialists were "as a matter of principle opposed to war, but it was a choice of evils and anything was better than an invasion of Russia."[15] In contradistinction, La Monte of the *New Review* considered the German socialists "craven chauvinists." Their actions during this war confirmed his worst opinions of the prewar SPD. La Monte hoped that the war would free the international socialist movement in the future from "the tyranny of the Prussian doctrinaire disciplinarians." With animosity, La Monte recalled that at Copenhagen in 1910 "the average American delegate" to the International Congress (including Hillquit) "was unable to discover his own thoughts on any subject until he had first found out what the Germans wanted. Then he said 'Amen'."[16]

Hillquit was sensitive to these charges of pro-Germanism from members of his own party. However, in the hope of salvaging what remained of the ideals of international socialism, he thought it best to refuse to declare himself an opponent of the SPD. Writing to the

British Marxist H. M. Hyndman on December 31, 1914, he said, "My sympathies in this war are not pro-German as far as the Social Democracy is concerned." He admitted to Hyndman that there was "legitimate room for discussion as to whether the Socialist members of the Reichstag have been justified on the ground of principle, policy or wisdom to take the stand they did, but I cannot join you or my numerous other friends in the Socialist movement. . .in branding the conduct of the German Socialists 'traitorous'." Hillquit thought the Germans acted in about the same manner as the other socialists in the warring countries and thus should not be singled out as exceptional. Hillquit wanted to look forward to the future. He told the Englishman, "I sincerely hope that whatever the German Socialists do after the war, they will take a firmer stand than ever against their government and purge their own ranks of their weak brethren." However, he wrote, "I am not ready to throw the entire Social Democratic movement of Germany into the scrapheap. I believe that after the war is over and its memories have died out, the International will find itself again and the German Socialists will continue forming part of it."[17]

Hillquit's defense of the Germans, especially the SPD leaders, grew more positive with time. By April 1915 he explained to his Rand School audience that the conduct of the German deputies who voted for war credits was determined not by their own volition but by the will of the majority opinion. He blamed the socialist support of the war on the German workers and Socialist voters who spontaneously supported their country as soon as war was declared. According to Hillquit, the leaders "had no opportunity for mutual consultation. They acted on impulse, which broke through with elemental force. It was not a decision, not a policy—it was history, and history cannot be scolded or praised; it must be understood."[18] This impulse to which Hillquit now referred was nationalism. For the first time in his career as a Marxist theoretician, he took serious cognizance of this sentiment and characterized it as a force powerful enough to divert the course of international socialist solidarity.[19]

By the beginning of 1915, pressure within the Party mounted to have the leadership formulate a specific policy and program toward the war. A. M. Simons, the Chicago socialist, wrote Hillquit in mid-November 1914 that "I think it is time we began to work out some sort of definite policy. The rattleheads and the pseudo-Specialists have all had their say and it is time the party found out where it stood." Simons also was apprehensive lest the American government begin preparations for war—even though the United States had made a declaration of neutrality. "I am of the opinion that we could exercise considerable influence on the final peace policy if we began our agitation now . . . ," Simons wrote. "I am certain that if we do not take action we are going to see a big increase in armaments in this country and much militarism."[20]

With the idea of an early and quick settlement of the war and with the hope of forestalling American commitment to what soon came to be called "preparedness," the NEC, under Hillquit's guidance, developed a substantive war policy which was published in the *American Socialist* on January 9, 1915. The peace program blamed the European capitalists and imperialists for the war and, by implication, affirmed the solidarity of interests of the workers in countries at war. The program included such planks as no indemnities, no annexations without popular consent, an international court to settle disputes and an international league to keep the future peace, internationalization of strategic waters, and neutralization of the seas. The program also called for the extension of democracy through "social changes in all countries to eliminate the economic causes of the war." These were to include socialization of national resources, public utilities, and basic industries; elimination of unearned income; and the immediate and progressive amelioration of conditions of labor. Two other planks were aimed at keeping the United States out of the war. One, written by the 1916 Socialist presidential candidate Allen Benson, called for a constitutional amendment requiring a popular referendum in order to declare future "offensive" wars. The other section asked for a disarmament program which would require freezing armaments at present levels until an international police force had enough power to enforce total disarmament.[21]

The proposal met with criticism from several prominent socialists who wanted to alter its planks before a vote by the National

Committee formally adopted the program. For example, Simons, who later supported American entrance into the war, thought the socialists ought to denounce not only "offensive" but also "defensive" wars.[22]

The left-wing critics of the NEC peace proposal immediately attacked the program as lacking in an adequate economic analysis of the origins of the war and for failing to take a stand for militant opposition to American actions favoring preparedness. Louis Boudin, in the *New Review*, claimed that the NEC's anti-militaristic and antiwar stands were insincere and only another trick by which "our opportunistic leaders and leaderlets" maintain their power over Party decision making.[23] *New Review* writer Louis Fraina also warned against the menace of American militarism. He accused Hillquit of not taking an adequate position against armaments and militarism in the NEC program. In fact he condemned the NEC, especially Berger and Hillquit, for being "in full agreement with the reactionary elements of Bourgeois progressivism."[24]

Although the NEC policy was approved in May 1915,[25] this did not terminate the differences of opinion over the Party's war and preparedness policy which continued to rage. In particular the left wing expressed dismay at the lukewarm opposition offered by the national leaders to growing militaristic sentiment in America. Hillquit was singled out for this failure to oppose preparedness directly. In an April 1915 debate with Massachusetts Congressman A. P. Gardner, who led the fight for increased armaments in Congress, Hillquit had avoided taking a principled stand against preparedness. Instead he argued that the United States did not need to arm since this country was immune from attacks by European or Asian powers.[26]

Hillquit's antiwar leadership also became suspect among left-wingers because of his rejection of one of the most popular planks of the Party's war program—a national referendum of all citizens to be held before a war was declared. He thought this idea, which virtually catapulted its author Allen Benson into the Socialist presidential nomination, "perfectly wild." He wrote Thompson that he thought the referendum idea "would only serve to embarrass the party."[27]

Hillquit continued to express his disdain for war and preparedness. Audaciously, he did this in front of mass audiences composed mainly of workers. He openly criticized Samuel Gompers for jumping on the Wilsonian preparedness bandwagon. In the past Hillquit had consistently objected to Gompers's conservative leadership of the AFL. Their differences on preparedness now evoked the bitterest of quarrels. Gompers refused to attend antiwar demonstrations called by the socialists. He said he objected to Hillquit's pronouncement that there be "peace at any price." He told the press that while he stood for peace, he favored only peace with honor. At a mass meeting against the war, attended by more than two thousand people on June 21, 1915, Hillquit replied to Gompers:

> Let me say that there is no such thing as war with honor and there is no such thing as peace with dishonor. There cannot be such a thing as war with honor as there cannot be murder with honor, pillage with honor, fiendish devastation with honor, arson with honor, or rape with honor.

Furthermore, Hillquit would not modify his position on peace. He wanted it understood that "we are for peace at any price." He said, "It is true of me and it is true of Socialists in general."[28] But only a few weeks later Hillquit made it clear that he was not a pacifist. On July 15 he was quoted as saying, "But I mean peace at any price under the present circumstances. If I had been alive in 1860 and had felt slavery could be abolished only by fighting, I would have fought."[29]

In late December 1915 Hillquit, James Maurer, and Debs were appointed by the NEC to present the Party's antiwar and peace proposal before President Wilson. In his autobiography Hillquit recorded the interview. The President, he wrote, "looked preoccupied and tired" but "as we proceeded with our argument he became interested and animated . . . ." Wilson gave the delegation to understand that he favored US neutrality and that he agreed with the Socialists' peace proposal, especially the platforms of no annexation and no indemnities. Hillquit quoted Wilson as saying, "I am more often accused of being influenced by radical and pacifist elements than by the capitalist or militarist interests."[30]

The war placed Hillquit in a prominent public position. He tried to capitalize on this during the 1916 election. New York socialists were elated that Meyer London had won a seat in Congress from the predominately Jewish lower East Side district. London had run on an antiwar platform. In 1916 Hillquit ran for Congress from the Twentieth Congressional District, a somewhat more prosperous Jewish, Italian, and Irish neighborhood than the lower East Side. Hillquit took a strong antiwar and anti-preparedness stand during this campaign despite pressure brought to bear upon him by prominent Jewish leaders who feared anti-Semitic responses. Hillquit almost won the election and, in fact, the Party claimed he did win by 800 votes but that the Republicans stuffed the ballot boxes.[31]

The left wing of the Party continued to be critical of Hillquit's war position. The future Russian revolutionary, Leon Trotsky, who was living in New York in the spring of 1917, wanted the American Socialist Party at its coming special convention at St. Louis not only to proclaim its opposition to the war but also its support of militant resistance against government policy, even if this involved civil war. The tactics which he advocated, at a meeting on March 4, 1917, at the Lenox Casino in Manhattan, were "to resist all efforts at recruiting, by means of mass demonstrations, street demonstrations and educational propaganda, and by other means in accordance with socialist principles and tactics." Trotsky also recommended "strikes against the mobilization of industry during wartime." Hillquit expressed the majority opinion of this meeting when he recommended that the coming St. Louis convention make "a forthright statement against the war." He also suggested that the socialist stand be taken "strictly on American lines" and be expressed "exclusively in the tradition of American parliamentarianism."[32]

In later years Trotsky recalled this meeting and his impression of Hillquit and the American socialists. The Russian's comment has often been quoted by Hillquit's detractors. Trotsky wrote that American socialists are "simply variants of 'Babbitt' who supplements his commercial activities with dull Sunday meditations on the future of humanity. . . ." Furthermore, he commented that "a Babbitt of Babbitts is Hillquit, the ideal Socialist leader for successful dentists. . . .Hillquit's art lay in keeping Debs on his left flank while he maintained a business friendship with Gompers."[33]

The Socialist Party, which was planned to define the Party's position on America's participation in the war, opened on April 7, 1917, a day after Congress declared war on Germany. Several groups were represented at St. Louis, for example, pacifists, pro-German or pro-Allied elements, right and center-wing antiwar socialists who were cautious when it came to "tactics," and a new leftwing which had been developing since 1914 and which based its main support on an advocacy of militant antiwar tactics. The left-wingers dominated the convention in number and spirit.

As the historian Theodore Draper wrote, "Hillquit outdid himself at St. Louis."[34] Swayed by antiwar feelings and by the strong left-wing tenor of the convention, he opened the first meeting with a rousing keynote addess which pleaded with all Socialists to stand by the Party and construct a plan for the future. "We are the only force in America now with clear vision," he said, "and it remains for us to protect it against the butchery that has deluged Europe with blood." He told the audience, in a radical-sounding tone, that he had "no desire to steer a middle of the road course." The March uprising ". . .was the social revolution that overthrew the Russian autocracy. . . . And soon there will be a revolution in Germany and in Austria-Hungary. A rebellious working-class will end war by social revolution."[35] The assembled delegates wildly cheered Hillquit, who for once seemed to be advocating revolution.

At St. Louis Hillquit willingly collaborated with the left wing of the Party in the formulation of the "Proclamation," the official Party position. Drawn up by Algernon Lee, Charles Ruthenberg, the Cleveland left-winger,[36] and Hillquit, the majority report[37] rejected the concept of "defensive warfare" and stated that those who favored United States entrance in the war were "instigated by the predatory capitalists in America." The Proclamation warned that "American participation would give the powers of reaction in this country the pretext for an attempt to throttle our rights. . . ." The most important part of the Proclamation—and where the left wing revealed its influence—was in the proposed course of action. First, the socialists pledged "unyielding opposition to all proposed legislation for military and industrial conscription" and urged "continuous efforts for the repeal of such laws." Second, the Proclamation proposed "continuous active, and public opposition to the war, through demonstrations, mass petitions. . . ." Third, the socialists urged "vigorous resistance to all reactionary measures such as censorship of press. . .rights of free speech, assemblage and organization, or compulsory arbitration and limitation of the right to strike."[38]

One can interpret Hillquit's unified front with the left wing in at least two ways. Perhaps he hoped to forge a new relationship with a growing power in the Party. Or, as was more commonly contended, he wished to outmaneuver the left. He wanted to make it impossible for the left wing to emerge at the convention as a fully developed independent political force. In the long run, the Proclamation accomplished neither of these tasks.

The most immediate effect of the St. Louis Proclamation was to drive a significant group of pro-war socialists out of the Party. This had been anticipated. Writing in his diary in 1916, Algernon Lee, for example, observed: "It seems that, once a country is involved in a serious war, few of its people, and least of all its intellectuals, can escape the infection of chauvinism."[39] However, the exodus from the Party of pro-war intellectuals was particularly painful for Hillquit since several of them had been close associates and because Hillquit had placed so much hope in forming a Socialist Party of intellectuals. For example, John Spargo was an old friend and one of the important figures in the New York Party. Spargo led the pro-war faction at the St. Louis convention. Later he wrote pamphlets in which he made guarded references to Hillquit as the infamous "spokesman of American Socialism upholding the impudent claims of the guilty Hohenzollern dynasty."[40] Spargo also participated in the American Alliance for Labor and Democracy, an organization formed to counteract the activities of the Hillquit-led antiwar People's Council for Peace and Democracy. Hillquit did not comment publicly on his friend's behavior. However, Spargo said, in an interview in the 1950s, that Hillquit refused to see him or correspond with him after mid-1917.[41]

The pro-war socialists were not alone in criticizing Hillquit and the St. Louis resolution. By June the left wing had regained its balance and began to reject the united front it had formed with the "majority" resolutionists. Hillquit became a target for left-wing dissatisfaction. It was claimed that at St. Louis he had made insincere promises in regard to militant attacks against the war and the draft. Boudin and others accused Hillquit of immediately reverting to a "policy of equivocation," especially in not supporting antidraft measures and mass strikes.[42]

Despite the attacks from pro-war socialists, antiwar left-wingers, and assorted non-socialist patriotic groups, Hillquit pursued an energetic antiwar program. In mid-May of 1917 Algernon Lee, Berger, and Hillquit were chosen by the Party to attend an international socialist meeting at Stockholm. This meeting had been called to discuss issues arising out of the March revolution in Russia. Secretary of State Lansing denied the Socialists passports and characterized the conference as a "cleverly directed German move."[43] Hillquit argued that the Socialists in Stockholm wished to discuss peace demands—that socialists were the harbingers of a peace settlement. Although Samuel Gompers called the conference a piece of "insidious pro-Kaiser propaganda" and former left-wing Socialist leader W. E. Walling characterized the conference as "the most dangerous of all the Kaiser's plots," Hillquit's public advocacy of the conference enhanced the Party's image as peacemaker.[44]

World War I was a turning point in Hillquit's relations with reformers. Before the war he had supported such reform legislation as woman's suffrage and child labor laws, but he had not joined non-socialist organizations with specific political or social goals. He remained faithful to his anti-fusionist position. The war and especially the consequences of the Party's antiwar stand had a strong effect upon him. He was drawn into a more formal alliance with those in the liberal camp who were also fighting America's entrance into the war. Although in 1917 Hillquit did not yet suggest that the Socialists form a coalition with other parties, he, Scott Nearing, and other socialists who opposed the war became active in the pacifist People's Council for Democracy and Peace. Hillquit, in fact, became one of the founders and prime movers of this ill-fated organization.

The People's Council was first organized in May 1917 as a peace movement whose immediate goals were to oppose conscription and the suppression of civil liberties and to encourage a negotiated peace.[45] It drew into temporary alliance reformers, social workers, single-taxers, antiwar Socialists, pacifist intellectuals who had not as yet identified with a political cause, and leaders of unions with large immigrant membership such as the ILGWU, the ACWA, and the United Cloth Hat and Cap Makers Union. The council was dominated by the socialists and, in fact, the very concept of a people's council was in imitation of the Russian Soviet.[46] Although some of the members of the Council, for example, the young rabbi Judah Magnes,[47] took its revolutionary aims seriously, others favored playing them down. Another member of the organizing committee, Gilbert E. Roe, a friend of Progressive Senator Robert M. La Follette, warned that "The People's Council of America should not be patterned too much after the Russian Council.[48] On August 11, 1917, Berger wrote Hillquit that the "People's Council should not expect to equal the Russians' achievement because there the soviets control the unions and the soldiers."[49]

Hillquit thought it inadvisable to press the council leftward. He did not suggest that it adopt a socialist as well as antiwar position. He was content with the enthusiastic response given the antiwar issue and the council by "no less than 284 organizations. . .of these 93 were trade unions, while the rest were local Socialist groups, peace organizations and fraternal societies."[50] He was anxious that the council appeal to as wide a range of people as possible. On June 15, 1917, at the eighth meeting of the organizing committee, he even expressed the opinion that a political program (that is, a specific radical platform) now "would be fatal for the movement." He believed the council ought to enlist all parties of all creeds, some of which might not endorse a political program. His suggestion was that "our chief function should be to influence public sentiment." Gilbert Roe, taking a more aggressive position, replied to Hillquit that "public sentiment would be of little value unless we are to be known as a political force."[51]

The People's Council never became such a force. Its failure was in part due to its inability to attract a large enough following among radicals. But equally important it was harrassed by the hostile propaganda of the AFL-organized American Alliance for Labor Democracy and by the kind of government interference which prevented its constitutent convention from meeting. Hillquit pointed out that although the council continued in existence until the end of the war, government opposition made in impossible to organize an extensive peace movement.[52]

In the summer of 1917 Hillquit began his famous election campaign for mayor of New York. He was able to draw together a remarkably diverse coalition of supporters for his candidacy.[53] The major portion was drawn to him because of his opposition to America's role in the war and his insistence on a speedy and just peace. In addition to Socialist Party members, Hillquit was supported by pacifists and pro-war liberals, some of whom had been "Progressive" reformers in the prewar years. The pacifists campaigned for him through the People's Council. The pro-war liberals, including Amos Pinchot, Dudley Field Malone, and Harry Hopkins, endorsed his campaign as a protest against the government's espionage and sedition policy which was meant to restrict freedom of the press. Pacifists and liberals also agreed with the Socialist demand for peace without annexation and indemnities.[54] Significant among Hillquit's supporters was the organized Jewish labor movement: the *Jewish Daily Forward* and several powerful unions including the ILGWU, an AFL affiliate, and the Amalgamated Clothing Workers, a radical, dissident anti-AFL union. The fact that the unions backed Hillquit was a departure from the general pro-war policy followed by the major portion of organized labor.[55]

Most left-wing socialists supported Hillquit during the 1917 campaign—he was not attacked by them during this period. Afterwards, Ludwig Lore even paid tribute to Hillquit's antiwar militancy in the left-wing *The Class Struggle*. However, Hillquit soon again became a target for left-wing criticism of the Party's policy.[56]

One of Hillquit's most unexpected admirers was the anarchist Emma Goldman. She commented in her autobiography that the "frenzied attacks" on Hillquit by "our common enemies and erstwhile comrades bridged the chasm of the past as well as our theoretic differences." Goldman admitted that "I felt much closer to Hillquit than to many of my own comrades whose social vision had been gassed." She was certain Hillquit's campaign had great antiwar propaganda value. Goldman maintained that Hillquit's campaign presented the only opportunity for people to hear some freedom of speech in a hysteria-crazed country. "As an experienced orator and clever lawyer," she wrote, "Morris Hillquit knew how to steer safely between dangerous patriotic cliffs."[57]

Despite this wide coalition of allies, Hillquit failed to win the New York mayoralty election in 1917. But he did receive 21.7 percent of the New York vote which represented a nearly fivefold increase over the normal Socialist vote. For the first time the New York Socialist Party put seven candidates on the Board of Aldermen. Socialists were also elected to the Assembly and to a municipal judgeship.[58]

The 1917 election represented a high point in Hillquit's career. From the onset of the war until this election, he enhanced the Party's prestige and he helped, at least temporarily, to unify most of its membership around an antiwar position. After the election Hillquit's ability to maintain a cohesive party was diminished by the November Bolshevik Revolution and by the intense persecution of radicals in the United States.

Notes

1. Alexander Trachtenberg, ed., *The American Socialist and the War* (New York, 1917), pp. 47-48, quotes Lenin's position.

2. Patterson (N.J.) *Press,* August 17, 1914, Clippings, Hillquit Papers.

3. Julius Braunthal, *The History of the International,* 2 vols. (New York, 1967), 1:355.

4. Morris Hillquit, "Socialist View of the War and Why They Failed to Stop It," Omaha *News,* September 6, 1914, Clippings, Hillquit Papers.

5. Hillquit's speech at the first demonstration of Socialists against World War I in New York City at the Harlem River Casino on September 21, 1914, Writings, ibid.

6. Morris Hillquit, "To the Socialists and Workingmen of the Warring Countries of Europe," September 22, 1914, ibid.

7. William D. Haywood, "Jaurès and the General Strike against the War," *International Socialist Review* 25 (September 1914).

8. Letter from Morris Hillquit to Walter Landferseik, September 21, 1914, Correspondence, Hillquit Papers.

9. Letter from John Spargo to Morris Hillquit, November 13, 1914, ibid.

10. See letters from Morris Hillquit to Walter Landferseik, November 21,

1914; to the NEC, December 28, 1914, and to Thornwald Stauning, December 28, 1914, ibid.

11. Ibid.

12. Letter from Morris Hillquit to Carl D. Thompson, January 6, 1915, Socialist Party Papers, Duke University.

13. Morris Hillquit, "Socialist Neutrality," *American Socialist*, January 9, 1914, Writings, Hillquit Papers.

14. Letters from George Herron to Morris Hillquit, November 3 and November 9, 1914, Correspondence, ibid.

15. "American Socialists and the War," *New Review* 2 (October 1914), 10:613-19.

16. Robert R. La Monte, "The War: Personal Impressions," ibid., 2 (November 1914), 11:639.

17. Letter from Morris Hillquit to H.M. Hyndman, December 31, 1914, Correspondence, Hillquit Papers.

18. Morris Hillquit, "How the Socialists Met the War," Part 4 in Rand School lecture series "Socialism and the War," March-April 1915, Writings, ibid.

19. See criticism of Hillquit's nationalism in Louis Fraina, "The Future of Socialism," *New Review* 3 (January 1915), 1:16.

20. Letter from A.M. Simons to Morris Hillquit, November 18, 1914, Correspondence, Hillquit Papers.

21. Hillquit claimed to have written the "manifesto." See his *Loose Leaves*, p. 160.

22. Letter from A.M. Simons to C.D. Thompson, January 20, 1915, Socialist Party Papers, Duke University.

23. Louis Boudin, "Let Us Take Ourselves Seriously," *New Review* 3 (January 1915), 1:365.

24. Louis Fraina, "The Menace of an American Militarism," ibid., 3 (March 1915), 3:135.

25. *American Labor Year Book* (1916), pp. 125-26.

26. New York *Call*, April 11, 1915.

27. Letter from Morris Hillquit to C.D. Thompson, January 30, 1915, Socialist Party Papers, Duke University.

28. Gompers was quoted in the Louisville (Ken.) *Post*, June 30, 1915, Clippings, Hillquit Papers.

29. *Outlook*, July 15, 1915, ibid.

30. *Loose Leaves*, p. 161.

31. New York *Call*, November 11, 1916, Clippings, Hillquit Papers. The 1916 campaign is discussed at length in Chapter 13.

32. Louis Waldman, *Labor Lawyer* (New York, 1945), pp. 67-68. Trotsky's position had been worked out by European socialists at a recent conference in Zimmerwald, Switzerland.

33. Cited in Robert Iverson, "Morris Hillquit, American Social Democrat: A Study of the American Left from Haymarket to the New Deal" (Ph. D. dissertation, State University of Iowa, 1951, p. 165, from Leon Trotsky, *My Life*).

34. Theodore Draper, *The Roots of American Communism* (New York, 1957), p. 92.

35. New York *Call*, April 7, 1917.

36. For a left-wing study of Charles Ruthenberg, see Melech Epstein, "Ruthenberg," New York *Freiheit*, March 5, 1927.

37. The St. Louis Emergency Convention as well as the majority and minority reports are described by James Weinstein, *The Decline of Socialism, 1912-1925* (New York, 1967), pp. 126-27.

38. See Fine, *Labor and Farmer Parties*, pp. 310-16.

39. Algernon Lee, "Diary," dated January 29, 1916, p. 7, Algernon Lee Papers, Tamiment Library.

40. John Spargo, *The Pro-German Cry of 'No Indemnities'* (New York, n.d.), p. 7.

41. Spargo, Oral History Research Project, Columbia University.

42. See Ray Ginger, *The Bending Cross* (New Jersey, 1949), pp. 349-50.

43. *Loose Leaves*, p. 156.

44. Gomper's comment cited in Merle Fainsod, *International Socialism and the War* (Cambridge, 1935), p. 145, and W.E. Walling quoted in the New York *Times*, May 24, 1917.

45. *Loose Leaves*, p. 172.

46. Ibid., p. 173.

47. Minutes of the Ninth Meeting, June 21, 1917, p. 3, People's Council Papers, Swarthmore College.

48. Minutes of the Eighth Meeting, June 15, 1917, p. 2, ibid.

49. Letter from Victor Berger to Morris Hillquit, August 11, 1917, Berger Collection, Milwaukee County Historical Society, cited in Sally Miller, *Victor Berger and the Promise of Constructive Socialism* (Westport, Conn. 1973), p. 176.

50. *Loose Leaves*, p. 172.

51. Minutes of the Eighth Meeting, June 15, 1917, p. 2, People's Council Papers, Swarthmore College.

52. *Loose Leaves*, p. 179.

53. The Hillquit campaign was followed in the *New York Times Index*, October-December 1917, pp. 174-75. Also see Hillquit's chapter "The

Mayoralty Campaign of New York," in *Loose Leaves*, pp. 180-210. This campaign has been examined in historical studies including Zosa Szajkovski, *Jews, Wars and Communism*, 2 vols. (New York, 1972), 1:141-61; Iverson, "Morris Hillquit," pp. 180-218, and Weinstein, *Decline of Socialism*, pp. 149-55.

54. New York *Times*, October 13, 27, and 29, 1917.

55. See New York *Jewish Daily Forward*, July-November 1917. Joseph Schlossberg, the left-wing socialist and secretary-treasurer of the Amalgamated Clothing Workers campaigned in favor of Hillquit's mayoralty candidacy. For a discussion of the 1917 election and the Jewish issues see Chapter 13.

56. Ludwig Lore, "The New York Mayoralty Campaign," *The Class Struggle* 2 (November-December 1917), 4:100-6, and "The Elections," ibid., 2 (December 1918), 5:621.

57. Emma Goldman, *Living My Life* (New York, 1931), pp. 637-38.

58. New York *Call*, November 8, 1917.

The Russian Revolution and the Communist Split

Chapter 12

Before the Russian Revolution of March 1917, Hillquit had absolutely nothing good to say about Russia. Like most socialists of the Second International period, he understood Russia to be one of the most politically reactionary and economically backward countries of the world. Since he believed that socialism would be realized in an advanced industrial country, Hillquit had little interest in the Russian potential for revolution. When Maxim Gorki, the famous Socialist novelist and playwright, came to the United States to raise money for the Russian socialists after the 1905 revolution, Hillquit told Gorki that he personally had a definite distaste for Russian society. The Riga-born Hillquit was especially condemnatory of the Russian government's support of pogroms against Jews.

More than most American socialists, Hillquit kept in touch with events in Russia during the several years between the 1905 and 1917 revolutions. He and Gorki became good friends while the Russian was in New York. Afterward, when Gorki left the United States, Hillquit acted as his literary agent. He was also employed by other Russian socialists, such as the Jewish Bundist and Menshevik Raphael Abramowitsch, to act as literary agent and lawyer in the United States.[1]

When the first revolution occurred in March 1917, Hillquit expressed his approval. However, as he told a Madison Square Garden audience on March 21, he hoped the next revolution in Europe would overthrow the Kaiser in Germany.[2]

The first Russian controversy to divide American socialists

focused upon whether or not the Russians ought to conclude a separate peace with the Germans. As early as April 1917, there were rumors in the press that the Russian government planned to sign such a peace. The United States had just entered the war. This supposed separate peace was taken to signify Russian desertion of the Allied cause and a rapprochement with the Germans. Several American socialists, who discarded their antiwar stand once the United States entered the battle, joined the government in trying to keep the Russians from withdrawing from the war.

The American government enlisted the aid of two prominent New York socialists—Meyer London who had been reelected to Congress on the Socialist ticket in 1916 but was an opponent of the militant-sounding St. Louis Proclamation[3] and Charles E. Russell who began to support American involvement in the war because of what he called the "democratic principles at stake."[4] On April 18, 1917, London and Russell cabled N.C. Tscheidse, socialist leader of the Duma, and Kerensky, respectively, urging the Russian socialists not to conclude a separate peace with Germany. This cable was signed by eleven American socialists including John Spargo.[5]

As International Secretary of the Party, Hillquit affirmed its "faith in the ability of the Russian comrades to solve their own problems in the furtherance of peace, democracy and international socialism."[6] On April 20 he cabled Tscheidse that the London-Russell cable was unauthorized and did not represent the American Party's views.

The American government was not willing to sit back complacently. In late April President Wilson selected conservative Republican Elihu Root, a Wall Street lawyer, to go to Russia to convince the socialist government not to sign a separate peace. Hillquit protested Root's appointment[7] and he warned the American government that the socialists in Russia would be fully informed about Root before he arrived.[8] American socialists were not appeased when Russell was added to the Root mission as a representative of their point of view.[9] In fact, while Russell was touring Russia in June and misrepresenting the American socialist view by telling the Russians to remain in the war, Hillquit had him expelled from the Party.[10] More than a year later, in December 1918, while Hillquit was recovering from his second major bout with tuberculosis, Algernon Lee sent him a sarcastically humorous description of Russell's behavior in Russia. According to Lee's report, Russell, the socialist, did not feel comfortable when the Root mission was "wined and dined by all sorts of eminently respectable clients." He therefore came to Bessie Beattie's room and begged her "to dig up a piece of red ribbon, a red silk neckercloth." An hour later she saw Russell on the street "with a flaming scarlet necktie and a red rosette in his coat lapel." However, these symbols did not seem to have the right effect. According to Lee, "ignoring these manifestations of his revolutionary soul, the heathen Bolsheviki snubbed him as cruelly as the rich bourgeois."[11]

At the opening meeting of his mayoralty campaign Hillquit interpreted the Russian Revolution as a triumph for international socialism.[12] The day following the November election, the Bolsheviks took power in Russia. In December 1917 President Wilson espoused the Socialist principles of no annexation and no indemnities and in his January 1918 Fourteen Points he suggested that the treatment of Russia by her sister nations would be the "acid test" of their abandonment of self-interest for the principle of free determination. In March 1918 the Russians accepted the harsh terms of the Brest-Litovsk treaty and withdrew from the war.

These events had a major impact on the American socialists. First, the Bolshevik Revolution evoked wholehearted enthusiasm for the Russians. "The hope of world revolution ran high in radical circles during 1918," wrote Joseph Freeman. "Even the cautious Morris Hillquit discreetly declared that the revolution in Russia would be of greater importance than the World War itself."[13] Actually, Hillquit went further. At the May 1918 ILGWU convention, he saw Russia standing "in the vanguard of democracy, in the vanguard of social progress, in the hands, all through top to bottom, of the people themselves, of the working class, the peasants."[14]

President Wilson's plans for peace and the treatment of the Russians by the Germans also affected the American socialists' position on the war. As Hillquit noted, "a large section of the Socialist movement was beginning to feel a certain change of heart on the question of supporting the war." "German militarism," he wrote, threatened the revolutionary government of Russia. Wilson's plans for "generous and progressive peace terms with their haughty rejection by the government of the Kaiser, had combined to arouse a sentiment of greater friendliness to the cause of the Allies. . . ."[15]

Hillquit's change of heart came to light in January 1918 when he publicly approved of Wilson's declared peace aims. In February, after the signing of the Brest-Litovsk treaty, Hillquit volunteered to investigate labor unrest in Germany and Austria in order to end the war. "It is now clearer than ever before that autocracy and militarism in Germany and Austria must be put down," he said. He suggested that "there is at least one branch of war service into which you [socialists] can enter with all your hearts and souls to aid our president in bringing about his ideals of peace. That branch of the war service is the work of scattering propaganda among the laboring classes of Germany. . . ."[16]

This suggestion met with more enthusiasm than Hillquit expected. Dr. Benjamin Saphir, a socialist and journalist on the Yiddish *Der tog*, requested that the Party recruit an American guard for active military service in Russia with Hillquit as its commander.[17] At a mass meeting on February 28, 1918, Hillquit said that such an idea was impractical and "very romantic." He wryly declined the command of a "Red Guard" on the grounds that "I have no previous military experience." The idea of an American Red Guard was taken up at this meeting by Louis Fraina, a strong Hillquit critic and left-winger, and by IWW leader Arturo Giovanitti, who cabled President Wilson asking for permission to recruit such an army.[18] Nothing came of it.

Hillquit's protective and pro-Russian feelings became more intense by the spring of 1918. When his friend Job Harriman, a staunch anti-Bolshevik, asked him what he thought of the Bolsheviki, he replied on April 30, 1918:

> I do not accept all [their] social theories. I am not convinced that they will succeed in a substantial realization of their. . . program, and I do not know how long they will maintain themselves in power. But I believe they have rendered a tremendous service to our movement and to the general cause of social progress by shaking up the old world. . .I believe the world will never be the same after the Bolsheviki experiment.

However, Hillquit told Harriman, "the immediate future of Russia, and for that matter the world, seems to me more uncertain now than ever. . . ."[19]

Uncertainty seemed to be the tenor of the times. By the spring of 1918 while Wilson expounded on his plans for peace and settlement, the general press expressed fear and distrust of the dangerously radical Bolshevik regime, which now also was considered pro-German because the Russians had left the war.[20] Left-wing socialists such as Fraina and Boudin, however, wanted the Party leadership to make a strong public stand in favor of the Bolshevik Revolution. The Left imagined it was possible to take advantage of the war crisis as Lenin had done in Russia and use it to sharpen the class struggle in the United States.[21] Moreover, the left wanted the NEC to reaffirm the provisions of the St. Louis Proclamation which called upon socialists to obstruct war measures.

The majority of the Party's leaders, including Debs, Berger, and Hillquit, were undecided in their approach to the revolution and to the question of resistance against the war effort in the United States. While these socialists were impressed with the Bolsheviks they were, at the same time, reluctant to appear to be in accord with violent Bolshevik methods. And while Hillquit and the other members of the NEC wanted the United States to leave the war, they did not want to appear to be undermining the U.S. war effort. Consequently, the NEC behaved ineffectually. The Russians were lauded but no conclusions for American socialism were drawn from the Russian experience. Furthermore, the NEC members neither advocated militant resistance to the war nor did they revise the St. Louis Proclamation.[22] Instead, from mid-1918 on, Hillquit stressed the issues of peace and postwar international harmony.[23] He claimed that a discussion of controversial matters was impossible.[24]

To an extent Hillquit was correct. The Party's chances of developing a militant antiwar program were seriously hampered by government harrassment, censorship, and arrest. Congress had passed the Espionage Act in June 1917 which exacted stringent penalties for causing subordination in the armed forces. The 1917 act also conferred on the U.S. Post Office Department broad powers to exclude from the mails all matters violating the provisions of the Espionage Act or advocating treason, insurrection, or forcible resistance to law. In June 1918 this act was drastically amended to include such non-military offenses as "profane, scurrilous and abusive" language about the government and Constitution of the United States, "or saying or doing anything" to obstruct the sale of government bonds.[25]

Beginning in June 1917 Hillquit acted as the defense lawyer for socialist papers and periodicals which were either totally excluded from the mails or deprived of the privilege of lower postage rates usually accorded such publications. He defended these papers sometimes because of their opposition to American participation in the war and sometimes because their social, economic, or political views failed to meet the approval of the U.S. Post Office authorities, particularly the approval of Postmaster General Albert Burleson.[26] These papers represented various wings of the Party, from the personal journalism of Frank Harris's *Pearson's Magazine* through the official and semi-official papers of the Socialist Party like the *American Socialist*, the *Call*, the Milwaukee *Leader*, and the *Jewish Daily Forward* to the avant-garde the *Masses*.[27]

In all these cases Hillquit argued that the socialist press was truly "American" and that a socialist definition of patriotism included the right of freedom of speech and the right to criticize a democratic society. He seemed genuinely shocked by the curtailment of these rights and he acted in court as though all that was needed was a clear didactic lecture on civil liberties. But most of all he was anxious to convince the juries and the press that Socialists were loyal to their country—something he found more difficult to accomplish as the war continued.

Government persecution of socialists was intense. Just before the new 1918 Sedition Law went into effect, Hillquit lashed out against the measure. He characterized it as "the nationalization of the private institution of lynching."[28] At a May 10 dinner given in honor of the *Masses* editors by the Liberty Defense Union and attended by radicals such as John Reed and reformers such as Amos Pinchot, Hillquit condemned the law with sarcasm: "Congress, it seems is trying to give us speakers a little vacation." And he noted that once the law went into effect in June, "by the provisions of this law which forbids criticism of the Constitution, the army, the navy, the uniform of the army...I shall be unable to explain this law, as I am now doing."[29]

In the summer of 1918 Hillquit had another attack of tuberculosis. He rejected the advice of his doctors that he withdraw from active life for two years. Forced by ill health to be away from the city periodically, he still ran for Congress in the New York 1918 election. His espionage cases were taken over by the socialist-lawyer Seymour Stedman and, as Hillquit said, "their outcome was predetermined by the fixed state of the judicial and public mind."[30]

The pressures of the war, the temporary collapse of international socialism, the growing disharmony in the American Socialist Party, and the persecution of radicals all contributed to Hillquit's second physical breakdown. He was unable to cope with the tensions of the situation. Although intellectually he had worked out rational arguments to deal with the war, the Russian Revolution, and the future of socialism, his body reacted negatively to all the irreconcilable aspects of the new circumstances. From a psychological standpoint, it is possible to conjecture that while Hillquit avoided indictment and prison, his illness was a way of sharing this experience with men like Debs whom he admired. His autobiographical statements about the breakdown seem to point to such an interpretation. "I was myself rather puzzled by my unindicted state," he wrote rather shamefacedly. He learned that the government dropped proceedings against him "on taking counsel with certain influential advisors."[31] Instead of going to jail he devoted himself to the defense of other socialists. But just when his "whole mind was absorbed by...pending espionage laws, the cases of my friends and comrades for which I had assumed prime responsibility," he became incapacitated. And he thought, "No prison sentence could have struck me such a heavy blow....There I was torn out of life and activity without warning, and consigned to the impotent and useless existence of an invalid....I was despondent and in black despair...."[32] Hillquit likened his illness to a rude arrest in the middle of the night.

Hillquit retreated to Saranac Lake in northern New York's Adirondack Mountains where he convalesced and where he followed the sedition cases and the developments within the Party through newspapers and private correspondence. In his autobiography he claimed that "after the first shock was over, I soon developed a realistic sense of proportion and values in life." He became reconciled to the fact that "the world was moving along its tortuous and irrational course without me, as well or badly as it had been doing with my active and ardent participation."[33]

Actually, Hillquit's stoic resignation, as expressed in the autobiography, was not corroborated by his behavior during the subsequent course of events. Despite his bedridden condition, he exercised a significant influence upon the American Party's policy-making processes.

When Hillquit became ill in the summer of 1918, the membership was moving decidedly leftward. Boudin, Fraina, and John Reed, in particular, were providing articulate leadership for a burgeoning left wing which openly criticized the Party's leaders and its cautious policies. The left wing identified with the militant actions of the Russian Revolution and held high expectations of implementing revolutionary changes in the United States. Leftist party sections were created in Boston, Chicago, and New York.[34] In addition, the composition of the Socialist Party was changing as Russian, Ukrainian, Finnish, Lithuanian, and Lett immigrants, recent arrivals to the United States, joined the Party's foreign-language federations. These new socialists, who by the end of 1918 made up more than half the Party's membership, tended to support left-wing enthusiasms and were oriented toward homeland or Soviet policies. Hillquit, who never approved of foreign-language federations on principle, was even more dismayed by these new recruits. He described them as "Bolshevik to the core" and he feared they would make the Party less American since they would accept "everything emanating from Moscow unquestioningly. . . ."[35]

Yet the threat of an actual left-wing takeover of the Party's machinery—the NEC or the official party press—did not seem to have worried Hillquit, or at least not until the spring of 1919. As late as April 1919 Hillquit wrote Adolph Germer, the Party secretary, that he thought the Socialists ought to take "a more aggressive policy" and perhaps incorporate some of the left's ideas. Germer did not agree. He told Hillquit that the left would not capture the

Party but that they had "succeeded in converting our most active locals into mere debating societies with the result that attendance at meetings is getting smaller and membership is decreasing."[36]

The success of the left wing in capturing twelve of the fifteen NEC seats and four of the five delegates to the International in May appeared to have been the decisive factor in causing Hillquit to change his mind about the left's threat to the Party. He now became convinced that the left intended to wrest the Party from socialists like himself, who had built and sustained it for nearly two decades. On May 21 his editorial "Clear the Decks" was published in the New York *Call*. In it Hillquit openly took a stand against "The Left Wing" and in so doing set the tone for the national leadership to follow.[37] The arguments he employed were to remain basic to his stance for years to come.

In his opening statement Hillquit admitted that the present-day socialist movement suffered from a "sad paradox" because it believed that European socialists had deserted the cause of international working-class solidarity. According to Hillquit, this was not true. The European socialists did not lead the workers astray. "It was the economic organization of the European workers," Hillquit wrote, "and the pressures of their immediate economic interests (as understood by them) that broke the solidarity of the Socialist International." In exonerating the European socialists from the "crime of the war," Hillquit also excused their prewar tactics. Thus he argued it was wrong to accuse the prewar socialists, as the left had done, of becoming too "constructive" or of being corrupted by bourgeois parliamentarianism. "It was not parliamentarianism which was primarily responsible for the mischief," he wrote.

Organized labor, not the socialists, was to blame for the workers' failure to remain faithful to their class interests. "The fundamental weakness of the organized labor movement," Hillquit wrote, "was that it was a movement of 'a class within a class'—a movement for the benefit of the better situated strata of labor, the skilled workers." Organized labor created a psychology of "craft solidarity" which excluded the majority of the working classes and consequently left the workers at the mercy of nationalistic sentiments at the time of the war. Hillquit suggested a remedy which sounded more radical and ambitious than an IWW program. Organized labor ought to be reorganized along "broad class lines, not only nationally but internationally. . .not as trade unions, nor even as mere industrial unions, but as one working class union."

Yet from an immediate, practical point of view, Hillquit advised that socialists in America bide their time. Socialists ought not to commit themselves to any program and least of all to the new Communist Third International. The Communists in Moscow, he warned, "make the mistake of attempting a sort of dictatorship of the Russian proletariat in the Socialist International." Instead, American socialists should wait for the right time when a new International would be created.

Hillquit now turned his attention directly to the left wing of the American Party. "The Left-Wing movement, as I see it, is a purely emotional reflex to the situation in Russia," he wrote. The American situation is totally different. Revolution in America was not possible because the United States "was now the strongest capitalist country in the world. . . [and] also because the power of capitalism has been less shaken in the United States than in any of the advanced countries of Europe." Therefore, Hillquit opposed the left "not because it was too radical, but because it is essentially reactionary and non-Socialistic; not because it would lead us too far, but because it would lead us nowhere." "To prate about 'dictatorship of the proletariat' and of 'workers' soviets' in the United States at this time," he continued, was to deflect the Socialist propaganda from its realistic basis, and to advocate "the abolition of all social reform planks in the party platform. . . ."

Now Hillquit had come to the point in his editorial where he was ready to excommunicate the left. Fully blaming them, he wrote: "The Left does not want to convert their comrades—they want to 'capture' and establish a sort of dictatorship of the proletariat (?) within the party." Therefore, he concluded, "it would be futile to preach reconciliation and union where antagonism runs so high." Sounding like a biblical prophet, Hillquit passed his sentence:

> Let them separate, honestly, freely, without rancor. Let each side organize and work in its own way. . .Better a hun-

> dred times to have two numerically small Socialist organizations, each homogeneous and harmonious within itself, than to have one big party torn by dissensions . . . an impotent colossus on feet of clay. The time for action is here. Let us clear the decks.[38]

At a special meeting of the old NEC in Chicago at the end of May, the seven foreign-language federations affiliated with the left wing were suspended, the entire state organization of Michigan expelled, the recent elections to the NEC declared null and void on the grounds that irregularities had occurred in the tabulation of the vote.[39] Although Hillquit indirectly inspired these actions through his "Clear the Decks" editorial, there is evidence that he did not know the NEC would employ an expulsion tactic. On June 2 Germer informed him of the event.[40] Hillquit never replied, for at the time he had suffered an attack of appendicitis and underwent surgery just when the expulsions took place.

The late spring and early summer of 1919 was a period of extreme agitation for the Party leadership. In June Algernon Lee informed the ailing Hillquit that at least in New York the left had taken the expulsions with equanimity.[41] But in July Germer wrote Hillquit that he feared the Chicago headquarters might be taken over as in the De Leon days and he planned to spend several nights guarding the office.[42] In August Hillquit, Lee, and Germer were hard at work on preparations to keep the left from interfering with the coming special national convention.[43]

The Left began to launch a serious counteroffensive. The New York *Communist*, a recently created left-wing paper, threatened in May 1919: "When the time comes for clearing the decks, we will handle the mop."[44] Thus during late August and early September a series of conventions and emergency meetings were held in Chicago which resulted in the split of the socialist movement into three distinct parties: the Socialists, the Communists, and the Communist Laborites. Hillquit was still in Saranac Lake.[45] His first public statement in reaction to these events was published in the *Call* on September 22. His words were conciliatory. He appeared, at least on the surface, to promise a potential unification. Yet it must have been difficult to take him seriously when he wrote, "The division was not brought about by differences on vital questions of principles. It arose over disputes on methods and policy. . . ." It was even harder to believe his statement that the separation of the Party into three organizations "need not necessarily mean a weakening of the Socialist movement as such." One wonders how the left responded to his contention that "our newly baptized 'Communists' have not ceased to be Socialists even though in a moment of destructive enthusiasm they have chosen to discard the name . . ." or his hope that "when the hour of the real Socialist fight strikes . . . we may find them again in our ranks."[46]

Hillquit proved to be incorrect. By the end of 1919 the Socialist Party of America was seriously weakened by loss of membership and a reintegration of the departed left wing never came about. The 1919 split marked the end of an era.

Whether Hillquit could have prevented the final split with the left is a moot but intriguing question. Responsibility ought not to be placed totally upon his shoulders. Certainly he, as one among many Party leaders, could not have alone prevented the factional strife. Furthermore, although the expulsions of June 1919 significantly reduced Party membership, after June an important number of left-wing members departed on their own.

Why then did the leaders panic, use semilegal methods, and act in such haste to expell the left wing especially if, as Hillquit thought, the ideological differences between the Party and the left were not significant? There were two central reasons. First, there was a power struggle within the Party, that is, the election to the NEC of a majority of left-wing members. Second, such a struggle might not have resulted in such measures had the American government and press in 1919 been less of a threat to the Party's survival. The government attacked the Socialists as an anti-American force within society.

Hillquit had spent more than a decade building his conception of an American socialist party. Although during the war he took a position counter to the government, he did so essentially on the grounds that the Party followed a "higher" but still American ideal of civil liberty. He thought that the best and perhaps only defense for the beleaguered Socialist Party was to prove that it had firm American roots.

The left weakened Hillquit's defense. As Eastern European immigrants joined the Party in large numbers, he could no longer say that it was predominately American-born. As the left-wing leaders claimed their ideological foundations were derived from the Soviet experience, Hillquit's argument that socialism in America was rooted in the American experience lost much of its credibility. Thus in order to preserve as much of an American image for the Party as he could, Hillquit agreed to the ouster of the left.

Notes

1. The letters from Abramowitsch to Hillquit are dated November 1, 1907; July 6, September 14, October 12, and November 26, 1908; December 8, 1909; November 1, 1910, Correspondence, Hillquit Papers. Letters from Gorki are translated into English in ibid. and include 27 letters written between 1906-1913.

2. New York *Times*, March 21, 1917.

3. For Meyer London see Rogoff, *An East Side Epic*, pp. 106-7.

4. For Russell see Ronald Radosh, "American Labor and the Root Commission," *Studies on the Left* 3 (1962), 1: 89-93.

5. New York *Call*, May 10, 1917, Clippings, Hillquit Papers.

6. New York *World*, April 21, 1917, ibid.

7. New York *Times*, April 30, May 2, and May 4, 1917.

8. Max M. Laserson, *The American Impact on Russia-Diplomatic and Ideological, 1784-1917* (New York, 1950), p. 413.

9. For Wilson's attitude toward socialists on the Root mission see Ray Baker, *Woodrow Wilson: Life and Letters*, vol. 7 (New York, 1939), p. 29.

10. Radosh, "American Labor," p. 91.

11. Letter from Algernon Lee to Morris Hillquit, December 17, 1918, Correspondence, Hillquit Papers.

12. Morris Hillquit, "Opening Speech to the 1917 Mayoralty Campaign," Writings, ibid.

13. Joseph Freeman, *American Testament* (New York, 1926), p. 144.

14. Morris Hillquit, "Labor's Progress in Spite of the War" (address to the International Convention of the ILGWU, Boston, Mass., May, 1918). Quoted in *The Ladies Garment Worker*, June 1918.

15. *Loose Leaves*, p. 235.

16. Hillquit's January and February statements were published in newspapers throughout the United States and collected in Clippings, Hillquit Papers.

17. New York *Tribune*, February 28, 1918, ibid.

18. Cincinnati (Ohio) *Enquirer*, February 28, 1918, ibid; New York *Evening Globe*, March 1, 1918, ibid.

19. Letters from Job Harriman to Morris Hillquit, April 12 and May 14, 1918, and letter from Morris Hillquit to Job Harriman, April 30, 1918, Correspondence, ibid.

20. In this period Hillquit was also called a Bolshevik by the conservative press. For example, see New York *Evening Globe*, November 1, 1918, Clippings, ibid.

21. For the left-wing view see Louis Fraina, "Problems of American Socialism," *The Class Struggle* 3 (February 1919), pp. 24-26, and Louis Boudin, "St. Louis—One Year After," ibid., 2 (May-June 1918), pp. 338-41.

22. For Debs's view see New York *Tribune*, May 14, 1918, Clippings, Hillquit Papers, and Ginger, *The Bending Cross*, pp. 352-53. For Berger see Miller, *Victor Berger*, pp. 233-53, and letter from Victor Berger to Morris Hillquit, August 20, 1919, Correspondence, Hillquit Papers.

23. See Chicago *Tribune*, May 8, 1918, Clippings, ibid.

24. *Loose Leaves*, p. 235.

25. Ibid., p. 211.

26. Ibid., p. 212.

27. The *Masses* trial is covered in Clippings, Hillquit Papers, (April 5-June 8, 1918).

28. Salt Lake City *News*, May 10, 1918, ibid.

29. New York *Tribune*, May 10, 1918, ibid.

30. Hillquit discusses these cases in *Loose Leaves*, pp. 235-45; the cases are also covered in Clippings, Hillquit Papers, (March-June 1918).

31. *Loose Leaves*, p. 234.

32. Ibid., pp. 240-41.

33. Ibid., p. 241.

34. For the development of the left wing see, for example, Weinstein, *Decline of Socialism*, pp. 177-96, and Shannon, *The Socialist Party*, pp. 126-35.

35. *Loose Leaves*, pp. 290-91.

36. Letter from Adolph Germer to Morris Hillquit, April 17, 1919, Correspondence, Hillquit Papers.

37. See, for example, Melech Epstein, *Profile of Eleven* (Detroit, Mich. 1965), p. 216.

38. Morris Hillquit, "The Immediate Issue" (1919), Writings, Hillquit Papers. Reprint of Hillquit's "Clear the Decks" editorial published as "The Socialist Task and Outlook" in the New York *Call*, May 21, 1919.

39. See Weinstein, *Decline of Socialism*, p. 198.

40. Letter from Adolph Germer to Morris Hillquit, June 2, 1919, Correspondence, Hillquit Papers.

41. Letters from Algernon Lee to Morris Hillquit, June 6 and June 8, 1919, ibid.

42. Letter from Adolph Germer to Morris Hillquit, July 14, 1919, ibid.

43. Letter from Algernon Lee to Morris Hillquit, August 6, 1919, ibid.; letter from Morris Hillquit to Adolph Germer, August 9, 1919, ibid.; letter from Morris Hillquit to Algernon Lee, August 9, 1919, ibid.

44. New York *Communist*, May 24, 1919.

45. Letter of the National Convention of the Socialist Party to Morris Hillquit, August 31, 1919, Correspondence, Hillquit Papers.

46. New York *Call*, September 22, 1919. Hillquit restated this position in his "We Are All Socialists," *Eye Opener*, October 1, 1919, in Eugene V. Debs Scrapbook, SB 1, vol. 1 ov., p. 144, Tamiment Library.

Chapter 13
Hillquit and the Jews, 1909-1930

Before examining Hillquit's role in the Socialist Party in the 1920s, it is important to note one special aspect of his political behavior—his relationship with the Jewish community. In the war years, Hillquit, although a self-styled "cosmopolitan," openly expressed Jewish loyalty. In fact he was drawn closer to the Jews and, even before the war, visibly championed the Jewish worker in the United States and the Jews in Europe.

The militant strikes of the ILGWU and the Cloakmakers' Union of 1909 and 1910 revitalized Hillquit's activities among Jewish workers. During the strikes Hillquit was a legal representative of the ILGWU. He also delivered rousing speeches to hundreds of striking shirtwaistmakers commending the Jewish and Italian women for their bravery and for their help in awakening the dormant social conscience of New York's non-working-class citizens.[1]

In 1915 Hillquit became a hero when he successfully defended seven Jewish officials of the Cloakmakers' Union charged with murdering a strikebreaker in 1910. The case had been originally dismissed as "cause unknown" but its revival, five years later, was considered an attempt by garment employers to discredit the reputation of the union.[2] Many Jews feared the trial would provoke anti-Semitism. Hillquit's defense presented Jews sympathetically. He was identified with the famous trial lawyer who had recently defended Mendl Beiless, the unfortunate Russian Jew who had been tried for "blood libel" in Russia.[3]

Just after the outbreak of World War I, Hillquit shared the alarm felt by American Jews over the fate of their kinsmen in Europe. The war had a particularly harsh impact upon the already disintegrating Jewish communities of Eastern Europe. Starvation, random looting by soldiers, and pogroms had left one out of every six Jewish families homeless. By November 1914 a coalition of wealthy, influential American Jews of German background and some leaders of New York's orthodox Jewish community had established an American Jewish Joint Distribution Committee for the Relief of War Sufferers. The leaders of Jewish labor, both Zionist and socialist, were dissatisfied with the narrow, philanthropic policy of the JDC. They wanted to provide European Jews with more than just means of survival. In 1915 a coalition of Jewish labor and socialist groups formed the People's Relief Committee which promised rehabilitation and industrial training for European Jews. Hillquit participated in this committee.

That same year Jewish socialists launched their own campaign to win equal rights for Jews in Eastern Europe. A National Workman's Committee was organized, composed of the United Hebrew Trades, the Jewish Socialist Federation of America, the Workmen's Circle, the Forward Association, the Socialist Territorialists, the Jewish National Worker's Alliance, and the Poale Zion. The *Call* and the Yiddish *Jewish Daily Forward* explained that the NWC proposed to reveal the extent of persecution suffered by the Jews in Eastern Europe and the committee offered a postwar program which included a set of political and cultural rights for "National Minorities."[4]

Hillquit acted as liaison between the Party and the NWC. Early in 1916 he wrote a peace program which the Party then urged the American government to adopt in anticipation of the coming end of the war. One of the program's projected resolutions for a durable peace in Europe was "the removal of political and civic disabilities of the Jewish people."[5] Hillquit, Meyer London, and James Maurer, leader of the Pennsylvania Socialist Party and president of the Pennsylvania Federation of Labor, interviewed President Wilson in January 1916 on behalf of the Socialists proposal which also was supported by the NWC. The *Jewish Daily Forward* lauded

Hillquit's role in making the President aware of the "cry of suffering of the dispossessed Jews of the war countries."[6]

In February 1916 Hillquit, London, and Maurer were again sent to Washington. This time the men spoke before a congressional committee on foreign affairs. Hillquit's speech emphasized the needs of the oppressed peoples of Europe. He singled out the Jews for special mention: "The 7,000,000 Jews in Russian-Poland who are outlaws to-day in the eyes of their Government . . . are hunted from place to place, without civic rights, the prey of every brutal soldier. . . ."[7]

When Hillquit ran for Congress again in 1916, his opponents no longer accused him of lacking concern for Jewish affairs; not only was he the lawyer for major Jewish unions in New York but he had joined Jewish socialists and non-socialists in activities intended to protect the worldwide Jewish community. In fact, Hillquit focused his campaign on Jewish interests. For the first time, instead of apologizing for him, the Yiddish socialist papers defended him with vigor.

The contest took place in the Twentieth District, Harlem, a predominantly Jewish neighborhood. According to Hillquit, there were 14,000 voters of whom 2,500 were Irish and American, 2,000 were Italian, and 500 were German. The rest were Jewish.[8] Both Hillquit's Democratic and Republican opponents were Jewish and *Yidishkeit* dominated as a campaign issue.

The *Jewish Daily Forward* ran lengthy articles, written either by its caustic editor (and Hillquit's old friend) Abraham Cahan or by the young staff writer and later editor of the communist *Frieheit* Moishe Olgin, comparing the qualifications of the candidates. Their general thrust was that Hillquit's opponents were poor politicians and therefore would be unable to defend Jewish interests in Congress.[9] The *Forward* writers saved their special invective for the Democrat Rosenblatt whose candidacy was supported by the New York *Times*. Rosenblatt appealed to the voters as a Zionist. Olgin asked, "Has Tammany Hall become kosher?"[10] Cahan reasoned that "just because the candidate is a Zionist and is running on a Tammany ticket, therefore all Zionists and intelligent people should not vote for him."[11] The Poale Zion's *Yidisher kaempher* corroborated the *Forward's* antagonism to Rosenblatt. Their most celebrated theoretician, Ber Borochov, who had acquired an international reputation on the basis of his intellectual synthesis of Zionism and socialism, attacked Rosenblatt and commended Hillquit in a preelection article, "Socialism and Tammany Hall."[12] He praised Hillquit's attitudes toward Jewish nationalism while condemning Rosenblatt's Zionism as a cheap opportunistic distortion of the highest ideals of the Jewish people.

In 1916 Hillquit was unusually outspoken in his assertion of his personal Jewish identity and ethnic pride. He criticized intolerance toward Jews in America. He claimed that the new war spirit in American life fostered racial and religious prejudice. Militarism, he said, was destroying the dream of the melting pot. While in former years the United States "was glad to serve as an asylum for the persecuted. . .," now, "the leading political parties and their candidates vie with each other in their insults of foreign born citizens, whom they contemptuously brand as 'hyphens'."[13]

In late October Olgin interviewed Hillquit on Jewish issues. Olgin's article in the *Forward* stressed Hillquit's appreciation of Jewish cultural nationalism. Hillquit argued in the Mazzinian fashion that nationality was a fact. "Each nation contributes something worthwhile toward the general human culture," Hillquit told Olgin. "The Jewish nation is also a fact. Jews have separate psychological identities—a special past, a special feeling of relatedness one to the other, up to a point, a special language (or rather special languages: Yiddish and Hebrew) and elements of a special Jewish culture." Furthermore, Hillquit thought that since Jews did not have their own homeland they had developed along two lines—those which bound them together and those which tied them to the country in which they lived. Not all Jews were alike and the strength of these bonds differed from country to country. Yet he insisted that Jews must have "nationality rights":

> In a State where two or three nationalities reside, and if non-Jewish nationalities have national rights like the right to have their own schools in their own language and culture then the Jews ought also to have the same national right. Whether

> they use this right or not, whether they sustain another culture or not . . . they must have guaranteed national rights.

Olgin questioned Hillquit about the use of Yiddish in schools, universities, and government institutions. Hillquit replied that he thought the Yiddish language should be taught and used wherever Jews desired its employment. Olgin quoted him as saying, "I am a Socialist and Socialists are for freedom. Freedom means that people should develop themselves as far as they are able. The right to use the mother tongue is most important . . . ." And again, pressing closer to home, Olgin asked Hillquit, "If 100,000 Jews wrote a petition to the New York legislature demanding the government to open a Yiddish language school, would you support the petition?" According to Olgin, Hillquit agreed to do so on the grounds that other nationalities were also granted special nationality rights. "It does not concern me whether America becomes a country of one language and one culture or multi-lingual and multi-cultural," he said. The interview ended on a light note. Olgin asked Hillquit, what "if the same . . . petitions were to ask for Yiddish language, literature and history [to] be taught in the public schools and high schools?" The wily Hillquit answered, "This is quite another thing. The Jews have the right as taxpayers. And if they hired me as a lawyer I would defend them."[14]

Hillquit lost to the Republican incumbent Siegal. Since the election returns were extremely close, the Party accused the Republicans of resorting to corrupt Tammany Hall techniques, that is, to fraudulent practices at the polls. The case was brought before the New York Supreme Court. Siegal's victory was upheld.[15]

In 1917, the year of the Russian Revolution and America's entrance into World War I, Hillquit moved his electioneering out of the Jewish neighborhoods and into the wider New York City scene. He ran for mayor in a four-cornered race against Tammany Hall Democrat Judge John F. Hylan, the incumbent mayor and reformer John Purroy Mitchel, and William M. Bennett, a Republican. Hillquit was conspicuous among the candidates his Jewish origin, his antiwar position and his enthusiasm for the Russian Revolution (still in its first stage). During the campaign the Party, seeking

Morris Hillquit, 1915 or 1916. *Courtesy of State Historical Society of Wisconsin.*

working and middle-class support, emphasized municipal reform, that is, medical care, municipal nurseries, better schools and more teachers, meals for poor children, tuberculosis centers, a free beach at Coney Island, and municipal ownership of street railways and subways. The stationery of the "Hillquit Non-Partisan League" carried the slogan, "Hillquit and 5 cent Bread."[16]

The repressive actions of national and local authorities against opponents of the war were important political issues and the role played by Jews in support or opposition to the war dominated the campaign battles. For the Socialists, according to historian Melvyn Dubofsky, the Hillquit campaign was "the climax of the Socialist and needle trades' crusade to keep America out of the war and to obtain a just and negotiated peace."[17] For Hillquit this campaign also brought to fruition his antiwar stand.

Many non-socialist Jews favored America's entrance into the war. They feared Hillquit's so-called pacifist campaign in New York would cast doubt upon Jewish loyalty to the American war effort, be considered pro-German, and stimulate anti-Semitic responses. Hillquit's most persistent critic was Louis Marshall, a lawyer and leading member of the wealthy German-Jewish community and a self-appointed champion of Jewish respectability. Marshall had gone out of his way to defend the socialistic *Jewish Daily Forward* against exclusion from the United States mail in an effort to shield the reputation of the Yiddish-language press.[18] Hillquit's antiwar speeches, appealing to New Yorkers to elect him as a mandate from the voters calling upon the government to withdraw from the war, struck Marshall as an attempt to undermine the safety of American Jewry. "The American government will investigate this election and find out which nationalities supported opposition to the war," Marshall threatened in his article in the *Tageblatt*, "Morris Hillquit's Campaign: The Danger for the Jews of New York and America."[19] In an open letter to the *Jewish Daily Forward* editor on the eve of the election, Marshall claimed that "an endorsement by the Jews of a candidate who boasts of his refusal to subscribe even $50 for a Liberty Bond, and who cries for an untimely peace, will be interpreted in a manner which will not redound to our advantage."[20]

Hillquit did not answer his critics; he was unwilling to be intimidated by the generalized hysteria and the type of paranoia which had taken hold of many Americans, Jews and non-Jews. Accustomed to taking "unpopular stands," he did not believe vague threats of anti-Semitism warranted his apologies. He was confident in the moral superiority of his opposition to the war. In another sense, he did not fear the ambiguity brought about by the war situation. "I am a Jew, a Socialist, a Russian, an American, a lawyer, a lecturer . . . ," Hillquit said in 1917. "As a lawyer I have one sort of interest, as a Jew another, as a Socialist—another. . . . As you see, it is not so easy, either for you or me to explain the way one should act . . . ."[21]

Many of Hillquit's supporters believed he was acting in the highest spirit of Jewish tradition by opposing the war. Abraham Liessin, the Yiddish poet and journalist, upbraided Marshall because he played on the fear of anti-Semitism in America. Liessin wrote, "Wild accusations against foreigners and the defenseless have always been the beloved tactic of the tyrant. In this way the tyrant seeks to divert the dissatisfaction of the *folk*-masses from their real enemy, the tyrant himself."[22] Furthermore, Liessin thought that voters who elected Hillquit were acting in the tradition of the Jews who fought in revolutionary Russia.[23]

Another of Hillquit's supporters was Rabbi Judah Magnes, a pacifist who had former ties with the wealthy uptown, pro-war German-Jewish community.[24] This young American-born rabbi actively participated with Hillquit and other socialists in the formation of the People's Council of America, which, in May 1917, fixed upon the peace terms—no forced annexations, no punitive indemnities, self-determination for all nationalities—as the basis for immediate peace negotiations. The council called upon America to support Russia in repudiating the imperialistic aims and the intransigence of the ally as well as the enemy. Rabbi Magnes, who headed the council, enthusiastically endorsed Hillquit's mayoralty campaign on the basis of the socialist's pacifistic "Jewish" position. Speaking at a private supper for socialist campaign workers at the Little Hungary restaurant on October 18, 1917, Magnes said:

> . . . since the outbreak of the war my affection for the Jewish people has been deepened immeasurably. This hatred

> of all the arts of soldiering, this repugnance to war, this abhorrence of blood spilling, that has characterized the Jewish masses is nothing more or less than a continuance of the great Jewish tradition which exalted the spiritual life....
>
> I am not nearly so much interested in the fact that Mr. Hillquit will doubtless make a very efficient administrator as Mayor....What I am interested in is this: That your campaign is but one phase of the great democratic movement that is now sweeping the world and that can be kept alive only if your forces and the liberal and democratic and radical forces throughout the world will not abate their activities....[25]

Louis Marshall upbraided Magnes for his support of Hillquit and his stand against the war. In a letter to Magnes, Marshall wrote menacingly, "I trust that you do not wish to occupy the theatrical position of becoming a martyr to a cause in which Scott Nearing and Hillquit and Berger and Emma Goldman...are fellow-martyrs."[26]

Another issue divided the Jews of New York during Hillquit's campaign in 1917—the meaning of the Russian Revolution, especially its bearing upon the status of Russian Jewry. The wealthy German-Jewish community in the United States had no sympathy for revolutionary Russia and was anxious to disassociate any Jewish connection with either the revolution itself or with the Russian withdrawal from the war. Nevertheless, leaders such as Marshall and Schiff were concerned with the safety of the Russian Jews. They hoped to achieve minority rights for Eastern European Jewry at the peace conference after the war.

In contrast, the Socialists greeted the Russian Revolution with enthusiasm. The fact that the new Russian government moved quickly to grant civil and political equality to Russian Jews strengthened their faith in the revolution (pre-Bolshevik). Thus many Jewish socialists were persuaded that the Jewish problem in Eastern Europe was well on its way to being solved.[27] The socialist coalition to which Hillquit belonged, the NWC, announced that the revolution in Russia had transformed the question of Jewish rights into a domestic issue which could be resolved not through "international politics but by inner struggle within Russia itself."[28] Hillquit expressed sentiments shared by many Jewish socialists when, as NWC representative to the American Jewish Congress, he said that he did not believe "in seeking to accomplish the emancipation of the Jewish race by stratagem or diplomacy. . . ." He explained that "the emancipation of the Jew abroad is a problem of democracy. . . . a process of gradual elimination of class and caste distinction."[29] For Hillquit and many other Jewish socialists of 1917, the new Russian government was well under way in its democratic efforts. In fact, the NWC formally dissolved in the belief that its mission had been accomplished.

The optimism of socialists in regard to the fate of Eastern European Jews particularly disturbed the Zionists. Previously, in 1916, American Zionists had successfully unified the uptown German Jews, Socialists of the NWC, and various Zionist groups into a coalition organization, the American Jewish Congress. The Zionists hoped that at the coming peace conference the AJC would press not only for Jewish minority rights in Europe but also for recognition of a Jewish national interest in Palestine. Zionists were disappointed when in May 1917 Hillquit, as the representative of the NWC to the Executive Board, withdrew from the AJC.[30] Nevertheless, the Poale Zion, the most radical Socalist-Zionist group, urged its members to vote for Hillquit in the 1917 election. David Pinski, a noted Yiddish novelist and playwright, asked readers of the *Yidisher kaempher* to bury differences with Hillquit and support socialist unity.[31]

Hillquit was not elected in 1917 although he received more than 20 percent of the vote. Interviewed by the New York *Call* Hillquit said his large showing rebuked American militarism.[32] To what extent Hillquit's vote was Jewish has still to be determined. It is possible that he failed to mobilize significant Jewish backing during the 1917 election campaign.[33]

In the last sixteen years of his life, during which Hillquit remained an important leader of the Socialist Party, he rarely championed Jewish causes and his image as a Jewish leader faded, especially among Jewish socialists. During the 1920s he did not think Jewish issues appealed to the American Jewish voter. He avoided confronting the problem of developing a special ethnic identity for Jews in America. His vision for European Jewry returned to the cosmopolitan model he had maintained from childhood.

He did not try to strengthen his ties with the Jewish Federation of the Socialist Party although the federation was one of the few foreign-language groups which remained in the Party after the Communist split in 1919. When the federation itself split in 1921 over the issue of affiliation with the Third International, Hillquit supported the right-wing Verband (the group which remained within the Party). Although his essays, *From Marx to Lenin*, with a special Yiddish introduction, were serialized in the Verband's new weekly *Veker* beginning in October 1921, Hillquit did not go out of his way to support the views of the Verband.[34]

Zionism, however, continued to plague Hillquit. The Balfour Declaration of 1917 promising the Jews a national homeland in Palestine stimulated Zionist dreams in the post-World War I period. The Poale Zion, which had supported Hillquit since 1908, continued to expect reciprocity from him. For example, in October 1922 he was invited by the Poale Zion and the Palestine Foundation Fund to speak at a dinner in behalf of Colonel Joseph Wedgewood, the British Socialist MP. The New York *Call* reported that "earlier in the evening a number of the audience hissed Morris Hillquit when he welcomed Wedgewood. . . .Hillquit had declared, 'I cannot claim fellowship with you in the Zionist movevent,' when shouts of 'Why not?' came from various parts of the audience. Chairman Samuel Untermeyer rapped for order, but before the disturbance subsided Hillquit declared with a smile, 'because the Socialist movement, to which I give all my energies covers the whole field of the struggle of human liberty and emancipation!"[35]

In a 1926 speech, "Socialism and Zionism," Hillquit made an even stronger statement regarding the Zionist ideology:

> Personally I am not a Zionist. I doubt the possibility of recreating a Jewish state in Palestine and am not convinced that the Jews as an organized nationality can make a distinct and valuable contribution to the world's culture.
>
> But I am not an anti-Zionist. . . .A movement may be utopian from the point of view of practical politics yet it may exert a potent spiritual influence and. . .affect the course of human progress.

> Zionism makes a strong sentimental appeal to me, chiefly as a manifestation of awakening national self respect of the Jewish people. . . . Zionism, like all other national movements, must guard itself against the danger of degeneration into jingoism. If it ever develops in that direction, it will forfeit all claims to Socialist sympathy.[36]

Toward the end of his life, Hillquit was still critical of Jewish nationalism. He showed insight into the actual problems facing Jews who intended to settle Palestine with the support of the British government. In his 1930 Rand School lecture on "Problems of World Socialism," he maintained that the Balfour Declaration was originally a war measure, designed to get Jewish support for the Allied war effort and that the British government had since then found it more politically expedient to support the Arab population. Hillquit cited Arab riots and British attempts to limit Jewish immigration into Palestine as clear signs of their hostility to the ever-growing increase of the Jewish population. Hillquit expressed sympathy for the Arabs although he deplored the riots of the 1920s which he compared with pogroms in Russia during the 1880s. Yet he was unable to reconcile the mutual claims to the rights of self-determination and national independence proffered by Arab and Jew. "Very candidly," he said, "I really don't know." However, it appeared to him that several aspects of the Arab-Jewish issue had to be considered:

> One thing seems clear to me. Palestine cannot be handed over by the British to the Jews or by anybody outside of the people of Palestine to anybody else. Any arrangement that may come and that may bear fruit must be one voluntarily arrived at between the Arabs and the Jews. Anything else will be not only oppressive and unjust, but it will be built on a very shaky foundation.[37]

Notes

1. Morris Hillquit, "Speech to the Striking Shirtwaist Makers," January 2, 1910, Writings, Hillquit Papers.
2. *Loose Leaves*, pp. 130-46.

3. James Oneal, *History of the Amalgamated Ladies Garment Cutters' Union* (New York, 1927), pp. 176-77.

4. New York *Call*, April 13, 1915; New York *Jewish Daily Forward*, April 11, 1915.

5. "Congress of Neutral Nations Hearing before the Committee on Foreign Affairs, House of Representatives," Febraury 24, 1916, box D49, Meyer London Papers, Tamiment Library.

6. New York *Jewish Daily Forward*, November 4, 1916.

7. "Congress of Neutral Nations," pp. 7-8.

8. New York *Evening Globe*, October 26, 1916, Clippings, Hillquit Papers.

9. "Morris Hillquit un zein tzvey gegnor," New York *Jewish Daily Forward*, October 27, 1916. Also see laudatory articles by Moishe Olgin, "Morris Hillquit," ibid., September 30, 1916, and "Genosse Morris Hillquit," New York *Naye velt*, October 13, 1916.

10. New York *Jewish Daily Forward*, November 4, 1916.

11. Ibid., November 3, 1916.

12. Ber Borochov, "Sotzializm un Tammany Hall," New York *Yidisher kaempher*, November 13, 1916. For the Poale Zion's endorsement of Hillquit see "Editorial," ibid.

13. New York *Call*, September 3, 1916, Clippings, Hillquit Papers.

14. Moishe Olgin, "Vi Morris Hillquit kukt oif di yidishe frage," New York *Jewish Daily Forward*, October 25, 1916. For a surprised response to this interview see A. Livak (pseud. Amuk), "Fun tsaytungen un journalen," New York *Naye velt*, November 3, 1916.

15. New York *Call*, November 11, 1916, Clippings, Hillquit Papers.

16. Szajkowski, *Jews, Wars and Communism*, 1:142.

17. Melvyn Dubofsky, "Organized Labor and the Immigrant in New York City, 1900-1918," *Labor History* 2 (spring 1961), p. 191.

18. Szajkowski, *Jews, Wars and Communism*, 1:145.

19. New York *Tageblatt*, October 31, 1917. See also Louis Marshall, "Morris Hillquit un di yidishe vuters," ibid., November 14, 1917.

20. New York *Jewish Daily Forward*, November 3, 1917.

21. H. Burgin, "A Short History of the Jewish Workers' Movement in the United States," in *Tenth Year Jubilee of the International Workers' Order* (New York, 1940). Yiddish pamphlet in the Bund Archives.

22. A. Liessin, "Di yidishe issu in di yitztiche kampayn," New York *Jewish Daily Forward*, November 3, 1917.

23. A. Liessin, "Kampayn notizen: Morris Hillquit," *Zukunft* 22 (October 1917), pp. 555-57.

24. Arthur Goren, *New York Jews and the Quest for Community: The Kehillah Experiment* (New York, 1970), p. 232.

25. Judah Magnes, "Remarks at Private Supper for Socialist Campaign Workers," October 18, 1917, pp. 1-2, Judah Magnes Collection, Hebrew University, Jerusalem.

26. Charles Reznikoff, ed., Louis Marshall, *Champion of Liberty: Selected Papers and Addresses,* 2 vols. (Philadelphia, 1957), 2:973.

27. Hertz, *Di yidishe sotzialistishe bavegung,* p. 163.

28. Mark Wischnitzer, "The Impact of American Jewry on Life Abroad," in *The Jewish People Past and Present,* 4 vols. (New York, 1946-1955), 4:249.

29. Morris Hillquit, "What Can Be Done to Aid the Emancipation of the Jews Abroad?," March 1916, Writings, Hillquit Papers.

30. Wischnitzer, "The Impact of American Jewry," p. 245.

31. David Pinski, "Shtimpt for Hillquitn," New York *Yidisher kaempfer,* November 2, 1917.

32. New York *Call,* November 7, 1917.

33. Szajkowski, *Jews, Wars and Communism,* 1:154.

34. Morris Hillquit, "Fun Marx biz Lenin," translated into Yiddish by D. Kaplan. It began in the New York *Veker* on October 1, 1921, and was serialized weekly until December 10, 1921.

35. New York *Call,* October 9, 1922.

36. Morris Hillquit, "Socialism and Zionism," April 12, 1926, Writings, Hillquit Papers.

37. Morris Hillquit, "Problems of World Socialism," December 17, 1930, ibid.

International Socialism in the 1920s

Chapter 14

"Unlike most Americans," Charles Beard wrote in 1934, Hillquit

> . . . had a wide knowledge of the labor and socialist movements of the Old World. His vision took in the Continent of Europe. . . . He belonged to Western Civilization rather than any national segment. . . . He was one of my few acquaintances in New York whom I could truly call "civilized"—civilized in the wide range of his interests and knowledge and sympathies.[1]

Beard was not the only one to remark upon the uniqueness of Hillquit's interest in the international socialist movement.[2] Before World War I, other American Socialist Party leaders seemed to be singularly disinterested in international relations. The Party concerned itself almost entirely with domestic issues. Not one of the Party platforms from 1904 through 1912 contained a single proposal for international affairs. Party theoreticians, such as Spargo or Russell, devoted few pages to European socialism in their books on the socialist movement.

Occasionally, the Socialist periodical literature dealt with international subjects. For example, the left-wing *International Socialist Review* as well as the more center-right-wing New York *Call* and the Yiddish press continuously ran articles about European socialism in the pre-war years. While Hillquit was not alone, he was exceptional in his enormous enthusiasm for maintaining close and careful ties with the international socialist movement.

The books he wrote in the pre-war years were full of references to the Second International and those of its leaders he particularly admired—Keir Hardie, Jean Jaurès, Karl Kautsky, Auturo Labriola, Wilhelm and Karl Liebknecht, Rosa Luxemberg, and many others. In both a popular article that appeared in Funk and Wagnall's *Encyclopedia of Social Reform* (1908) and in *Socialism in Theory and Practice* (1912) he included a special historical sketch of the socialist movement in Germany, France, Russia, Austria, England, Italy, Belgium, Holland, and Scandinavia.[3]

Hillquit was a firm believer in the Second International; he had attended three International congresses before World War I: Amsterdam (1904), Stuttgart (1907), and Copenhagen (1910). He approved of the structure of the International which granted autonomous status to the national members. Its decisions were not binding upon the member countries and yet those resolutions which were passed at International congresses carried the weight of majority rule. Nina Hillquit wrote about her father's strong commitment to the Second International. She quoted him as saying, "Since my early years, I had followed the development of the Socialist movement in the different countries of the world with absorbing interest. To me, they were not merely kindred to each other because of the substantial identity of their aims and philosophy: They were one world-wide and indivisible whole of which our movement was an organic part."[4]

The disintegration of the Second International in 1914 was difficult for Hillquit to comprehend. He did not abandon hope for international socialism and instead pleaded for tolerance and for a renewed faith in the movement.[5] From the beginning of the war, he thought the international movement could be salvaged. He faced the growing resentment of many American socialists toward the Europeans by holding firm to his antiwar stance, by seeking what appeared to him to be logical explanations of European behavior, and by continuing a correspondence with Camille Huysmans, the secretary of the traumatized International Bureau of the Second International.[6] He spoke at the Rand School in favor of creating a new International.[7] With no success, he tried to attend conferences of socialists in Europe. The American government refused to issue passports to Party delegates.[8]

The American Socialist Party was unable to participate in the conferences held by European socialists between 1915 and 1920 which paved the way for a set of antagonistic international organizations: the reconstituted Second International, the Communist or Third International and the Two and a Half or Labor and Socialist International. However, the American Party reacted to the events in Europe. By 1920 the SP had decided preferences.

In the main, the American Party rejected realliance with the reconstituted Second International. It was too conservative. Even Victor Berger, hardly a radical socialist, was impressed by the tone of the postwar International. On August 20, 1919, he wrote to Hillquit, who was then in Saranac Lake, that he "...was cowed by the war patriots" and that he thought the Berne conference, held by the Second International, was "...completely dominated by English laborities—most of whom are 'weak sisters' and dull. The Berne aggregation was just as impossibly reactionary as the Spartacans were crazy revolutionary. The hope of the world is in intelligent action, not in violent insanity."[9]

Under Hillquit's direction, the American Party specifically broke off any kind of relationship with the Second International at its 1920 National Convention. Hillquit commented that one could not "...acquiesce in the passive and sterile conservatism of the Second International." Evaluating the postwar International he said that it was "morally bankrupt" and had lost prestige and authority and had forever ceased to be a directly inspiring force in the world.[10]

However, the American Party did not join the Communist or Third International although membership became an issue of heated controversy. The Third International was founded in March 1919, a few months before the first communist split in the American Party. At the founding congress assembled in the Kremlin, thirty-five parties and organizations accepted a set of principles prepared by Lenin and Chicherin and drafted by Trotsky. The aim of the Third International was the immediate and universal establishment of the dictatorship of the proletariat in view of the impending dissolution of capitalism throughout the world. Its other provisions included the conquest of state power, the destruction of the bourgeois state machine, the replacement of parliamentary democracy by "self-rule by the masses through their own elected organs," the expropriation of capital, and the abolition of private ownership of means of production and its transfer of state ownership. This first congress of the Third International also declared its enmity toward the socialists of the former Second International, "the social-patriots who have gone over openly to the bourgeois camp."

In September 1919 the famous Twenty-One Points refined this latter point. As a condition for admission into the new International, socialist or communist national parties were required to expel from their ranks party leaders suspected of reformism or "center sympathies." The Twenty-One Points specifically named for expulsion Longuet, Turati, Kautsky, Hilferding, and Hillquit.[11]

Hillquit was enthusiastic about the Russian Revolution in 1917. Even earlier, in September 1915 after the Zimmerwald conference and in April 1916 after the Kienthal conference, where a Russian-led left-wing militant opposition to the war was formed, Hillquit supported the Russians.[12] Although his critics in the American left-wing *New Review* doubted his sincerity as a militant, Hillquit appreciated the Zimmerwald Manifesto which denounced the war as imperialistic and he concurred that a permanent committee be formed with the task of reuniting the Socialist parties of the world. The American SP endorsed the Zimmerwald program.[13]

Even the development of a strong, left wing in the American Party during the spring of 1919, a left wing which articulated the desire to imitate Soviet revolutionary style, did not dampen Hillquit's loyalty to the Russian efforts. A May Day Manifesto, issued under Hillquit's signature as International Secretary of the American Party, greeted the Socialist Soviet Republic of Russia "which is so valiantly upholding the lofty international proletarian ideals in the face of the combined military, economic and political attacks of reactionary powers, and in spite of the systematic campaign of libelous misrepresentation on the part of the lying capitalist press of the world." He also sent greetings to "the workers of Hungary on the establishment of a free communistic workers' republic upon the ruins of the predatory monarchy of their exploiting and land-monopolizing rulers." Hillquit concluded his manifesto with the familiar: "Long live the international of the Proletariat!"[14]

But which International? On May 29, 1919, the NEC, under attack by the growing left wing, came out with a "Statement of Party Policy" which was probably written by Hillquit. The statement rejected affiliation with the Third International.[15] In August 1919 the first major split between communists and socialists occurred. The Communists founded their own party, two in fact, and desired affiliation with the Third International.

A significant left wing which also wanted affiliation remained within the Party. Although the NEC opposed joining the International, the left was conciliated by a "Manifesto" which stated that "the world crisis brought on by the war and the quickened pace of the Socialist and labor movements in all parts of the world impose upon the party the duty of adopting more energetic action and more resolute methods. . . ."[16]

The left wing within the Party continued to urge affiliation with the Third International. But the Party leaders and particularly Hillquit, who was the international policymaker, became increasingly opposed to such union. When in September 1919 the International had declared its Twenty-One Points, Hillquit said that this document labeled "your humble servant in America" a traitor because he does "not wish to lead the struggle for the soviet power of the proletariat."[17] Hillquit felt personally attacked. The January 1920 trial of the five New York assemblymen in Albany reinforced Hillquit's rejection of the Communist alliance. In Albany Hillquit had to fend off accusations by conservative politicians that the Party belonged to an "invisible empire." He spent considerable time convincing the trial committee and the press that it was not affiliated with international Communism.

At the May 1920 National Convention the left again urged affiliation with the Third International. Hillquit took the position that "we draw a clear and distinct line between our relations to Soviet Russia and our relations to the Third or Moscow International." He supported the Soviet Union but declined to "blindly accept every formula, every dogma coming from Soviet Russia as holy, as a Papal decree." Furthermore, Hillquit criticized the concept of the "dictatorship of the proletariat" claiming that it did not exist in Russia. Russia was a "limited democracy" which excluded "from its ranks non-producing classes, just as democracy in the United States at one time excluded non-propertied classes." Hillquit concluded his discussion on dictatorship by affirming its inappropriateness to the American situation and stating that the term implied "the disarming, the disenfranchising and the outlawing of the bourgeoisie. . . . In countries of democratic and parliamentary traditions the Socialist movement cannot consistently employ or advocate such methods. . . ." American socialists, he said, cannot revert to "the old methods of street barricades" but rather should pursue "a political fight with the weapons and methods of political democracy."

Not wishing to completely alienate the left wing, Hillquit admitted that at present the Third International "represents after all the best spirit in the Socialist movement. . . ." He promised the convention that "we will work towards the creation of a larger International on the basis of the Third. . . ."[18] The American Socialist Party applied for affiliation with the Third International. In October 1920 Hillquit announced that "from late unofficial reports the Moscow International has rejected the conditional affiliation of the American SP and the latter is at this time not attached to any international organization."[19]

But there were postmortems. Hillquit was assailed by Socialists within the Party and by communists who found fault with his handling of the international question. Almost immediately after the May convention, Eugene Debs, the presidential candidate for 1920, disagreed with Hillquit's lack of confidence in the Communist International. On June 30, 1920, Hillquit wrote Debs a letter. "Like you," he said, "I am a determined and enthusiastic supporter of the Soviet Government of Russia." But he insisted that the "Communists of Russia have done certain things which their own desperate conditions have probably forced upon them." Therefore, the Russians could not be trusted to take control of the international socialist movement. Hillquit advised Debs that "we have a voice in the formulation of the basis of . . . unity, and we reserve the principles of self-determination. . . ." Hillquit expressed confidence in the future. "Personally I am strongly inclined to think that such action will bring about a sane, healthy Socialist International. . . ."[20] Theodore Debs replied to Hillquit's letter after a conversation with his brother who was still imprisoned in the Atlantic Penetentiary. On July 12 Theodore wrote that "Gene says he notes with special interest what you have to say about the Third International."[21] Ultimately Debs concurred with Hillquit.

By November 1920, in his journalistic debates with communists, Hillquit began to argue that the socialist revolution may assume different political forms in different countries and that the Bolshevik Revolution was not necessarily a socialist one. For example, he contrasted the Russian situation with the attempt at revolution in Germany in 1918. In Hillquit's interpretation the Germans were not as successful because Germany was more industrialized, its political institutions more democratic, and its masses less docile. In contradistinction, the Russians, with their agricultural economy, autocratic political institutions, and naïve citizens, had succeeded in overturning their system. Hillquit implied that this Russian Revolution in an agrarian, non-industrialized, and non-democratic society was not socialistic.[22]

In late 1920 Hillquit quarreled with Max Eastman, the editor of the *Liberator*. Eastman, now a communist, contended that the specific issues of affiliation with the Communist International and of the appropriateness of soviets in America were merely manifestations of a broader and older problem. "The split in Socialist parties has always been the same—on the one hand revolutionary Marxians, on the other reformists and diluters of Marxian theory." Furthermore, Eastman dated authentic American Marxism to the 1915 days of the *New Review* and the work of Fraina and Boudin. He implied that Hillquit's socialism was diluted and "insincere."[23] Hillquit, who had defended Eastman against antiwar charges in 1918, answered in a personal way and with more than his usual invective. He accused the *Liberator* and its editor of ". . .flirting with every new name and notion that happened to be in vogue, from Woodrow Wilson to Nietzsche, from birth control to communism."[24] It is interesting that years later, when Eastman left the Communist Party, he was particularly contrite about doubting Hillquit's sincerity. In his autobiography *Love and Revolution* Eastman apologized. "I did not mean to call Hillquit insincere; nothing was remoter from my mind. . .," he wrote in 1964.

> But his political lieutenant, Algernon Lee, denounced and scourged me for this in a long article. . .making me feel that

> an uncrossable personal rift had opened between me and my friend and one-time legal defender. To a true-blue Bolshevik this was as it should be, but I never was as good a Bolshevik as that. I liked and admired Morris Hillquit. He had the faults, I suppose, as well as the virtues, of a skilled politician but there was a character both firm and tender behind those strong jaws and bright dark-gleaming eyes.[25]

By late 1920 Hillquit began a serious attack upon American Communists. "In the United States," he wrote, the split in the Socialist Party "has resulted in the creation of a perfectly ineffective and impotent Communist party, a weakened Socialist party and a strengthened capitalist reaction." He predicted that "for some time to come the glamor and fascination which naturally attach to struggles of the Russian Soviet Republic will carry away large bodies of emotional Socialists everywhere." But he thought that "eventually a sobering process will set in. The Socialists will learn to distinguish between their just sympathies for the Russian proletarian government and the exotic methods of revolutionary struggle sought to be forced upon their own country."[26] Hillquit was convinced that communism was inappropriate, harmful, and a foreign import into American radical life. He never changed his mind.

The 1921 National Conference in Detroit concluded the controversy over affiliation. Again there was a motion that the American Party affiliate with the Communist International. Illinois left-winger William F. Kruse supported the motion by saying. "We can't swallow the Twenty-One Points but we can petition again for admission. . .on a better basis." Hillquit answered that "the Third International doesn't want us . . ." and that affiliation with this International would be suicidal. Kruse reported that "it is also suicidal to join the capitalist anvil chorus condemning the Third International. The working class is leaning toward Moscow, whether you like it or not."[27]

The Detroit Conference decided to submit the issue of affiliation to a national referendum. The convention majority report, which was adopted by a 31 to 8 vote, proposed "to remain without international affiliation" until a suitable organization was found. The minority report, defeated at the convention by a 26 to 13 vote, proposed that the Party join the Communist International "but retain autonomy in matters of membership, organization and tactics in questions which are primarily of domestic concern."[28] The outcome of the national referendum was 2,517 for the majority and 675 for the minority.[29] The left-wing pro-Third Internationalists split from this already drastically diminished Socialist Party. The controversy was over.[30]

Although the American Party declared itself without international affiliation in June of 1921, Hillquit had already begun to open negotiations with a newly formed International, the Vienna International Working Union of Socialist Parties, founded in February 1921. The Vienna International, or the Two and a Half as the Communists derisively called it, was created in 1921 by a group of antiwar European socialists who wanted a more militant international organization than had been proposed by the Second International but were at odds with the Communist International. The leading figures were Adler, Bauer, Longuet, Kautsky, Wallhead, Crispien, Hilferding, Bracke, Renaudel, and Ledebour.[31]

In July, after the June 1921 National Party Convention, Hillquit was sent abroad as a representative "to study socialism"[32] and to look over the Vienna International. He sailed on the *Lorraine* with his wife Vera and daughter Nina. This was his first return trip to Europe since 1913. Subsequently, he spent almost every late spring and summer in France, Germany, England, and Italy. Through the 1920s he was the Party's major and sometimes sole representative in Europe and an interpreter of the European situation to American socialists.

On his 1921 trip Hillquit visited individual socialists whom he had known before the war. In Paris he spoke with Jules Guesde and Jean Longuet, Karl Marx's grandson. In Berlin he visited Kautsky and Ebert, the socialist president of the German republic whose support of the war and conservative behavior during the 1918 German uprising Hillquit did not condone. According to Nina, her father asked Ebert how he liked his new quarters as president of the German republic. "Not much. . .nor many things connected with it," was the German socialist's reported cryptic reply.[33]

During his trip to England Hillquit acquired a great respect for the British Labour Party. He especially admired such prominent

Labour Party leaders as Ramsey MacDonald, Snowden, Clynes, and Arthur Henderson, all of whom had served in Parliament. After the war the Labour Party had moved further to the left. Its new constitution, adopted in February 1919, turned the party from a loose federation of affiliated organizations (the trade unions and the various socialist societies) into a centralized party. There was party discipline but individual members belonged to their local branches. The trade unions were dominant both financially and numerically. The Labour Party put forward a socialist policy—though it still avoided the use of the word socialism.[34]

It would be fair to say that after his trip to England in 1921 Hillquit seriously planned to develop a Labor Party in the United States. This was a drastic departure; for more than twenty years he had insisted that the Party avoid political "fusion" with non-Socialist labor or reform parties. The change was a result of several factors including the unprecedented shrinkage in Party membership as well as the interest shown by a few important unions, especially the railway unions, for an American Labor Party in the early 1920s.[35] The British Labour Party's political success and its socialistic ideology encouraged Hillquit in his attempt to construct a socialist-labor political party.[36]

Hillquit wanted American socialists to see the British model of socialism as an alternative to the Soviet model. In July he wrote in the *Socialist World* that "the focus of international working-class interest is shifting from Moscow to London, from the Communist Party of Russia to the British Labour Party." And he noted, "As time goes on it becomes increasingly evident that the recent development of the British Labour Party is a more thoroughgoing revolution than the Bolshevik *coup d'etat* in 1917. The latter was a dazzling historic adventure, while the former is a solid historic event."[37]

When he returned from Europe in the fall of 1921, Hillquit recommended that the American Party join the Vienna International. At the 1922 National Party Convention, which the Communist press gleefully pointed out had only thirty delegates in attendance,[38] Hillquit asked for immediate affiliation. He told the convention, "The purpose of the International . . . is to infuse a little more revolutionary enthusiasm in the Second International, and to put a little more realism and sanity in the Third (Moscow) International." Furthermore, he assured the delegates that "the Vienna International represents the elite of the various socialist organizations of Europe."[39] The vote in favor of the measure was a close 11 to 10.[40]

Although at the 1922 convention the American delegates also voted for complete recognition by the United States of the Soviet Union,[41] Hillquit and the majority of the Vienna International leaders found it increasingly difficult to maintain any kind of relationship with the Communist International. For example, on April 4, 1922, a meeting took place in the Reichstag building in Berlin which was attended by the executive committees of the Communist International, the Second International, and the Vienna International. This was the last attempt on the part of European socialists and communists to form a united international organization.[42] The Berlin meeting failed to create unity. It was Hillquit's impression that the communists were at fault "partly because the trial of Socialists for treason in Moscow and partly because. . .the increasing dislike of the Russian officials by the Socialist leaders of other countries of Europe made unity impossible."[43]

A year later the Vienna International merged with the more conservative Second International to form the Labor and Socialist International. Although Hillquit praised the merger, he felt uneasy with those socialists of the Second International who had supported the war. At Hamburg where the union took place in May 1923, Hillquit told the more than 400 delegates that the "union is not so much a marriage of love as of convenience." He hoped that a great love and happy life would result.[44] On the same rather dismal note he wrote home from Hamburg to his old friend Job Harriman:

> The gathering was somewhat sad and depressed and not as inspiring as the pre-war congresses, but it accomplished the main object for which it was called and has re-established the machinery for international action between the Socialist Parties of Europe, which was so sadly needed.[45]

Between 1923 and 1931 Hillquit represented the American Socialist Party at three Labor and Socialist international congresses—

Marseilles in August 1925, Brussels in 1928, and Vienna in 1931. He also traveled to Europe to attend meetings of the International's Executive Committee and corresponded with dozens of the International's leaders. His involvement in those years focused around several issues: the persecution of socialists, Mensheviks and Social Revolutionaries in the Soviet Union; the plight of the German trade unions, and American imperialism.

The first two issues involved raising money. In 1924 Friedrich Adler, secretary of the International, informed Hillquit that a representative of the Central Committee of the Mensheviki had visited the executive offices in London and asked for financial aid. Adler wrote that "repeatedly we decided that it is an obligation of international solidarity to help the prisoners in Russia." Since Adler thought financial conditions in the United States were far better than in Europe, he advised American socialists to hold a funding drive.[46] The German trade unions, the Central Trade Organizations of the City of Berlin, and the General German Federation of Trade Unions also appealed for money. The appeal was made through Arthur Henderson of the British Labour Party. Hillquit was requested to organize a special committee to raise funds. On November 27, 1923, he wrote to Samuel Gompers trying to enlist help from the AFL for German workers:

> As you well know, the organized workers of Germany are desperately struggling on both fronts, in their economic organizations to maintain their daily lives and in their political organizations to preserve the Republic and the newly gained democratic institutions against the extreme right and the extreme left.[47]

Gompers agreed to help.

In May 1922 the Vienna International declared itself against Italian fascism.[48] That summer Hillquit visited Italy and his impressions of the Fascists were reported home in the New York *Call.* On October 9, 1922, the *Call* ran an article describing Hillquit's visit to the offices of *Avanti*, the socialist newspaper in Milan. This visit took place shortly after the Fascists had burned and machine-gunned the building. He was quoted as saying:

> The Fascisti are made up of army officers out of work, of landowners, of former left wing Socialists, of boys, kids, loafers, and of underworld elements. They overshadow every other power in Italy. They have dissolved Socialist municipalities. They have forbidden Socialist deputies to go home, threatening to kill their wives if they try to return.[49]

Opposition to fascism became intertwined with distrust of communism. For example, Julius Deutsch wrote Hillquit on September 8, 1926, inquiring whether "the so-called anti-fascist Alliance with Northern America is under communist domination." Deutsch said that the International would support this group only on the condition that "it had not been penetrated by communist cells."[50] In fact, by 1927 Hillquit blamed the Italian Communists for originating Italian fascism. Speaking at a Rand School lecture on the subject of "New Forms of Class Struggle—Political and Economic," he claimed that the communist experiment of "direct action" in Italy led to the fascist takeover. As he put it:

> ...the first definite experiment in direct action...took the shape of the workers in the leading industry in Italy—the metal industry—after a strike and a dispute with their employers, deciding to occupy the factories....They couldn't operate them....They withdrew. They left the entire working class in a weakened condition. And that seemingly heroic and romantic act undoubtedly has contributed a good deal to the rise and ultimate triumph of Fascism.[51]

In the early 1930s Hillquit also attacked German fascism, but in this case he attributed its success to the economic depression and the failure of political parties to offer constructive programs.[52]

While he interpreted the situation in Europe to Americans, he explained American circumstances to the Europeans of the Labor and Socialist International. In August 1925 at the Marseilles Congress, Hillquit launched a vigorous attack upon American foreign policy. He denounced the Monroe Doctrine and American capitalist designs on Mexican oil wells. He said that the "United States policy of isolation forced her to become imperialistic. The Monroe doctrine—the doctrine that America is for Americans—is now obsolete. Today it is North and South America for the United States."[53] This speech caused a great sensation in Marseilles. Hillquit was applauded wildly when he concluded his speech with "Capitalism is war! Socialism is peace!"[54] The New York *Times* reported that Hillquit said ". . .Mexico is now 'the prisoner of American capitalists, and in the Far East the same capitalists are moving toward war with Japan'."[55]

Both the capitalist and the communist press in the United States were delighted when on his return trip from Marseilles to New York, Hillquit sailed on a ship whose original crew was on strike. The Montreal *Gazette* ran an article with the headline "*Majestic* Jeered by Mob of I.W.W.—Hillquit also Target for Ribald Shouts by Reds."[56]

At the Brussels Congress in 1928 Hillquit's address surveyed the world political and economic situation. He explained the evil effects of reparations, deflation, and war debts. He denounced capitalist rationalization and warned those English labor leaders who were inclined to support rationalization that it was making slaves of the American worker. "Rationalization means the triumph of the machine over man," he said. "Socialism must make man triumph over the machine." Furthermore, Hillquit criticized the inhuman realities of economic imperalism. In a radical departure from his unpopular 1907 Stuttgart position twenty years earlier, Hillquit now pleaded for a world Socialist organization to include "the newly industrialized coloured workers of the East."[57]

Until the 1930s Hillquit's almost complete domination over the American Party's international relations went virtually unnoted. It was taken for granted that he represented the Party's views in Europe. However, by 1931, a left-wing group critical of Hillquit's actions abroad called the Militants had developed in the Party. Hillquit was called to task for what the Militants believed was his inadequate stand against disarmament after the Labor and Socialist Congress in Vienna in 1931. In fact, Dr. Louis Sadoff, a left-winger who also attended the Congress, criticized the lack of preparation with which the American delegates came to Vienna. He also objected to the methods by which delegates were chosen and asserted that in the future they should be elected rather than let the Party continue with the practice of allowing only "those comrades who could afford to make the trip to Europe. . . ."[58]

Notes

1. Charles Beard, "The Noblest Tradition of Manhood," New York *New Leader*, October 6, 1934.

2. See C. Roland Marchand, *The American Peace Movement and Social Reform*, 1898-1918 (Princeton, N.J., 1972), pp. 267-68, and Sally Miller, "Americans and the Second International," *Proceedings of the American Philosophical Society* 120 (Octobr 1976), 5:372-87.

3. Morris Hillquit, "History of Socialism," in *Encyclopedia of Social Reform* (1908), Writings, Hillquit Papers, and in his *Socialism*, pp. 320-56.

4. Nina Hillquit, "Morris Hillquit," p. 9.

5. See, for example, the letter from Morris Hillquit to the NEC, December 28, 1914, Correspondence, Hillquit Papers.

6. See letters from Camille Huysmans to Morris Hillquit, January 16, May 5, July 10, and September 9, 1915, and February 7, 1917, ibid. Also see letter from Pieter Troelstra to Hillquit, January 29, 1917, ibid., about the impossibility of holding a meeting of the International Bureau because of discord.

7. Morris Hillquit, "Socialism and the War" (May 1915), Writings, ibid.

8. For problems with passports as late as 1919 see the letter from Algernon Lee to Morris Hillquit, February 9, 1919, Correspondence, ibid.

9. Letter from Victor Berger to Morris Hillquit, August 20, 1919, ibid.

10. *Loose Leaves*, p. 287.

11. Braunthal, *History of the International*, 2:165.

12. *Loose Leaves*, pp. 153-54.

13. Lenin's suspicion of the American SP position on Zimmerwald is to be found in his letter to Kollontai on November 9, 1915, cited in O. Gankin and H. H. Fisher, *The Bolsheviks and the World War* (London, 1940), pp. 591-92.

14. Morris Hillquit, "May 1, 1919," Writings, Hillquit Papers.

15. *National Executive Committee of the Socialist Party: Statement of Party Policy*, May 29, 1919, ibid.

16. Morris Hillquit and Adolph Germer, "May 1, 1919, Manifesto," source unknown, ibid. Also see left-wing "Minority Report in International Relations," signed by Louis Engdahl and William F. Quick, Socialist Party Papers, Tamiment Library.

17. Morris Hillquit, "Dictatorship and the International," *Socialist World* (August 15, 1920), 1-4, Writings, Hillquit Papers.

18. Morris Hillquit, "The Socialist Party of the United States and the Moscow International," October 1920, ibid. By June 1921 Hillquit had redefined "dictatorship of the proletariat" to mean a workers' society "without suppression of minorities." See New York *Evening Globe*, June 28, 1921, Clippings, ibid.

19. See New York *Herald*, December 2, 1920, ibid., for the official announcement.

20. Letter from Morris Hillquit to Eugene V. Debs, June 30, 1920, Correspondence, ibid.

21. Letter from Theodore Debs to Morris Hillquit, July 12, 1920, ibid.

22. Morris Hillquit, "Again the Moscow International, Part I," November 15, 1920, Writings, ibid. He stated this thesis more directly in his anticommunist work *From Marx to Lenin* (New York, 1923).

23. Max Eastman, *Love and Revolution*, p. 213.

24. Morris Hillquit, "Again the Moscow International, Part III," November 16, 1920, Writings, Hillquit Papers.

25. Max Eastman, *Love and Revolution*, p. 212.

26. Morris Hillquit, "Again the Moscow International, Part III," Writings, Hillquit Papers.

27. "The Socialist Pin Wheel," *Liberator* 4 (August 1921), pp. 22-23.

28. *The Socialist World* (June-July 1921), p. 4.

29. Ibid., (October 1921), p. 8.

30. Coverage of the Detroit Convention included in Clippings, Hillquit Papers. In 1921 the reported dues-paying membership of the SP was 7,000.

31. Braunthal, *History of the International*, 2:232-36.

32. Letter form Party Secretary Otto Branstetter to Morris Hillquit, September 2, 1921, Correspondence, Hillquit Papers.

33. Quoted in Nina Hillquit, "Morris Hillquit," p. 39.

34. T. J. Jarmon, *Socialism in Britain* (London, 1972), p. 122.

35. See Chapter 15.

36. See New York *Times*, June 9, 1923, report that while in England Hillquit had consultations with Ramsey MacDonald and Philip Snowden and had drawn up plans for the formation of a political labor party in the United States similar to the one in England. Hillquit was disappointed in 1931 when MacDonald resigned as Prime Minister of the Labour government and formed a new coalition consisting of his own personal Labour supporters, Conservatives, and Liberals. See, for example, Hillquit's "MacDonald Forsakes Labor in Her Important Crisis," New York *New Leader*, August 29, 1931.

37. Morris Hillquit, "Moscow and London," *Socialist World* (July 1923), Writings, Hillquit Papers. Also see his "The Story of the British Labor Party," ibid., September, 1923, ibid.

38. New York *Freiheit*, May 2, 1922.

39. Springfield (Ohio) *News*, April 20, 1922, Clippings, Hillquit Papers.

40. Washington *Post*, April 30, 1922, ibid.

41. New York *Times*, May 3, 1922, ibid.

42. Braunthal, *History of the International*, 2:245-54.

43. Pittsburgh *Post*, September 10, 1922, Clippings, Hillquit Papers.

44. Chicago *Tribune*, May 22, 1923, ibid. For a verbatim report on Hamburg see Nina Hillquit, "Research," Writings, ibid.

45. Letter from Morris Hillquit to Job Harriman, June 27, 1923, Correspondence, ibid. Also see "From Hillquit's Report," May 1923, Socialist Party Papers, Duke University, where he wrote: "The Hamburg Congress was, to some of our delegates, a little disappointing. It was not in any sense of the term a deliberative body. None of the great problems confronting the world was taken up and discussed. It could have been a little more deliberative and democratic and allowed more room for discussion, but the desire of the delegates for unity overshadowed every other consideration.

46. Letter from Frederich Adler to Morris Hillquit, November 18, 1924, Correspondence, Hillquit Papers. For the Menshevik opinion of Hillquit see his obituary in *Socialistitcheski Vestnik* (Paris), October 25, 1933, and Raphael Abramowitsch, "A Bridge between America and Europe," New York *New Leader*, October 1934.

47. Letter from Morris Hillquit to Samuel Gompers, November 27, 1923, Correspondence, Hillquit Papers.

48. Chicago *Tribune*, May 22, 1923, Clippings, ibid.

49. New York *Call*, October 9, 1922.

50. Letter from Julius Deutsch to Morris Hillquit, September 8, 1926, Correspondence, Hillquit Papers.

51. Morris Hillquit, "New Forms of Class Struggle—Political and Economic," Rand School lecture, December 1927, Writings, ibid. However, in 1933, when the Communists proposed a "united front," Hillquit wrote Clarence Senior that "our International is at this time for a program of common action along certain lines." Letter from Hillquit to Clarence Senior, July 28, 1933, Socialist Party Papers, Duke University.

52. New York *Tribune*,September 27, 1930, Clippings, Hillquit Papers.

53. Quoted in the Pittsburgh *Sun*, August 25, 1923, ibid. See verbatim report of Hillquit's speech in the *Proceedings of the Second Labor and Socialist International*, Marseilles, August 1925, pp. 224-28, Hoover Library, Stanford University.

54. Quoted in *Le Petit Provençal,* ca. August 24, 1925, Clippings, Hillquit Papers.

55. New York *Times,* August 26, 1925, ibid.

56. Incident of the *Majestic* in Montreal *Gazette,* September 9, 1925, ibid; New York *Times,* September 2, 3, and 9, 1925, ibid., and New York *Tribune,* September 2, 1925, ibid.

57. Hillquit discusses Asian socialism in a Rand School lecture, "Socialism and the Development in the East," December 20, 1927, Writings, ibid. Also see the New York *New Leader,* August 10, 1928.

58. New York *New Leader,* September 19, 1931. See also Hillquit's speech at the Vienna Congress in *Fourth Congress of the Labour and Socialist International,* Vienna, July-August, "Reports and Proceedings" (London, 1932) 6:604-5, Hoover Library, Stanford University.

The American Party in the 1920s

Chapter 15

During the 1920s the dues-paying membership of the American Socialist Party continued to decline. In 1919, before the first Communist split, the Socialists numbered 118,000. Membership fell to 12,474 in 1923 and, following the La Follette debacle, dropped to 7,793 by 1928. The Party was no longer composed of a large American-born majority. More than 3,400 American Socialists in 1928 were in foreign-language-affiliated organizations. Nor were large numbers of Socialists to be found west of the Mississippi. Most of the membership was concentrated in the Midwest and in the East, especially in New York.[1]

In the mid-1920s Hillquit was recognized as the Party's major leader. Articles in the *New Leader* (which replaced the *Call*) such as William Feigenbaum's "Morris Hillquit: Pillar of Socialism," acknowledged his centrality to the Party's life.[2] A further testament to his importance was his continuous election as International secretary and as a member of the NEC as well as his elevation to the National Party chairmanship in 1929.

It would have been difficult for any individual to lead the Party in those years. Hillquit had specific personal problems and limitations. He had never been a warm, attractive, charismatic figure. Now in his late fifties and early sixties, having suffered serious bouts with tuberculosis, his personality was more brittle and sharper than before. An edge of pomposity crept into his relationships with fellow socialists.

After the 1919 Communist split and the continuous attack upon the Party by the American government, Hillquit developed more cautious attitudes toward the socialist role in American society. He attempted to "soften" socialism in the United States in order to make it more palatable to the American public.

The Albany trial was illustrative of Hillquit's post-split tactics. Although still not entirely well, in January 1920 Hillquit left his bed in Saranac Lake to defend five New York socialists who had been expelled from the Assembly. August Claessens, Louis Waldman, Charles Solomon, Samuel De Witt, and Samuel Orr were accused of having been elected on a platform which was inimical to the best interests of New York State and the United States. The enumerated charges were that the Party was not a regular political party, that it admitted aliens and minors into its ranks, that its elected officials were bound by instruction of the Party's Executive Committee, that it was disloyal during the war, and that it was in sympathy with the Communist International and its program of violence and civil war.[3] This Red Scare trial lasted from January through March 1920 and resulted in the Socialists' expulsion.

Hillquit saw this trial as an opportunity afforded socialists to explain their ideology to the general public and, consequently, as an important step also affecting the termination of Red Scare tactics. Therefore, in his speeches before the jury, Hillquit toned down issues of class war and revolution and stressed the democratic and hence American qualities of socialism. He argued that socialism was not only a respectable creed in and of itself but it represented the ideals of the United States Constitution; he felt that the Party would bring American democracy to fruition.[4] In his summation for the defense, which lasted three days and was later printed as a pamphlet entitled *Socialism on Trial*, Hillquit emphasized the political and evolutionary rather than the trade union or revolutionary nature of American socialism. He expressed the confidence American socialists had in the democratic ideals of their country and the vast separation which existed between American social democrats and the Communist Bolsheviks of the Third International. He reserved his harshest criticism, not for the capitalist system, but for the tactics of the Red Scare, "the peculiar psychology which has taken hold of the people in the country, largely on account of the war, the psychology of recklessness, of partisanship, of hate, of reaction and persecution."[5]

Hillquit was not troubled by the negative decision. On the contrary, he was impressed by the support given the Socialists by the press. He wrote that "the intoxicated forces of law and order had secured a decisive victory, but the general indignation which the disgraceful proceedings aroused throughout the country was such that. . .for at least some years to come no American legislative body will dare again to disenfranchise a legally constituted political party."[6]

Not everyone was satisfied with Hillquit's performance at Albany. When the Socialist Party Convention met in New York City in May 1920, there was a strong left-wing contingent from Illinois, led by Louis Engdahl, which came instructed to censure Hillquit and the other lawyers who defended the New York State assemblymen. But the left-wingers failed to carry a motion declaring that the legal defense at Albany did "not truly express the position of the National Socialist Party."[7]

The left wing also criticized the SP's new Declaration of Principles of which Hillquit was the sole author.[8] The declaration deleted such Marxist terms as "class struggle." It also presented a mild and unmilitant exposition of the future realization of socialism in America. "The Socialist Party seeks to attain its end by orderly and constitutional methods," the declaration stated.

A battle royal, lasting several hours and running into more than fifty pages of transcript, broke out at the convention on the question of the new declaration. Hillquit justified deleting the Marxist terms for the purposes of intelligibility and for the protection of the Party. "I do not believe that when it comes down to the actual reading and analysis of it they could point out a single statement there that is not good Orthodox Marxism," he said. He insisted that the declaration spoke "in plain American language" for the "average worker."[9] One left-wing delegate wryly remarked when he heard the declaration, "I had a peculiar sensation of being smothered by a feather pillow." He thought the concepts in the declaration and in the actual program "seemed to be to disguise the Socialist position in this campaign so that the Department of Justice could not discover it. Now, if the Department of Justice cannot discover it I think the vast majority of those to whom we seek to appeal cannot discover it either."[10] Later, in the left-wing press, Crystal Eastman, who had served on the People's Council with Hillquit,[11] wrote that "the Socialist Party leaders. . .abandoned their former economic viewpoint, ceased to criticize the political forms of democracy, and [have] taken refuge in pre-Marxian documents like the Constitution and the Declaration of Independence. They are the party of old-fashioned Americanism."[12] The declaration was accepted by a majority of the 1920 convention—an indication of Hillquit's influence over the national party.

Eugene Debs, who was chosen to be the Party's presidential candidate in 1920 although still incarcerated in the Atlantic Penitentiary, supported the left-wing position. He was quoted in the official Party *Bulletin* as saying that the platform could have been more effective if it had stressed the class struggle more prominently and if more emphasis had been placed on industrial organization. He also objected to Hillquit having deleted the traditional Marxist terms.[13]

Hillquit wrote Debs a long letter on June 30, 1920, in which he said that the Declaration of Principles was not drawn with a view to making the Party more respectable or more conservative. "It was my intention. . .to uphold the radical position which has characterized the party. . .and to surrender nothing." Furthermore, Hillquit told Debs that the "somewhat novel tone of the document" was determined by the fact that the war was over and "we cannot of course get anywhere as a party of mere perpetual negative protest." He thought "the constructive side of the Socialist movement must again be emphasized." Defending his systematic omission of "our favorite Marxian terminology," Hillquit, in a tone of frustrated anger, wrote, "It is perfectly useless to attempt to explain our conception of such terms as 'social revolution,' 'class struggle,' 'proletariat,' etc." He insisted that "to the unschooled mind the one always means a barricade fight accompanied by terrorism, guillotining, etc. . . ." He was convinced that "in order to get our message across we must divorce ourselves from the worship of phrases, and talk the plainest English."[14]

In the early 1920s Hillquit abandoned his staunch anti-fusionist position—as a way of attracting the "average worker" to socialism. In fact he became convinced that an American labor party, composed of a coalition of organized labor, political liberals, and socialists, could help salvage the remnants of the diminished Socialist Party. His model was the British Labour Party, now winning electoral gains in England, which had "no independent existence of its own. Rather it is in the nature of a joint political committee of trade unions, cooperative societies and socialist organizations, cooperating for the sole purpose of electing public officers and shaping or influencing the policies of their country along the lines of Socialist and labor programs."[15] Perhaps he envisioned the American Socialist Party to be the counterpart of the Independent Labour Party, the radical Socialist wing of the British Labour Party.

Hillquit's efforts to create a labor party began at the July 1921 Socialist Party National Convention in Detroit. He asked the convention to appoint a committee which would make a survey of "all radical and labor organizations in the country, with a view of ascertaining their strength, disposition and readiness to cooperate with the Socialist movement upon a platform not inconsistent with that of the party, and on a plan which will preserve the integrity and autonomy of the Socialist Party."[16]

The first opportunity to form an alliance with a farmer-labor group came in February 1922. Hillquit received an invitation to attend an organizing "conference of Progressives" in Chicago. The communication came from William H. Johnston, general president of the Machinists' Union, a former socialist whom Hillquit praised in his autobiography as "the highest type of trade union official."[17] To be present at this conference were the leaders of five other major railroad unions (whose aggregate membership was somewhere around 1.5 million workers), a few needle trades union leaders, and representatives of the National Non-Partisan League, the Farmers' Council, and the Women's Trade Union League.

Although Hillquit and many other socialists evinced high enthusiasm for the coming conference,[18] the organization meeting of the Conference for Progressive Political Action was a disappointment to them. The day before the opening meeting (February 20,

1922), he wrote his wife that the Socialist members of the conference (James Oneal, Otto Branstetter, Victor Berger, Daniel Hoan, and Bertha Hale White) held a special caucus with a number of Chicago socialists. The local Chicago men seemed to have little faith in the railroad union leaders. "They think it [the conference] will result in nothing more than another resolution 'to reward the friends and punish the enemies' of labor," he wrote. And he confided, "I hope they are wrong."[19]

The Chicago socialists proved to be basically correct in their evaluation of the union leaders. At the opening meeting, Hillquit made "an eloquent appeal for the outright formation of a political party which will be separate and apart from both of the old organizations . . . [which] have repeatedly betrayed the interests of the industrial and agricultural workers."[20] However, the railroad leaders clung to the nonpartisan policy of supporting the most friendly candidates on the old party tickets. The majority of the CPPA representatives were influenced by the powerful railroaders and viewed their new organization as a pressure group, spurring on both parties to nominate progressive candidates and keeping election representatives in line with an eye to reelection.

Hillquit's anger and disappointment at this turn of events was expressed in a letter to Vera:

> The conference had obviously been called with a purpose entirely different from what we of the Socialist Party had in mind, and with a cut and dry program. Johnston had completely veered around and there seemed to be a determination to ignore the Socialists entirely and to avoid even the mention of independent working class political action.[21]

Immediately following the conference, Hillquit urged the Party not to adopt the CPPA's principles since a new party was not to be launched.[22]

Despite the conference's conservative stand, the Socialist Party remained within the new organization.[23] Hillquit was appointed to the Executive (or National) Committee which included William Green, secretary-treasurer of the United Mine Workers; Fred

Howe, municipal reformer and former commissioner of immigration at the Port of New York; Edward Keating, former Colorado Congressman; Sidney Hillman of the Amalgamated Clothing Workers; Benjamin Marsh, managing director of the Farmer's National Council; Agnes Nestor, president of the Chicago Women's Trade Union League, and William Johnston. Hillquit was also made chairman of the yet-to-be-formed New York State CPPA. The conference sent out circulars which advised its members that it "agreed that the time was ripe for progressive political action, but that the organization of a new party should await developments." Immediate political action was urged upon individual states.[24]

Following the organizing conference in February 1922, Hillquit continued to urge the CPPA to form a new labor party. He wrote Fred Howe, chairman of the CPPA's state committees, that his own organizing efforts included special propaganda for a labor party. The Jewish socialistic fraternal order, the Workmen's Circle, had been sent literature on the CPPA. "I . . . laid particular stress upon the phase of our activity which . . . will appeal to them most strongly, i.e., the effort to organize the forces of labor and farmers for united political action on a permanent basis," Hillquit wrote Howe. He also advised Howe against permitting the Farmer Labor Re-Construction League of Oklahoma, a CPPA affiliate, to work toward capturing the state's Democratic Party. The Socialists, Hillquit reminded Howe, decided to cooperate with the CPPA in all states in which the conference planned to organize for independent political action. "We did not believe that Socialist locals anywhere would participate in attempts to capture old party primaries." Summing up, he said:

> Personally, I have not the slightest faith in that policy [capturing the Democratic Party] and am convinced that the organizations represented in our Conference will discard it for straightout independent political action after some practical experiences.[25]

At the May 1922 Socialist Party National Convention in Cleveland, Hillquit actively sought to convince its delegates of the potential promise of the CPPA. As he told a New York *Call* reporter after the convention, he was satisfied the Party ". . .would be willing to co-operate politically with any group with a working class program not inconsistent with that of the SP." He also thought that at the Cleveland convention "the party has for the first time since the war been able to ignore all controversial matters and settle down to clear the way for the constructive work of rebuilding the party."[26]

By June 1922 Hillquit was hard at work bringing together New York City labor unions in the hope of laying the groundwork for a statewide CPPA organization. He and Algernon Lee, representing the Socialist Party, and Maurice Williams and Ben Howe, representing the Farmer-Labor Party, issued a call for a meeting of a "Joint Committee for Independent Labor and Political Action to Organize Labor in New York City" to take place on June 21, 1922. An impressive number of the city's labor union leaders agreed to attend including representatives from the Master, Mates and Pilots; International Jewelry Workers; Mine, Mill and Smelter Workers; Typographical Union; Joint Board of Cloakmakers' Union; Painters' Local; Teachers' Union; ILGWU; Carpenters' Union, and Fancy Leather Goods Workers' Union. A program drawn up before the meeting stated an ambitious wide-reaching set of demands, seemingly designed to satisfy the tastes of socialists, trade unionists, and farmers. Specifically, the program demanded public ownership and democratic control of public utilities and natural resources, local and national, especially the transportation system and mines; a forty-four-hour week with social insurance and the right of workers to organize, bargain collectively, strike, and picket; repeal of all taxes on articles of consumption and a high tax on inheritance and land; the establishment of a Housing Commission; the creation of an elected and paid Board of Education; creation of a Farm Production Commission; immediate withdrawal of the United States from imperialist interference in Haiti, Santo Domingo, and recognition of the governments of Mexico and Russia; and the immediate restoration of full freedom of speech, press, and assembly and the liberty of all persons imprisoned for their political beliefs.[27]

Hillquit was excited by the favorable outcome of the meeting—the founding of the New York City American Labor Party, an affiliate of the CPPA. On June 26, 1922, he wrote Howe that "...we have an unequalled opportunity in this city not only to secure concrete and big results in the coming election, but also to build up a strong and permanent political party of labor which may serve as a model in other industrial centers." He also told Howe that the leaders of this new organization hoped to put up more than fifteen candidates for the state legislature and a half dozen representatives for Congress. However, competition was looming; an independent move to organize for nonpartisan political action in the coming election was initiated by the New York Railway Union.[28]

In October 1922 a combined Socialist and Farmer-Labor ticket[29] offered the New York voters a slate which ran several old-time Socialists: Edward Cassidy of the Typographical Union for governor; Charles F. Steinmetz for state engineer; Meyer London and Abraham Lefkowitz for Congress, and Harriet Stanton Blatch for the Assembly.[30] The campaign was backed heavily by the New York City unions, especially the needle trades. Hillquit made vigorous speeches in behalf of the candidates but he emphasized the need to create a political labor organization on a state and national basis. He drew comparisons between the British Labour Party and the newly formed CPPA to show that American labor unions must act independently in order to safeguard their own economic and political interests.[31]

The prospect of a viable, socialist-led Labor-Farmer political organization was seen as a threat by the conservative New York railway unions. In 1923 the railroad brotherhoods based in Albany and led by Thomas Ryan, chairman of the New York Brotherhood of Locomotive Firemen and Enginemen, attempted to wrest control of a growing New York CPPA from the New York City radicals. At the first statewide organizational meeting of the CPPA, the railroad union representatives refused to work with the Socialists and the American Labor Party. They formed their own New York CPPA which espoused the old philosophy of nonpartisan politics.[32]

Again Hillquit was deeply disappointed with what he termed "the politically less advanced groups of organized labor." On July

31, 1923, in the New York *Call*, he excoriated the behavior of this group:

> The average organized worker of America is politically a generation behind the workers of the advanced countries of Europe and the average American labor leader is so thoroughly committed to old party politics that the ideal of independent working class action appears as a mere chimera to his strophied political vision. It would be futile to attempt to reach the masses over the heads of the leaders or to win over the leaders if the masses are not prepared to follow. The rank and file of the labor movement and its leadership are all of one piece.[33]

Railroad union opposition continued to plague Hillquit's and the Party's efforts to transform the CPPA into a permanent labor party. Yet he tenaciously clung to the idea that the unions could be swayed. By the end of 1923, he placed his hopes for a labor party in the upcoming 1924 presidential election. On November 9, 1923, he wrote William Mahoney, leader of a radical Minnesota Farmer-Labor group, that "personally I have not illusions about the sentiment of the leadership in the Conference toward independent politics but there is still a widespread feeling that the fast moving political developments may shape themselves in a way to force the Conference to make independent Presidential nominations."[34]

Hillquit attended the St. Louis CPPA meeting in February 1924, where he again pressed for the formation of a third party. When the convention adopted a temporizing resolution calling for a national CPPA meeting in Cleveland on July 2 "for the purpose of taking action on nomination of candidates for the offices of President and Vice-President of the United States," Hillquit seconded the motion declaring, "America is ready to follow labor's lead in England and turn the government to the producers instead of the exploiters of wealth."[35]

By the time of the July convention, it was all but settled that the CPPA including the Socialist Party would endorse the senior senator from Wisconsin, Robert La Follette, for the presidency and that La Follette would accept the nomination.[36] Hillquit, like most socialists, had mixed feelings about La Follette. Although Hillquit thought "he had no special philosophy beyond the immediate and specific problems of the day, and his political conception moved wholly within the orbit of the existing economic system," La Follette had mitigating qualities. He had suffered persecution for his pacifist antiwar stand and in domestic politics "he consistently took the side of the underdog and was the recognized and trusted champion of the farmer and the worker as against 'vested' interests and the 'power of privilege'."[37]

Hillquit also considered La Follette's open rejection of Communist support a definite attribute. During May Hillquit and Job Harriman had corresponded about the possible sponsorship of La Follette by the Communists in the Minnesota Farmer-Labor Party. Harriman warned Hillquit that the Communists at the St. Paul Farmer-Labor Convention in June ". . .control the convention and nominate La Follette and adopt his platform and go in a body to Cleveland."[38] No doubt Hillquit was relieved when, in an open letter printed in the New York *Herald Tribune* on May 29, La Follette stated that he would not accept the endorsement of the Minnesota Farmer-Labor Party because of the Communists in that organization. Their ultimate aim was not democracy, he wrote, "but a soviet form of government and the dictatorship of the proletariat."[39]

Hillquit came to Cleveland hoping that La Follette would not only accept the CPPA nomination but proclaim his support for a third party. He also wished that the conservative railroad leaders on the National Committee of the CPPA would somehow alter their nonpartisan position. Hillquit spend hours with the National Committee trying to convince its members that it was shortsighted to unite all progressive elements on the presidential ticket, but leave them to work within the old parties in congressional, state, and local campaigns. This tactic if proposed by the conservatives, wrote Hillquit, "would take the soul out of the movement."

Hillquit related in his autobiography how during the Cleveland Convention he had an opportunity to go over the heads of the committee directly to those delegates who voiced a decided sentiment for organizing an independent political party. His appearance on stage was the signal for "a spontaneous and lusty ovation.... Delegates and visitors stood on chairs, waved and cheered and shouted for many minutes...." He interpreted this demonstration as "popular acclaim" for his stand. "Had I at that moment proposed the immediate organization of a new party," Hillquit recalled, "the proposal would have been carried by an overwhelming vote." Hillquit realized the psychological importance of the moment but he was incapable of seizing it.

Perhaps it was one of Hillquit's greatest failings as a political leader that he could not act on mass response even when that response coincided with his own deepest beliefs and ambitions. Instead he resisted the temptation to appeal directly to the convention and justified his failure to act with the argument that it would have been disloyal to force a decision from the floor before the National Committee reached a conclusion. Moreover, he thought that the majority of the delegates did not represent the railroad workers, who were the backbone of the movement and who stood behind their conservative leaders.[40]

The moment passed. Although later Hillquit tried to stay the conservatives on the committee by legalistic tactics, Robert La Follette ran (by his own volition) as an independent presidential candidate and the CPPA was not formed as a third party at Cleveland in July 1924.[41]

Nevertheless, Hillquit and the Socialist Party vigorously supported the La Follette campaign. Hillquit even served on the La Follette-Wheeler Joint Executive Campaign Committee.[42] His dogged optimism was apparent in his letter to Frederich Adler, the secretary of the Labor and Socialist International, in which he said, "Our hope is, that through daily cooperation between Socialist and organized workers and farmers in the campaigns, a permanent political unity between them will eventually be established.[43]

Although few socialists placed hope in stemming the process of disintegration which overcame the CPPA after the La Follette defeat, Hillquit made a last attempt to form a labor party at the CPPA convention held in Chicago on February 21, 1925. The CPPA was attacked by the Communists—although they had not pursued their original intention to back La Follette. "What is the

CPPA?" asked Alexander Bittleman in his ascorbic article, "A Conference of Progressive Reactionaries." "It is the tailend of the La Follette movement," he wrote, answering his own question. "It is a conglomeration of a certain brand of trade union bureaucrats, bankrupt socialists, active petty-bourgeois politicians of the La Follette type with an admixture of liberal busybodies of every kind and sort." In general, Bittleman thought Hillquit and the Socialists were wasting their time. "Just now," he contended, "the most burning issues in the life of the labor movement are: to resist wage cuts by strikes, to fight against child-labor exploitation, to secure relief for the unemployed...to unite the workers and poor farmers around the banner of class struggle, under the leadership of a revolutionary political party of the working class."[44]

However, the railroad brotherhoods had no intention of going so far as to support a new third party at Chicago. Hillquit and Eugene V. Debs, who died in 1926, urged them in February 1925 to recoup their losses by reforming the CPPA into an American Labor Party. Their speeches were emotional.[45] The irony in the situation was not lost on Hillquit. As he pointed out, Debs had been a founder of the railroad union. "And now," Hillquit remembered in his autobiography, "as he stood there, tall, gaunt, earnest, and ascetic, before the well-groomed and comfortably situated leaders of a new generation, he seemed like a ghost of reproach risen from their past and calling them back to the glorious days of struggle, suffering and idealism."[46] The Chicago convention ended when the railroad brotherhoods withdrew to form a separate CPPA. L.E. Shepard, president of the Railway Conductors, presented the motion for adjournment with the statement that the brothers held no prejudice toward the Socialists but that they were committed to a Gompers-type program of nonpartisan politics.[47]

These arduous attempts to create a third party and its subsequent failure dampened Hillquit's conviction that such a party could reinvigorate the Socialist Party and offer a focus for workers' protest. Perhaps he ought to have been more aware that the railroad leaders' conservatism would create an impass. Moreover, the anxiety over communist infiltration was another central factor; Hillquit and other Socialist leaders were apprehensive lest the Communists use the CPPA for what was believed to be "their own purposes." As a result, the Party did not seek left-wing support and Hillquit himself toned down a direct, militant appeal to workers who might have been more attracted to a radical labor party.

After 1925 Hillquit no longer believed in the possibility of developing a political labor party. He returned to his prewar anti-fusionist stand.

Notes

1. Bernard Johnpoll, *Pacifist's Progress: Norman Thomas and the Decline of American Socialism* (Chicago, 1970). Statistics are cited on p. 50.

2. William Feigenbaum, "Morris Hillquit: Pillar of Socialism," New York *New Leader*, September 21, 1929.

3. *Loose Leaves*, p. 247. For a specific enumeration of the charges see Boston *Evening Transcript*, January 21, 1920, Clippings, Hillquit Papers.

4. Newspaper reports of Hillquit's arguments at the Albany trial, for example, in New York *Call*, January 23, 1920, ibid.; New York *Tribune*, January 25, 1920, ibid.; New York *Post*, February 17, 1920, ibid.; San Francisco *Chronicle*, February 18, 1920, ibid.; New York *Evening Post*, February 18, 1920, ibid.

5. Morris Hillquit, *Socialism on Trial* (New York, 1920), p. 72.

6. *Loose Leaves*, p. 275.

7. Crystal Eastman, "The Socialist Party Convention," *Liberator* 3 (July 1920), p. 28.

8. *Proceedings of the National Convention of the Socialist Party of 1920*, p. 75. Pagination from the copy in the Duke University Library. Also see letter from Morris Hillquit to Algernon Lee, August 24, 1919, Algernon Lee Papers, Tamiment Library, about the tentative draft of the declaration.

9. *Proceedings. . . 1920*, p. 42.

10. Ibid., pp. 54-57.

11. Letter from Crystal Eastman to Morris Hillquit, August 15, 1917, Corresondence, Hillquit Papers.

12. Crystal Eastman, "The Socialist Party Convention," p. 28.

13. Letter from Morris Hillquit to Eugene V. Debs, June 30, 1920, Correspondence, Hillquit Papers.

14. Ibid.

15. *Loose Leaves*, p. 301.

16. "Minutes of the National Convention in Detroit, June-July, 1921," *The Socialist World* (July 1921), p. 26

17. *Loose Leaves*, p. 306.

18. New York *Call*, February 8, 1922.

19. Letter from Morris Hillquit to Vera Hillquit, February 19, 1920, Correspondence, Hillquit Papers.

20. New York *Call*, February 21, 1922.

21. Letter from Morris Hillquit to Vera Hillquit, February 20, 1922, Correspondence, Hillquit Papers. Hillquit gives a somewhat different version in *Loose Leaves*, pp. 310-11.

22. New York *Call*, February 22, 1922. However, see Hillquit's reserved praise for the conference in the *Call*, February 25, where he said that the united parley is a stride forward but "we must maintain our integrity as the Advance Guard of the Worker's Movement."

23. Conference for Progressive Political Action, enclosure from William H. Johnston, Correspondence, Hillquit Papers. There is a discussion of Hillquit's active role in the CPPA in Scott Doran Johnston, "The Socialist Party in the Conference for Progressive Political Action" (Ph.D. dissertation, University of Minnesota, 1952).

25. Letter from Morris Hillquit to Fred Howe, April 6, 1922, Correspondence, Hillquit Papers.

26. New York *Call*, May 12, 1922.

27. "Joint Committee for Independent Labor Political Action to Organize Labor of New York City," June 21, 1922, Correspondence, Hillquit Papers.

28. Letter from Morris Hillquit to Fred Howe, June 26, 1922, ibid. For an impression of Hillquit's work in the American Labor Party see "Reminiscences of Benjamin F. McLauren," Oral History Research Project, Columbia University.

29. A Farmer-Labor Party existed in New York. The American Labor Party was not on the ballot but this newly created party endorsed the combined SP and Farmer-Labor ticket.

30. New York *Call*, October 14, 1922.

31. Ibid., October 19, 1922.

32. Newspaper reports of the Albany Conference collected in Clippings, Hillquit Papers, include New York *Times*, July 30, 1923; New York *World*, July 30, 1923; Brooklyn (N.Y.) *Standard Union*, July 31, 1923; New York *Tribune*, July 31, 1923.

33. New York *Call*, July 31, 1923.

34. Letter from Morris Hillquit to William Mahoney, November 9, 1923, Correspondence, Hillquit Papers.

35. Cleveland *Times*, February 13, 1924, Clippings, ibid.

36. *Christian Science Monitor*, June 1, 1924, ibid., quotes Hillquit: "If Senator La Follette is chosen as the presidential candidate of such a party, he will be acceptable to us."

37. *Loose Leaves*, p. 315.

38. Letter from Job Harriman to Morris Hillquit, May 1, 1924, Correspondence, Hillquit Papers.

39. Text of La Follette's letter to Herman L. Ekern, attorney general of Wisconsin, May 29, 1924, released in the New York *Herald Tribune* is cited in Weinstein, *Decline of Socialism*, pp. 313-14.

40. *Loose Leaves*, pp. 317-19.

41. Newspaper reports of Hillquit's tactics at the Cleveland Convention are covered in Clippings, Hillquit Papers.

42. Letter from Morris Hillquit to Bertha Hale White, August 22, 1924, Correspondence, Hillquit Papers.

43. Letter from Morris Hillquit to Frederich Adler, September 13, 1924, ibid.

44. Alexander Bittleman, "A Conference of Progressive Reactionaries," *Worker's Monthly* (February 1925), pp. 166-67.

45. Muskogee (Okla.) *Phoenix*, February 22, 1925, Clippings, Hillquit Papers.

46. *Loose Leaves*, p. 322.

47. New York *American*, February 22, 1925, Clippings, Hillquit Papers.

The International Ladies Garment Workers' Union: Union Leaders and Manufacturers

Chapter 16

Hillquit was retained as one of the chief labor lawyers for the ILGWU in 1914. It was a professional position which went far beyond a simple attorney-client relationship. He negotiated with manufacturers and represented the union in major court disputes; he was also expected to formulate union demands and in this capacity was an intimate advisor to the union's national leadership. Furthermore, he interpreted this policy to the union members and to the public.

By 1914 the ILGWU was one of the largest and most radical unions in the AFL with a membership of about 70,000; by 1920 membership had reached 105,400. After the internecine warfare and disastrous strikes of the 1925-1926 period, membership dropped precipitously.[1] A large portion of the ILGWU and almost all of its national leaders were influenced by socialistic ideals. After 1919 a radical pro-Communist left wing developed in the union. Underlying all of Hillquit's work in the International was the fact that he represented the Socialist Party in the union; the Party expected him to set the tone of the socialist program within the union. It was assumed that he would maintain amicable ties between the Party and the ILGWU.

Hillquit worked closely with the New York-based ILGWU leadership. He was chosen as the union's lawyer by the incoming new executive, Benjamin Schlesinger, the president, and Morris Sigman, the secretary-treasurer. He replaced Meyer London who had been elected to Congress on the Socialist Party ticket. Schlesinger, Sigman, and Hillquit shared a common background and, for the most part, a similar outlook on union matters. The three men were close in age and were Eastern European Jewish immigrants to the United States; all were seasoned participants in New York-centered radical politics. Since their adolescence all had worked within Jewish garment workers' unions as union leaders. They were socialists. Like Hillquit, Schlesinger had been a member of the SLP in the 1890s and had entered the Socialist Party mainly to oppose De Leon's tactics. In 1903, for one year, Schlesinger had been president of the ILGWU. In the period immediately preceding his presidency in 1914, he was business manager of the *Jewish Daily Forward*, a newspaper which consistently supported the Socialist position. Sigman's labor background was more militant than either Hillquit's or Schlesinger's. He had been an anarchist in his youth. As the leader of the Independent Cloak Pressers' Union in 1904, Sigman joined the De Leonite Socialist Trade and Labor Alliance, which in 1905 helped form the Industrial Workers of the World. Sigman became the organizer for the Cloakmakers' branch of Local 59, IWW. He later left the IWW and joined the Socialists. Immediately before his 1914 appointment as secretary-treasurer of the ILGWU, Sigman was an official of the Joint Board of the Cloakmakers' Union, one of the most powerful sections of the ILGWU, which he had helped to organize in 1909.[2]

As socialists, leaders such as Schlesinger and Sigman shared with Hillquit a deeply engrained critical attitude toward the American capitalist system and a compassion for the immediate plight of workers in the garment industry. Their variety of socialism, however, made them regard the union's purpose as primarily ameliorative; the union ought to improve the workers' lives and, only indirectly, should it act as a vanguard for societal change. Furthermore, they accepted the need for the union to operate within the established American capitalist socioeconomic institutions. However, they wanted to alter this structure. Their strategy for integrating the union into the garment industry economy was through rationalizing factory processes, developing collective bargaining techniques, and creating a mass union whose power could be juxtaposed to the well organized employers' association. Philosophically, Hillquit composed the guiding principle of the union upon which he thought all alterations of the economy's structure should be based: "...that industry is a social function rather than a purely private concern, and that the workers have certain inherent rights in its operation...."[3]

The union's officials with whom Hillquit became associated shared a major apprehension that the union might disintegrate under the pressures of hostility from without and divisiveness from within. They were proud that the union had survived and they regarded themselves as guardians of this burgeoning institution which they had actively watched grow from a sickly infancy. Their paternalism made them place a high value upon cautious behavior.

Schlesinger, Sigman, and Hillquit shared a willingness to use the capitalist institutions to ward off employers' threats to the union's existence. In fact, they had been deeply impressed by the Protocol of Peace, a system of collective bargaining which was in operation between 1911 and 1916. The Protocol created a set of permanent governing boards for the women's garment industry (that is, a Board of Arbitration, a Board of Grievances, a Joint Board of Sanitary Controls) which were designed to lessen intense friction through a continuing process of mediation, arbitration, and internal legislation. Theoretically, the worker, the employer, and an impartial representative of the "public" were equal in this innovative form of collective bargaining. To disarm both sides, the workers were enjoined to relinquish their right to strike while the employers were forbidden to use the lockout. Union leaders believed that under this system working conditions would improve; there would be an immediate rise in union membership and, above all, the union would enhance its position by acting within an institutional framework. Hillquit was appointed as union representative on the Protocol's most prestigious example of industrial "self-government"—the Board of Arbitration.

Finally, Hillquit shared with Schlesinger and Sigman a deep distrust of the left wing, the more radical element of the ILGWU. Although after 1914 most of the union leaders were avowed socialists, large and articulate groups existed in the union which were considered far more militant and more democratic than their leaders. The left wing protested the Protocol, mainly because it outlawed strikes but also because it was slow in hearing grievances and failed to provide for worker control in the factories. The left also accused the union leaders of paternalism and the use of undemocratic methods. After the system was disbanded in 1916 and even before the rise of a pro-Communist left in 1919-1920, the left elements in the ILGWU expected Hillquit and the others to be more militant in their attitudes toward strikes, more sympathetic to worker control in the union and in the factories, and less willing to accept government and employer pressures.

The left wing was disappointed and isolated attacks were launched against the leaders by individuals such as Moishe Rubin of the renegade Cloakmaker's Local 1 and journalists Tzivion and Salutsky of the Socialist Party's Jewish Federation weekly *Naye Velt.*[4] When a definite and growing pro-Communist group was created in the ILGWU, the union leaders faced intensified criticism of their policies by an unrelenting Communist press, particularly the daily Yiddish *Freiheit*, the Yiddish *Hamer*, and the English *Daily Worker.* The left planned to unseat and eliminate the leaders from their positions of power. Hillquit, Schlesinger, and Sigman, often the special targets of left-wing criticism, appeared to share the conviction that the maintenance of their position meant the survival of the union. Consequently, they felt it justifiable (although occasionally against the expressed wishes of many union members) to employ such tactics as disbanding and reorganizing dissident locals, or using New York State courts to prosecute "libelous" accusations made by detractors. On occasion they disguised terms of negotiations to avoid criticism leveled at the kind of agreements they had reached with employers.

From 1914 until his death in 1933 Hillquit remained on friendly terms with the upper echelon of the union's bureaucracy. He was admired by Schlesinger and others for his shrewd insights into union politics, his formidable private legal career, and especially for the agility he demonstrated in negotiating union demands with manufacturers. He was respected because of his important position on the executive of the Socialist Party. The union leaders also assumed that Hillquit lent the union an air of respectability. He was on friendly terms with many New York lawyers and prominent state officials who were involved in developing labor legislation and arbitration procedures. The union hierarchy imagined that these liaisons would enhance the union's chances of obtaining specific labor goals as well as contribute positively to building a public image of the ILGWU as an organization of responsible, co-operative unionists.

By the mid-1920s Hillquit's relationship with the union's bureaucracy had solidified into a pattern. He represented the older generation of entrenched leadership; he expressed satisfaction with the way the internal affairs of the union were managed. He thus approved of arbitration, especially under government supervision, as an alternative to strikes or any other form of labor militancy. Like this older generation, he had long ago come to reconcile his kind of socialism with the kind of unionism provided by the ILGWU.

Almost in the same way that Hillquit maintained good relations with the union's national leadership, he encouraged little personal friction between himself and the garment manufacturers with whom he negotiated. In fact, he was considered by manufacturers' lawyers as an exceptionally able opponent. The "impartial" mediators appointed by the governor, men like Felix Adler and Louis Brandeis, acknowledged his objectivity and fairness.

Certain aspects of Hillquit's cultural background and lifestyle made him especially attractive and acceptable to the manufacturers. Many of them and their representatives were first or second-generation Americans of German-Jewish descent who were anxious to fit themselves and their Russian-Jewish workers into American life as inconspicuously as possible. Like Hillquit (who also identified with the heritiage of German language and culture) they valued respectability, order, efficiency, and a moderate amount of social change. At negotiation sessions, before 1916, Hillquit's socialism tended to be conveniently overlooked. He was regarded as one who shared their concern for the industry and who could therefore be trusted to accurately relay their point of view to the workers. After 1916 the relationship between Hillquit and the manufacturers became more openly distrustful when the Protocol system was disbanded and the war issue introduced a new note of disagreement.

The manufacturers' relationship with Hillquit is reflected in the tenuous friendship that existed between Hillquit and Julius Henry Cohen, the manufacturers' major legal representative throughout the heated period of negotiations with the ILGWU (1913-1916). Cohen, who was four years younger than Hillquit, was born of German-Jewish parents in Brooklyn, New York. Like Hillquit he was a wealthy, established attorney and a respected urban reformer beyond the confines of the garment industry. A prewar Progressive, Cohen acted as the lawyer for the Transit Reform Committee of 100, assisted in the prosecution of a corrupt district attorney, and investigated the New York City Department of Street Cleaning. Cohen, like Hillquit, was an assimilationist and belonged to the Ethical Cultural Society founded by Dr. Felix Adler.[5] The society, composed primarily of educated, middle-class Jews, preached a mild social reform philosophy without a specifically Jewish content.

Cohen admired Hillquit. His letters in 1914-1915 revealed his wish to maintain a close ideological as well as professional relationship with his adversary at the bargaining table. For example, Cohen wrote Hillquit on October 28, 1914, that he planned to quote him on the subject of equipping the worker for his work in life. Cohen's purpose was "to show that the Socialist view is not inconsistent with the view of true efficiency in life and primarily to show that, in working to develop the protocol, you and I occupy common ground." In this same letter Cohen gingerly suggested they coauthor a "lawyer-like digest of the 'Law of the Protocol'." He flattered Hillquit by saying, "I am sure that your collaboration would be a guarantee, not only of your own efficiency, but mine as well."[6] In his autobiographical account of the Protocol years, Cohen lauded Hillquit's foresight. He wrote, for example: "The governing law of industrial relations, Hillquit believed was not the commercial law he practiced in behalf of his business clients. It was law *still in the making*—new law born out of the industrial needs of the time."[7] Julius Cohen showed his appreciation of Hillquit in March 1915, when he gathered more than thirty letters from New York lawyers recommending Hillquit's admission to the Bar Association of the City of New York.[8]

However, after America's entrance into World War I, Cohen's ardor seemed to have cooled (especially since he was working for the Draft Board). On September 13, 1918, he wrote the ailing Hillquit a letter which revealed the ambivalence in their present relationship. "I never could understand how you managed to carry your large work and responsibility without showing signs of physical impairment, and I am quite sure that your zeal for causes in which you believe (and in which, I must say, I do not) led you beyond the limitations your fine judgment would prescribe," he admonished his sick colleague.[9] Almost a year later, on July 4, 1919, Hillquit who was still recovering from tuberculosis at Saranac Lake, wrote Cohen a rather ascerbic letter, reviewing a recent book written by his friendly enemy. Hillquit said to Cohen:

> You don't of course expect me to accept your stand on all social and economic theories. We have always been on opposite sides, shaking friendly hands...over a deep chasm of conflicting interests and viewpoints. But I will say this for you, that if you are to be classed as a Bourgeois, in the modern political vernacular, you are one of the most enlightened and progressive of the species. Your advice is good, but unfortunately for the ruling classes, they never have taken good advice, and never have been known to make substantial concessions, until it was too late, and the concessions had no effect.[10]

Hillquit tried to gain substantial concessions for the workers. Consequently, his relationship with the garment manufacturers went through several stages, beginning with an uneasy unity of goals in the 1914-1916 period and terminating in the 1920s and 1930s with mutual hostility. In late 1914 when he became the union's negotiator, he was an ardent defender of the Protocol. He stood in agreement with Protocol employers, the Manufacturers Protective Association, and the Ladies Dress and Waist Manufacturers Association in seeking ways to control the chaotic conditions prevalent in the garment industry. Like these employers he also wanted the kind of industrial efficiency which would eliminate the cutthroat competition of subcontractors and jobbers, standardize wages and hours, and avoid anarchical and violent class warfare. He antagonized employers with his claim that job security and a limited control of the work situation by the employee would contribute toward establishing industrial efficiency. In December 1914 he presented the Board of Arbitration of the cloak, suit and skirt industry with his most radical demands, later known as Hillquit's "right to the job" philosophy. The demands consisted of three stipulations which controlled the employers' right to discharge, their right to reorganize shops, and their right to distribute work.[11]

In May 1915 the Manufacturers' Protective Association decided to break with the ILGWU and the Protocol. There were many reasons. For example, the industry trade paper, *Women's Wear Daily*, reported that the manufacturers desired "to eliminate the radical element which think it can dictate to us how we shall conduct our business."[12] Admittedly, workers in the industry were class conscious, their leaders were overtly Marxist, and the employers were unable to recognize that organized labor had an equal stake in the industry's efficient operation. But the union leaders were moderate in their demands and conciliatory in their manner. The employers, in fact, created work problems which generated anger and led to spontaneous strikes. They then could charge that the anarchical behavior of the workers under the Protocol was intolerable.[13]

When the manufacturers abrogated the Protocol in 1915 Hillquit tried to salvage the machinery of the Protocol and convince the association that they needed the union to insure the stability of the garment industry. Tactically, Hillquit's and Schlesinger's first move was to maneuver the manufacturers into agreeing to participate in a special Council of Conciliation called by New York mayor John Mitchel and presided over by mediators from outside the industry. Favorable press coverage, which expressed sympathy for the union, helped the union leaders pressure the manufacturers into this further arbitration.

At the meetings of the council, which lasted from July 14 to July 23, Hillquit argued the union's case.[14] He maintained that the manufacturers' repudiation of the union, through their rejection of the Protocol system, ruined the chances of developing a stable industry. "Our union is a national organization," he told the council on July 14, ". . .and it is the only factor which unites the industry all through the country. It is the only factor which at least potentially has the power of developing uniform standards all through the country."[15] Furthermore, he claimed that the union had succeeded in organizing most workers in the industry and in raising standards generally. Efforts to standardize conditions in order to bring about fair and reasonable competition ". . .and not a cut-throat competition, came from the Union and not the employers."[16] But, Hillquit argued, employer cooperation was essential since the "standards set in the shops of this Association are generally recognized and made binding upon all manufacturing establishments in the industry."[17]

Hillquit used all kinds of arguments to bring about a reconciliation. He even appealed to the sense of ethnic solidarity between the employer and the worker. For example, on July 14, he mentioned that just prior to the meeting someone had made a statement that the ILGWU was not an "American Union." His reply to this accusation stressed both the existing rapport and the degree of interchangeability between owner and worker. Thus he told the council members that ". . .nothing should be easier or more natural than for the men and the employers in this industry to arrive at an understanding. . . ." He reasoned that the ILGWU

> . . .was not an American Union in the sense of its members consisting very largely of foreigners, overwhelmingly Jews, with a considerable percentage of Italians; and the Employers' Association is made up of exactly the same elements and materials—and it is good material. They understand each other perfectly well. The workers sometimes develop into manufacturers; and some of the more successful manufacturers have come from the ranks of the workers. They know the business; they have the same notions; they know all the shop difficulties; and I say they understand each other.[18]

In another argument for reconciliation (which might have antagonized the more militant rank and file of the union), Hillquit disavowed the strike as a union tactic and insisted that "our union has fully lived up to the covenant against striking and the industry has enjoyed a period of industrial peace quite unprecedented in the annals of its history."[19] However, he qualified this statement by insisting that in order to make the Protocol work, the employer had to be willing to surrender an "inalienable right"—the right to indiscriminate discharge.[20] "That was the sense of the protocol," Hillquit reminded the employers, "and that was the reason why the workers surrendered the right to strike against you." In a rare flash of anger, Hillquit threatened:

> The moment you will assume an unreasonable attitude, the moment you will expect us to work for starvation wages and treat us improperly, then we will rely upon our strength, upon the Union's strength, to correct the abuses; in other words, we will go on strike.[21]

However, Hillquit was unwilling to press this point of workers' resistance or to present himself and the other union leaders as "radicals." On the contrary, his strategy in the council meetings was to portray the union leadership as the legal moderator between the manufacturers who abrogated the Protocol and the rank and file who were chaffing under the infringements of Protocol rule. Therefore, he clearly denied any connection between the union's demands and any radical philosophy. Trying to reduce to absurdity the employers' accusations that union officials were advocates of the theory of force and syndicalism, he humorously claimed the employers had ransacked the Socialist vocabulary within the last two months, and that "we have heard no end of reproaches about radicals being in control of the Union now, and carrying on the protocol as a contention of their theory of a class struggle. . . ." With lawyer-like aplomb Hillquit appealed to the evidence:

> I beg to say that when it comes down to a question of class struggle and radicalism or conciliatory spirit, the record speaks for itself. If the present administration of the Union had stood for class struggle and nothing else, in their application to our relations, we would not be here before you gentlemen. It was we who maintained the protocol.[22]

The settlement on July 23, 1915, recommended that the workers receive wage increases, the old Protocol machinery be reestablished, and strikes and lockouts again be forbidden for the new agreement's two-year life. Hillquit's special report to the Committee of Conciliation (dated July 23) requested "that the principle of industrial efficiency and the principle of respect for the essential human rights of the worker must always be applied jointly, priority being assigned to neither."[23] Nevertheless, in the final agreement the employers were given the right to hire and fire without union authorization, but the union could take measures to forestall discrimination against workers and could protect union security.[24] In a sense, the reestablishment of the Protocol was a pyrrhic victory for Hillquit. The failure of the union officials to acquire "rights to the job" intensified rank-and-file opposition to a system which prevented them from striking but did not give them other forms of control.[25]

The new agreement of July 1915 also failed to cement what became a deteriorating relationship between the Manufacturers' Protective Association and the union hierarchy. Having been forced into arbitration by public opinion, engendered by the actions of Hillquit, Schlesinger et al., the association members grew increasingly distrustful of the Protocol system (now seen by them as a government-ILGWU coalition) and even hostile toward public censure. By April 1916 the system broke down entirely when the employers announced a lockout and, almost immediately, the union proclaimed a general strike affecting workers in all the city's cloak and suit shops. Hillquit still would have preferred a return to the Protocol system. But the Protective Association at first refused to arbitrate with the union under any circumstances. It was only after pressure was brought upon the employers by civic organizations, by prominent New Yorkers such as the wives of Benjamin Guggenheim, Learned Hand, and Willard Straight, by Ruth Morgan and Jacob Schiff who established a Citizen's Committee for the Locked-Out Cloak and Suit Makers, and by the intransigence of the workers that the Protective Association finally agreed to negotiate with the union and to accept Mayor Mitchel's intervention.[26] The employers could not have been happy to read in the *Ladies' Garment Worker* that Hillquit said, "It was, in the last analysis, the ever-increasing presence of public opinion which forced the employers of this industry into a fair settlement."[27]

The new 1916 agreement dismantled the Protocol in the cloak and suit industry. The boards and impartial arbiters were dismissed. The workers won increased wages, reduced hours, the retention of the preferential shop, and the guarantee of the right to strike against discriminatory layoffs and arbitrary shop policies. Publicly, Hillquit appeared to be pleased by the apparent success of the new contract. He justified the end of Protocolism in the cloak industry by declaring that this system had served its purpose. It had created a large and effective union. He wrote in the *American Labor Year Book* (1916) that "to-day the Union no longer requires the artificial stimulant of an elaborate outside machinery" and he suggested that a Protocol arrangement was ". . . very serviceable in industries and places in which our organizations are new and weak or in industries mainly composed of women and subject to frequent changes of the working force."[28]

But even at the triumphant October 1916 ILGWU Thirteenth Convention in Philadelphia where Hillquit complimented the workers for their independent spirit, he still emphasized the fact that the Protocol was a great advance over all other previous agreements in the garment industry. In fact, he told his audience that it was the Protocol which had altered the very foundations and philosophic premises of the factory system because ". . .it demolished the old, antiquated and reactionary notion that a shop or factory is the private property of the employer to be handled by him as he pleases, without any responsibility to his workers or the public at large."[29]

Hillquit declared that the Protocol had wrought a true revolution in the industry—the recognition of the workers' right to jobs. Thus despite his approval of the workers' fourteen weeks of militant behavior during the strike and their success, he was loathe to relinquish the machinery of formal arbitration.[30] By March 1916, lecturing at the Rand School on "Collective Bargaining and the 'Protocol' in the Garment Industry," he was again cautioning would-be militants that ". . .it is not the act of striking or the act of boycotting that determines the power of a union."[31]

Between 1917-1919 Hillquit's relationship with the employers reflected the generally more aggressive spirit of the union. New contracts were negotiated for wage increases to meet the rising cost of living and for shortened work hours. Also in this period, he took a strong didactic tone toward employers. He lectured them on industrial efficiency[32] and pressed for greater worker control in the factory, that is, union control which limited the employer's right to hire and discharge and to reorganize his business. By 1919 the ILGWU had virtually established strict union shops among the manufacturers with whom it negotiated. Although methods of settling grievances varied, Hillquit's hand could be seen in the extent to which Protocol-type arbitration boards with "impartial umpires" came to characterize the manner in which disputes were settled.

The 1917-1920 period was one of general prosperity in the garment industry. To some extent the pliability of the employers was based upon the favorable economic conditions which had been a result of accelerated war production and government contracts. However, in mid-1920 the garment industry faced a depression. In reaction, the manufacturers resisted further workers' demands and began to reject the "concessions" previously granted to the unions. The union threatened the manufacturers with a general strike.

In the late fall of 1921 the New York Cloak and Suit Manufacturers' Protective Association declared that as of mid November every member of the association would operate his factory on the piecework system (rather than the higher paying week-work system), would cut wages, and would extend working hours to forty-eight a week.[33] On November 14, 1921, about 55,000 workers in the New York cloak trades went out on strike.[34] Applying his customary tactic—the best defense is offense—Hillquit suggested the International obtain a temporary injunction against the Protective Association on the grounds that the association had broken the agreement which it made with the union in May 1919 for a three-year period and which did not expire before June 1, 1922. The association claimed that the agreement ceased to exist as of November 1, 1921.[35]

Before such an unprecedented injunction could be granted, the New York State Industrial Commission, headed by Henry D. Sayers, announced the appointment of a special board to conduct an inquiry into the strike-lockout situation. Although the Protective Association accepted this chance to mediate, the ILGWU (which in all its previous strikes had welcomed government intervention) at first refused to meet with the board.[36] However, on November 25 Hillquit and Samuel Untermeyer, the AFL lawyer who volunteered his services in this case, met with association lawyer Max D. Steurer and special board members John D. Higgins, Hugh Fraynem, organizers for the AFL, and Marcus M.

Marks, former president of the Borough of Manhattan.[37] Steurer told the board his clients would waive whatever doubts they had about the legality of the board, provided its members concerned themselves in a general investigation and did not specialize in inquiring into the union's claim that the employers arbitrarily broke an existing contract.[38] Hillquit unambiguously advised the board that it ought not expect to mediate differences until an investigation had been made of the manufacturers' violation of the contract. The Brooklyn *Standard Union* quoted Hillquit as asking the board, "Is it possible that the law upholds contracts only when they affect the laborer?"[39]

On November 26, the day following the hearing by the special board appointed by the State Industrial Commission, Hillquit announced that the union would file an injunction suit in the State Supreme Court, ". . . the same sort of sweeping injunction against the protective association as employers have been granted so often against the workers. The Courts have established an excellent precedent for us."[40] The threatened injunction appeared to have frightened a number of employers. For example, Reuben Sadowsky, whose business as manufacturer of suits and cloaks was rated in the press as the largest in the world, made an individual agreement with the ILGWU through his lawyer Louis Marshall (Hillquit's old adversary in the 1916-1917 loyalty-antiwar controversy).[41] On November 27 the New York *Herald* reported that nearly one-fifth of the workers in the cloak trade (about 1,100) were back in the factories.[42]

Three days later, on November 30, Justice Charles L. Guy granted the union a temporary injunction restraining the Protective Association from carrying into effect the establishment of piecework and the lengthening of work hours.[43] The New York press was favorably inclined toward the injunction. The *Tribune* commented that it was the first such attempt by a union. The editorial sympathized with the unions' charge that the employers chose to conspire against the workers at the end of a season when they could permit their plants to become idle without appreciable loss and thus "practically starve" the workers into accepting the new terms which they proposed.[44] On December 1 the New York *Evening Globe* editorialized that "the practical effects of the injunction will be to loosen the hold of the employers' organization over its members and probably hasten individual settlements with the union." "This is an outcome," wrote the *Globe*, "with which the public, which has reason to think the employers wholly wrong in their present intentions, is likely to be in sympathy."[45] The more conservative New York *Times* chastised Hillquit's legal style, saying it "smacks of the soap box," but nonetheless the paper supported his criticism of the injunction method of solving industrial problems. The *Times* editor explained, "Sooner or later government by commission must supplant government by injunction."[46]

The ILGWU also had another new ally, Samuel Gompers of the AFL, who only recently had been a foe. Gompers actively supported the ILGWU injunction efforts.[47] "You will win," Gompers told 30,000 striking cloakmakers at a mass meeting in January 1922. "The masses will no longer permit employers' exercise of autocratic power over our lives," he said.[48] His reasons were clear. The AFL was going through a period of economic depression and employers' offensives in the form of "American Plans" whittled away the federation membership. Gompers had been hostile to the "socialistic" spirit of the ILGWU. During the war years, he had not only denounced Hillquit and the union for its suport of the antiwar position, but he formed the American Alliance for Labor and Democracy which almost singlehandedly destroyed the chances of the ILGWU-supported People's Council for organizing a peace movement among organized workers. Now he was seeking allies among old enemies.

In the middle of December the manufacturers tried to prevent the temporary injunction from becoming permanent, as the union intended. Steurer argued that "the charges of conspiring is a mere smoke screen" and that "the union waged a campaign of sabotage against productivity by a series of shop strikes."[49] On December 10 the manufacturers' lawyer submitted a seventy-four-page document to the Supreme Court defending their actions. Hillquit was quoted in the *Tribune* as saying that after examining the document ". . .he was of the opinion that it was heavier in physical weight than in actual substance."[50]

But the manufacturers did not use only defensive tactics. They counterattacked on December 15 by filing their own injunction against the union.[51] Actually, there were two manufacturers' associations in operation in 1921: The Protective Association was composed of the larger manufacturers; the American Cloak and Suit Manufacturers' Association was made up of small manufacturers and contractors. Few of the small manufacturers had been able to operate since the strike was called. The ILGWU regarded the American Association as having the same status as the big manufacturers in the Protective Association. In fact, Hillquit insisted that the 20,000 workers in the American Association shops refuse to work since these shops serviced concerns against whom a strike had been called. It was the American Association to which Justice Alonzo Hinckley granted a temporary injunction on January 7, 1922, restraining the union from picketing, holding meetings, paying strike benefits, and from conspiring unlawfully to "injure the business and keep idle the shops of the plaintiffs."[52]

However, the manufacturers did not succeed in their counterattack. The ILGWU, with the aid of the AFL's New York City Central Trade and Labor Council, condemned this action as imitative, drastic, and "so much against the constitutional rights of the people that comment on it seems unnecessary."[53] Hillquit told the press that "the strike will go on just the same and this move of the employers will not interfere with its conduct."[54] Somehow the injunction became entangled in a legalistic web and was never put into effect. Instead, on January 10 Supreme Court Judge Robert Wagner granted the ILGWU a permanent injunction restraining the employers from combining to enforce a forty-nine-hour week and the piecework system in their shops.[55]

Samuel Untermeyer, Hillquit's associate throughout the battle, lauded the "justice, wisdom and efficacy of the injunction." Hillquit was considerably more reserved and, as always, tried to draw a didactic lesson from the proceedings:

> I have by no means been converted to the opinion that court injunctions are the proper method of adjusting industrial disputes. Injunction against employers can never be as drastic and deadly as those issued against workers. . . .
>
> One of the principal merits of the precedent established in the present suit is that it will tend to make injunction less popular with employers. I hope it will lead to a radical limita-

tion and eventually the complete abolition of judicial interference in labor disputes by means of injunction.[56]

The New York socialist press, in particular the *Call* and the *Jewish Daily Foward*, considered the injunction and the strike to have been a great victory for labor at a time when unions everywhere were beleaguered.[57]

In the long run, however, this novel injunction failed to stem the ILGWU's declining power in its relations with garment manufacturers. Throughout the 1920s business conditions continued to worsen. This gave the employers an edge in negotiation. The depression also bred small shops, increased the contracting system, and accelerated the growth of jobbers, especially out-of-town jobbers, who evaded responsibility for standardizing wages, hours, and general working conditions. Intense competition and insecurity made the large manufacturers of the "inside" shops reluctant to yield any control to the union or the workers in the factories. The employers refused to experiment with new forms of factory administration at a time when they were operating on ever smaller profit margins. In viewing the situation, Hillquit remained convinced that the salvation of the workers in the cloak industry resided in the cooperation of a strong union with the manufacturers' association and the elimination of "wildcat" shops.[58]

After the 1922 cloak and suit industry settlement,[59] Hillquit ceased to invent novel ways of pressuring employers. He relied upon tactics he and the union hierarchy developed from 1910 through the early 1920s. Thus the public image of the ILGWU's philosophy that the national executive of the union projected remained the advocacy of industrial efficiency coupled with industrial justice. Employers' associations were encouraged while jobbers and out-of-town shops were exposed in the labor press and legislated against in union-employer contracts. In general, their contracts were made on short-term basis—two years—and were arrived at through negotiation in the presence of impartial umpires. Higher wages, shorter hours, and Hillquit's "right to the job" position continued to be major areas of contention. The union welcomed governmental intervention to investigate conditions and to mediate whenever conflicts appeared to be irreconcilable (as they did in the 1925 strikes when Governor Alfred E. Smith mandated a special Advisory Commission to settle the prolonged dispute).[60] Hillquit persisted in trying to legally outmaneuver his opponents, the employers' association lawyers, in order to strengthen the union's position within the factories and to improve working conditions. When in the 1930s the government supported industrial codes, the aging and ailing Hillquit contributed his fund of knowledge and experience toward developing New Deal labor relations boards and legislation.[61]

Notes

1. Louis Levine, *The Women's Garment Workers: A History of the International Ladies Garment Workers' Union* (New York, 1924), p. 431.

2. Ibid., pp. 124-25. This author discussed Schlesinger's career in the ILGWU with his son Emil Schlesinger in an interview in May 1975.

3. Morris Hillquit, "Rise of the Russian Jew," Writings, Hillquit Papers.

4. Levine, *Women's Garment Workers*, p. 327, notes that in Rubin's attempt to wrest Local 1 from the jurisdiction of the National Executive Isaac Hourwich represented Local 1 while Hillquit represented the General Executive Board. For articles by Tzivion and J.B. Hardman (Salutsky), respectively, in the New York *Naye velt* see July 28, 1916, and September 1, 1916. Also see Morris Winchevski's article in ibid., August 9, 1917.

5. For the life and work of Cohen see Julius Henry Cohen, "The Revised Protocol in the Dress and Waist Industry," *Annals of the American Academy of Political and Social Science* 69 (January 1919), pp. 183-96; Cohen, *A League to Enforce Industrial Peace* (New York, 1916), pp. 35-36; "Julius Henry Cohen," *Who Was Who in America* (Chicago, 1960), p. 170.

6. Letter from Julius Cohen to Morris Hillquit, October 28, 1914, Corresondence, Hillquit Papers.

7. Julius Cohen, *They Builded Better Than They Knew* (New York, 1916), p. 204.

8. See numbers 662-92 of Corresondence, Hillquit Papers.

9. Letter from Julius Cohen to Morris Hillquit, September 13, 1918, ibid.

10. Letter from Morris Hillquit to Julius Cohen, July 4, 1919, ibid.

11. Morris Hillquit, "Before the Board of Arbitration in the Cloak, Suit and Dress Industry," December 19, 1914, Writings, ibid.

12. *Women's Wear Daily*, January 8, 1915.

13. For a treatment of the collapse of Protocolism see Melvyn Dubofsky, *When Workers Organize* (Amherst, Mass., 1968), pp. 86-101. Also see

Jesse Thomas Carpenter, *Competition and Collective Bargaining in the Needles Trades, 1910-1967* (Ithaca, N.Y., 1972).

14. The council was composed of Felix Adler, Louis D. Brandeis, George W. Kirchway, Judge Walter C. Noyers, Henry Bruere, and Charles Bernheimer.

15. *Minutes,* Council of Conciliation (women's coat and suit trade), July 14, 1915, p. 82, International Ladies Garment Workers' Union Research Library.

16. Ibid., p. 83.

17. Ibid., p. 13.

18. Ibid., p. 27.

19. Ibid., p. 22.

20. Ibid., p. 37.

21. Ibid., p. 38.

22. *Minutes,* ibid. (July 17, 1915), p. 77.

23. Morris Hillquit, "Report of Mayor Mitchel's Commission on Conciliation," ca. July 23, 1915, Writings, Hillquit Papers. For a favorable evaluation see New York *Jewish Daily Forward,* July 23, 1915.

24. Levine, *Women's Garment Workers,* p. 290.

25. See Hillquit's letter of thanks to Mitchel, July 26, 1916, John P. Mitchel Papers, Municipal Archives, New York City.

26. M. Kushner, *Thirty-Fifth Anniversary Jubilee Book,* 1910-1945 (New York, 1945, in Yiddish), p. 35, published by the Joint Board of the Cloakmakers' Union, notes that the union's strike fund came from the UHT, the Forward Association, and the Workmen's Circle. Even the French Tailor's Union sent one hundred francs as a symbol of international solidarity. Also see Chicago *The Tailor,* May 23, 1916. This official organ of the Journeymen Tailors' Union of America asserted that "public opinion stood by the workers. . . ."

27. *Ladies' Garment Worker* 7 (August 1916), p. 17.

28. *American Labor Year Book* (1916), p. 57.

29. *Report and Proceedings of the Thirteenth Convention of the I.L.G.W.U.,* October 16, 1916, p. 132.

30. Ibid., p. 133.

31. Morris Hillquit, "Collective Bargaining and the 'Protocol' in the Garment Industry," March 24, 1916, Writings, Hillquit Papers.

32. See, for example, *Minutes,* Arbitration Proceedings between the Ladies Dress and Waist Manufacturers' Association and the International Ladies Garment Workers' Union, January 20, 1917, pp. 14-20, ILGWU Research Library.

33. New York *Evening World,* November 21, 1921, Clippings, Hillquit Papers.

34. M. Kushner, *Thirty-Fifth Anniversary*, p. 37, states the union vote to strike was 38,672 to 162.

35. New York *Evening Mail*, November 22, 1921, Clippings, Hillquit Papers.

36. New York *Herald*, November 23, 1921, ibid.

37. Brooklyn (N.Y.) *Standard Union*, November 25, 1921, ibid.

38. New York *Sun*, November 25, 1921, ibid.

39. Brooklyn (N.Y.) *Standard Union*, November 25, 1921, ibid.

40. New York *Herald*, November 26, 1921, ibid.

41. New York *World*, November 26, 1921, ibid.

42. New York *Herald*, November 27, 1921, ibid.; New York *Tribune*, November 27, 1921, ibid.

43. New York *Evening Post*, November, 30, 1921, ibid.; New York *Tribune*, November 30, 1921, ibid. Also see New York *World*, November 30, 1921, ibid. for provisions of Judge Guy's injunction.

44. New York *Tribune*, November 30, 1921, ibid.

45. New York *Evening Globe*, December 1, 1921, ibid.

46. New York *Times*, December 1, 1921, ibid.

47. New York *Sun*, December 3, 1921, ibid., quotes "...the union has received from Samuel Gompers, Executive Council of the A.F. of L., unanimous endorsement of the strike and the way it has been conducted."

48. New York *Call*, January 5 and January 6, 1922.

49. New York *Tribune*, December 23, 1921, Clippings, Hillquit Papers.

50. Ibid., December 11, 1921.

51. New York *Tribune*, December 15, 1921, ibid.

52. New York *Call*, January 8, 1922, ibid.; New York *Times*, January 8, 1922, ibid.

53. New York *Tribune*, January 9, 1922, quotes William F. Kehow of the City Central Trade and Labor Council.

54. New York *Tribune*, January 8, 1922, ibid.

55. New York *Evening Post*, January 10, 1922, ibid.; New York Tribune, January 10, 1922, ibid.; New York *Call*, January 10, 1922, ibid.; Brooklyn (N.Y.) *Standard Union*, January 11, 1922, ibid.

56. New York *Tribune*, January 12, 1922, ibid. Also see Morris Hillquit, "Injunction May Lose Popularity if Used on Bosses," *Justice*, December 9, 1921, ibid.; for disagreement between Hillquit and Untermeyer see debate, "Shall Trade Unions Be Regulated by Law," 1923, Morris Hillquit Papers, Tamiment Library.

57. New York *Call*, January 13, January 19, and January 22, 1922, report on the commemorative dinner where Hillquit praised the workers and leaders who "outgeneraled the manufacturers."

58. John Dyche, "Salient Features in the Cloak Industry," New York *Evening Post*, December 12, 1921, Clippings, Hillquit Papers.

59. See, for example, *Minutes*, Conference between Committee of the Cloak, Suit and Dress Manufacturers' Protective Association and Committee of the International Ladies Garment Workers' Union, May 31, 1922, ILGWU Research Library.

60. See, for example, *Report*, New York State Governor's Advisory Commission on the Cloak, Suit and Shirt Industry, 1925, ibid.

61. For Hillquit's work on New Deal legislation see Carpenter, *Competition and Collective Bargaining*, p. 731, and New York *World*, February 23, 1930, Clippings, Hillquit Papers.

Chapter 17

The International Ladies Garment Workers' Union: Workers

Hillquit was never regarded as a charismatic leader among the rank and file of the ILGWU. Contemporary journalists and historians agree that he impressed the garment workers as clever and legally competent but they also considered him cool and remote. In the first two decades of the twentieth century, an estimated 80 percent of the garment workers in New York City were Jewish.[1] Hillquit's estrangement from this ethnic group made him appear culturally alien to the majority of Jewish workers who might have responded to a more Jewish-oriented politician. Nevertheless, from 1909 through the 1930s Hillquit was a visible, familiar figure to garment industry workers. He regularly addressed Socialist Party and ILGWU conventions. It was often his function to explain the progress and outcome of strike negotiations to the expectant strikers. His pronouncements were highly publicized in newspapers closely associated with the New York Socialist Party, especially the New York *Call* and the popular Yiddish *Jewish Daily Forward*. Hillquit's behind-the-scenes advisory role in the union was understood by the general public. Union members expected him to express the official position of the ILGWU leaders. Among his Jewish socialist critics he was called a *Forverts' mentsh.* Only rarely did he publicly disagree with Schlesinger, Sigman, or the other national officers of the union. As radical opposition against the union bureaucracy developed, Hillquit became a major target for the union's left-wing critics.

Left-wing opposition began in earnest before Hillquit became a member of the bureaucratic hierarchy of the union. It began in the Hourwich Affair, a reaction against Protocolism.[2] In 1913 Isaac Hourwich, socialist, lawyer, and economics professor who had been appointed chief clerk of the union and its negotiator with the employers, expressed dissatisfaction with the Protocol. His objections included opposition to the antistrike provision and the centralized control over strike action given to the New York Cloakmakers Joint Board, complaints of improperly observed wage scales and, most of all, dismay at the slowness and partiality shown by the Grievance and Arbitration Boards. Hourwich's supporters saw themselves as class-conscious militants who were being dominated and, in a sense, betrayed by their leaders. Although John Dyche, the general secretary-treasurer and Abraham Rosenberg, the president of the ILGWU, were socialists, they were believed to lack the necessary spirit of class war. By February 1914 the dissenters engineered a modest reform of the Protocol machinery. A special Committee on Immediate Action was created to deal with the growing numbers of unheeded grievances. Dyche and Rosenberg were removed from office and replaced by Schlesinger and Sigman who in turn retained Hillquit as the union's attorney. The Hourwich group imagined or hoped that the new leaders would be more in tune with radical demands. Disappointment soon set in; the problems and the discontentment which Hourwich originally identified persisted.

In his first years as the union's lawyer, Hillquit appeared to present its position with aggressive vigor. He became something of a hero in June 1914 when he obtained an injunction preventing Max Sulkes, a shady figure, from using the term *International* for a union he formed under the misleading title International Ladies Garment Workers of the World. Sulkes's intention was not to form a dual union but rather to discredit the ILGWU. In April 1914 he brought indictments against Sigman, the new secretary-treasurer of the ILGWU, and several other officers of the Joint Board of Cloakmakers on the charge that they were instrumental in causing the death of a strikebreaker during the 1910 general strike. Hillquit's defense and the subsequent acquittal of the union officials in the spring of 1915 assured Hillquit the respect and confidence of large numbers of garment workers, at least temporarily. He was even lauded uncritically by the conservative Jewish press who thought the trial of Jews for murder portended a coming wave of anti-Semitism.[3] Furthermore, in December 1914 Hillquit presented the Board of Arbitration with his plan for workers' rights to the job and equalization of work. Hillquit's relationship with the workers looked promising.

In May 1915, when the Protective Association abrogated the Protocol and arbitration broke down, Hillquit tried to save the system through reform. His conciliatory attitudes evoked criticism among militant cloakmakers and socialists. There was an outburst of anti-Protocol sentiment. The Party's left-wing weekly *New Review* rejoiced over the demise of the Protocol, "the pet child of the uplifters."[4] Even the official press of the ILGWU, the *Ladies Garment Cutter*, reported ". . .the Union does not shed any crocodile tears for the instrument that *kept them in subjugation for five years* without improving their conditions one iota."[5] The union leaders were especially singled out by the leftist press for their part in the failure of the Protocol. "It should have been clear to the leaders, who stand high in the councils of the class-conscious Socialist party," wrote Isaac Hourwich in the *New Review* on June 15, 1915, "that a labor union which existed merely through 'friendly cooperation' of the employers could not endure." Hourwich had no use for ". . .a new type of labor leaders [*sic*] who, after learning their catechism in the S.L.P., the S.P., and the I.W.W., or some Anarchist group, have taken a practical course in the training school of the Protocol."[6] Later, in July 1915, when the special Council of Conciliation was brought into existence by Mayor Mitchel (with the strong approval of Hillquit, Schlesinger, and other officials), Hourwich was puzzled by the naïveté of these leaders. On July 15 he wrote, "So sophisticated, however, seems to be the faith of the Socialist leaders of the Union in 'social justice' that they would readily accept 'any other person of recognized standing in the community' as arbitrator including Mayor Mitchel, who has exhibited his capitalistic bias against labor . . . ."[7]

Conflicts between manufacturers and cloakmakers remained unresolved. Opposition to the Protocol system among the workers grew even after Mitchel's Council of Conciliation revised it. In May 1916 the Protective Association again rejected the Protocol and called for a lockout in more than 400 of its shops. It was anticipated that the Protocol provisions would be entirely dismantled. In response to this action, 50,000 workers went out on strike.

The issues related to the termination of the Protocol and new work agreements were hotly debated in the Yiddish press where several points of view were clearly expressed. Hourwich, the spokesman for the union's leftwing, adamantly demanded in *Der tog* that the right to strike be returned to the workers.[8] Chicago cloakmaker, Abraham Bisno, *de facto* chief clerk of the Joint Board and a pure and simple unionist who thought "collective agreements were 'revolutionary' instruments which marked the transition from autocracy to constitutionalism in the industry," insisted the arbitration machinery remain intact.[9] His polemic against Hourwich and the strike position was printed in the *Jewish Daily Forward* which generally supported the continuation of the Protocol. The Jewish Socialists, at least those represented by the Party's Jewish Federation, expressed their opinion in the *Naye velt*. Their labor editor Salutsky was favorably disposed to the return of strike power but believed caution was necessary before dispensing with the arbitration system in its entirety.[10]

Hillquit wanted the Protocol to remain in force but he bent to majority sentiment within the union. The new agreement, which he helped write, removed the boards of arbitration and returned the workers' right to strike and the employers' right to reorganize the shops (although to some extent the employers were not permitted to fire workers at will). The machinery for arbitration was left in the hands of the union and the manufacturers. Subsequently, the Joint Board and the ILGWU Executive Committee claimed the right to call strikes in cases where union-employer arbitration failed.

On September 3, 1916, B. Levitan of the *Jewish Daily Forward* interviewed Hillquit about the cloakmakers' agreement and how it would work in practice. In this interview Hillquit appeared resigned to the elimination of formal arbitration boards. He expressed a faith in future harmonious relations between the bosses and the workers based on self-control. "After a while when both sides become accustomed to the new situation, they will realize that neither the bosses nor the workers ought to make use of these rights," he said.[11]

During the negotiations related to this 1916 strike, the cloakmakers expressed distrust of Hillquit and Schlesinger. Accusations circulated among the strikers that the negotiators had not disclosed the "real" provisions of the agreement and that the agreement contained secret and unfavorable terms. Thus the strikers refused to approve the final signing until questions of contract terminology were clarified to their satisfaction. The strike continued for two weeks while the matter was under investigation. Melech Epstein, who was then labor editor of *Der tog*, reported Hillquit's cynicism and initiated what was to become an archtypical tale among leftwing socialists and later communists. Epstein related how on the morning of the settlement he was "tipped off that one clause of the agreement was loosely formulated to hide a secret concession to the association." Epstein wrote an exposé in *Der tog* and when Schlesinger addressed the workers that evening at Arlington Hall, he had to leave the hall under police escort. Epstein recalled:

> Schlesinger took it as a personal blow, but Hillquit was overheard comforting him with his usual reassuring smile, "Don't worry, Ben, if an error has been made we will find enough expressions to satisfy each side"—and he did. The union leadership had no choice but to return the settlement and to persuade the association to change the wording of the clause. Only after a long speech in Yiddish by Morris Hillquit was the agreement approved by the shop chairman.[12]

During the 1916-1918 period Hillquit did not sympathize with those who wished to reform the ILGWU but he supported other kinds of radical positions. His stand against United States preparedness and then, in 1917, his position against the war favorably impressed even his leftwing critics.[13] Hillquit was, in fact, one of the few socialist and labor leaders who not only condemned the war but also warned the workers to be wary of capitalist appeals to their patriotism. At the May 20, 1918, ILGWU convention in Philadelphia he exhorted the workers: "We must not forget that the first duty to ourselves, to the labor population of the country, to the generations of workers to come, is to maintain and to improve the living standards of the workers in times of war, as well as in times of peace." Hillquit had no illusions about the intentions of the employers during the war. He told his audience,"...there is not one among our employers, as among the employing class generally, who is not ready to take advantage of the world-calamity to coin the misery of the war, the misery of his fellowmen into dollars and fortunes for himself, to accumulate vast fortunes...and at the same time try to hold down the workers to the lowest possible level on the plea of patriotic duty...." He warned the ILGWU convention that the employers would"...discourage and decry any effort on the part of the workers to barely maintain the pre-war standards, on the assumed ground that such an action would introduce disturbance in the industry during the war, while they themselves never hesitate to introduce any disturbance, any upheaval for the sake of their sacred profits."[14]

Along with his solid opposition to the war and his support of workers' rights during the war, Hillquit also came out enthusiastically in support of the Russian Revolution. In the initial months following the Bolshevik takeover, he shared the general optimism about a socialist future in Russia which pervaded radical circles in the United States. The large Russian Jewish socialist population of the ILGWU was especially susceptible to the news of a revolution in their former despotic homeland. The union's officers published a laudatory report on the progress of the Russian Revolution.[15] Hillquit, speaking at the same 1918 convention, assured the workers that "the revolution in Russia will be of greater importance than the entire war." But even in May, when most Socialists were still wildly praising the Russians, he was not willing to participate in blind hero worship nor did he want to single out the Russians as the sole revolutionary force in Europe. "The present regime in Russia may change," he noted. And he went on to say:

> It need not necessarily be Lenine and Trotzky forever. They are undoubtedly great leaders. But if Lenine had remained in Switzerland and Trotzky in the Bronx New York, the Russian revolution would have gone on just as well, and if there

> should be any change in the administration, one thing is absolutely certain, autocracy, capitalism, oppression are dead in Russia.[16]

Furthermore, Hillquit told the ILGWU convention delegates: "There are other revolutions. . . . less spectacular, less picturesque, less appreciated generally, but probably almost as significant. And that is, the revolution, the spiritual, moral revolution and the political revolution which has taken place in England, particularly among the working classes of England."[17]

However, after 1918 the success of the Russian Bolshevik Revolution caused extreme changes in the Socialist Party of America and directly influenced the future development of the ILGWU. In August 1919 the Party split; a Communist Party was formed. Hillquit approved the expulsion of the Party's dissident leftwing, including a majority of the foreign-language federations. From then on, he was personally attacked by the Communists who labeled him a reactionary. In 1920 Hillquit was ranked by Lenin in his Twenty-One Points along with Kautsky, Turati, Hilferding, Longuet, and MacDonald as a centrist and social traitor who paid lip service to the proletarian revolution. This document specifically excluded Hillquit from membership in the Communist International.

In general, the 1919 split in the American radical movement promised to provoke a Socialist-Communist civil war in the garment industry. When this conflict was still in its embryonic stage, between 1918-1921, Hillquit withdrew from public life and spent considerable time recovering from a physical breakdown caused by tuberculosis. When he returned to active work within the ILGWU in 1921, the union faced serious attempts by the employers to undermine the gains won over the past decade while the union hierarchy faced a Communist opposition which preached intraunion reform, labor militancy, and the ouster of the old leadership.

In 1921 the Communists in the ILGWU had a fresh yet experienced and vocal group of leaders as well as a large and growing rank and file. The Jewish Federation of the Socialist Party, one of the few foreign-language organizations to remain in the Party after the 1919 debacle and one which had great influence in the unions, also split in September of 1921. Those leaders who left the Party, such as Salutsky and Olgin, formed an independent party sympathetic to the Communists. Their founding declaration offered the following reasons for their abandonment of the Socialists. First, "we are leaving the SP not because it lacks revolutionary ideas but because under Hillquit it is inconsistent and vacillating." Second, they declared that the *Jewish Daily Forward* was "running the unions through its labor department."[18]

With ever increasing intensity Hillquit, between 1921 and 1926, antagonized the left-wingers by his insistence upon a cautious attitude toward the use of strikes, by his acquiescence to government-dictated arbitration agreements, and by his indifference to democratic reform measures within the union. For instance, at the 1922 AFL convention, Hillquit revealed his conservatism in union matters when he personally instructed the ILGWU delegates not to vote for John L. Lewis, a candidate for president on a militant platform against Samuel Gompers. Hillquit, who was then trying to form a socialist-labor coalition Labor Party in alliance with several conservative trade unions, sent Schlesinger, Cahan, and the other ILGWU delegates a telegram stating that it was the consensus "of the movement" that they should by no means oppose Gompers. Historian Melech Epstein, who was then a communist, noted that "the young radicals of the delegation were displeased by the wire, but they had to ask Lewis to release them from their pledge given him a day before. One of them, Mary Goff, of Local 62, tears in her eyes, refused to cast her vote for Gompers.[19]

After 1922 left-wing Communist power in the ILGWU became increasingly more significant. Communist leaders Louis Hyman and Charles Zimmerman could point to the acute problems in the industry and blame the traditional leadership for its failure to solve them. There was a decline of the cloak trade, a spread of the contracting system, and a movement of employers to nonunion shops away from New York. Unemployment was high and wages did not keep pace with the cost of living. By the end of 1924 Communists had won majorities on the executive boards of three large ILGWU locals. In 1925 the Communist left took over the biggest affiliate of the ILGWU, the Joint Board of the Cloak and Dress Makers. The attempts made by the national leadership on the General Executive

Board, especially by President Sigman, to expel Communist leaders from executive committees of locals and to reorganize locals failed to stem the tide of left-wing popularity among the union's rank and file.[20]

Until 1925 Hillquit remained on the sidelines. Unlike Sigman he was not ready to claim that the Communists "have only one purpose: to capture the existing trade unions and make them pliant tools of the dictatorship of the secret communist central committee, to destroy them entirely if they cannot be captured."[21] While Hillquit attacked the Communists in the Soviet Union and in the Third International, he did not have much to say publicly about the growing communist influence in the needle trades. In fact, when the Communists took over the single most important segment of the ILGWU in 1925, the New York Joint Board, with Hyman becoming general manager and Zimmerman head of the dressmakers' department, Hillquit was retained as the board's counsel.

However, he disagreed with the militant policy of the new leadership. This set the stage for an intense rupture between Hillquit and the Communists, a split precipitated by the conflict which occurred in 1925 between the union and the manufacturers. Since the union's position was weakened by internal battles, chronic problems in the needle trades economy, and the profileration of nonunion shops, the manufacturers had become especially stubborn in granting either new benefits or reforms in the factories. In general, during this period, the labor movement in America was on the defensive, and the employers in the garment industry hoped to capitalize upon the "spirit of the times."

In 1924 the ILGWU had opened negotiations with the manufacturers. The union demanded a forty-hour week, an increase in minimum wages, and a scheme for unemployment insurance. The manufacturers refused to negotiate. At this point, Governor Smith had appointed a special Advisory Commission to survey the possibilities of a settlement and to make recommendations to the employers and to the union. Hillquit, who argued the union's case, expected that the commission would decide in favor of the union.[22] But while the commission accepted the union's program and recommended the adoption of the wage increases, the forty-hour week, the unemployment program, and a plan for regulating employment in the shops, the employers rejected the recommendations. A short strike followed which ended in the employers' acceptance of the commission's recommendations with the provision that the advisors continue investigating the industry. The final report was to be submitted to the governor in May 1926.

Although Hillquit had faith that the Smith Commission could produce a workable solution, the Communist left did not. For them the central issue between employer and employee was worker control of the shops, that is, worker security in employment and worker self-government in the factory. The Communists knew that a government arbitration board would never grant these goals. They advised militant strike action.[23]

Hillquit, however, saw the workers' problem in a different light. For him it was not so much their lack of control in the shops but the methods of production in the industry that were at the root of the problems. Hillquit told the Smith Commission (and Sigman told the 1925 ILGWU Convention) that 80 percent of the manufacturing was now being done by a system of "outside shops," while only about 6,000 workers remained in shops under union jurisdiction. Sweatshop conditions and cutthroat competition among workers had returned to the garment industry. Hillquit wanted the commission to force the employers to reorganize their associations—to bring the "outside shops" under the jurisdiction of a broad Manufacturers' Association. Hillquit insisted that the manufacturers should regulate the number of shops, health conditions, standards of wages and hours, and work distribution. In other words, the thrust of Hillquit's argument was decidedly in the direction of manufacturers' rationalizing the garment industry and in their keeping a good deal of control—shared, to some extent, by the union.[24]

At the Eighteenth ILGWU Convention in 1925 Hillquit, a keynote speaker, urged the acceptance of arbitration and warned against the use of strikes. He said:

> And you may be Socialists and Anarchists and Communists, as much as you want to, and be as zealous and enthusiastic in your political beliefs as you want to be . . . but what I want to impress upon you is the thing that it seems to me you

> have forgotten . . . to serve the tens and thousands of men and women who have entrusted you with their power and responsibility . . . . You know it is easy to destroy, it is hard to rebuild.[25]

The left-wing leaders at the convention opposed Hillquit's solution. They suggested that arbitration was no solution. The answer to the proliferating small shops was a massive organizing campaign and an aggressive insistence upon the maintenance of union conditions in all shops. Let the bosses worry about how to organize the industry. If the union organized the workers, it could demand higher wages and better working conditions. In short, class struggle, not rationalization, was the key to workers' victory.[26]

When the commission submitted its final report on May 20, 1926, it made several suggestions about rationalizing the industry, but nothing was said about the forty-hour week, or about equalizing work during the slack seasons, or about guaranteeing minimum amounts of work or "the right to the job."[27] Although President Sigman urged that the recommendations be accepted because he feared a strike would be a disaster, the Joint Board ordered a general strike on July 1, 1926.

The strike was a disaster. Intense factionalism among the union leaders, the use of gangsters, and unclear union demands which were not understood by workers were only a few of the problems. When the strike was finally settled in November 1926, Hillquit negotiated an agreement with the manufacturers which was not appreciably better than what had been offered the union months earlier. The strike seriously damaged union morale and depleted its financial resources.

Hillquit blamed the Communist leadership. Reviewing the events of 1925-1926 before the Nineteenth ILGWU Convention in 1928, he said that at first he had been "benevolently neutral" toward the radicals because he recognized that the old leadership had become "a little lax, a little over confident, a little neglectful." But now he was convinced that the radicals were reckless, incompetent people who called a needless strike and squandered more of the union's money than "any old-style corrupt union leader."[28]

Hillquit was reviled by the Communist press for his part in

accepting the terms of the 1926 agreement and for "selling out the workers." But interestingly, he and other staunch anti-Communists were also criticized within the Party for the bankruptcy of the ILGWU policy toward the radical wing of the union. Norman Thomas, for example, wrote Hillquit on December 21, 1926, congratulating him "for the notable part you have played in clearing up the mess of this cloakmaker's strike. . . ." But he pointed out to Hillquit: "It is thoroughly unhealthy that the one issue on which a great many of our comrades tend to arouse themselves, the one thing that brings into their eyes the old light of battle, is their hatred of Communism. . . ." He warned that "a purely negative anti-Communist position will ultimately kill the Socialist Party body and soul." Rhetorically he asked Hillquit, "Is there to be no alternative in the United States between the crazy leadership from which cloakmakers have suffered and the selfish, calculating, plotting, unidealistic leadership of the average AF of L union. . . ?" Thomas wanted to know whether "it [would] be any help if we could get together a small group of people on your call to discuss the situation and what can be done within the Socialist Party and through the Socialist Party to remedy it."[29] Hillquit replied by complimenting Thomas's "keen perception of some of the vital problems which confront. . .practically all the Needle Trades Union."[30] The matter rested there.

After 1926 Hillquit personally suffered from that purely negative anti-Communist position of which Thomas spoke. The hostility was reciprocated. When in 1929 Hillquit, under the direction of the ILGWU's General Executive Board, converted the stock of the union's International Union Bank into cash to pay off union debts, the Communist press accused him of theft and of personally profiting from the transaction. Hillquit had a libel suit brought against the editors of the *Daily Worker* and the Yiddish *Freiheit*. It was a cause célèbre in the communist and socialist papers for months.[31] Eventually, Hillquit was instructed to drop these charges by Schlesinger, the president of the ILGWU. Schlesinger reasoned that the libel suit "would only serve to infuse a flicker of life into their dying movement and give them an opportunity to start out making collections of money to enable them to keep alive their army of professional hangers-on."[32] Hillquit dropped the charges.

Morris Hillquit, about 1929. *Courtesy of State Historical Society of Wisconsin.*

Hillquit's career as a labor lawyer in the ILGWU reveals the weakest aspects of his socialism. Since he emphasized the role of a political party and minimized the efficacy of trade unions as agents for societal change, his vision of the goals toward which unions ought to aspire was limited. Although he was not a bread-and-butter-type trade unionist and he framed such radical-sounding concepts as the worker's "right to the job," he did not expect the union to be revolutionary. He expected it to function within the confines of the established institutions. Moreover, he advised the union to accept guidance from capitalist governmentally appointed arbitrators and manufacturer-appointed lawyers. It is possible, using his evolutionary kind of socialist thinking, that he imagined slow reform, designed by socialist leaders and implemented by well-meaning middle-class reformers, would ultimately lead the needle trades into the socialist future.

At the root of Hillquit's reliance upon "progressive" government mediators, sympathetic manufacturers, and union bureaucrats was his distrust of the immigrant garment workers. The very basis of his Marxian ideology resided in his faith in a working-class movement; however, his experiences with workers, especially Jewish workers of the 1890s, made him fearful of militant strikes or even of democratic worker control in unions. When he became the lawyer for the ILGWU in 1914, he rationalized this contradiction. For workers he substituted the union bureaucracy. In his mind the Schlesingers and Sigmans knew what the workers needed and what they wanted. He thought that leadership "from the top" would eventually achieve socialist goals. Union control and rank-and-file-directed policies from the bottom would lead only to chaos. In the mid-1920s he dissipated a great deal of energy combatting the Communists who, in his opinion, represented the chaotic point of view.

It is more than likely that Hillquit singlehandedly could not have altered the direction taken by the ILGWU leadership between 1914 and 1930. But his career in the union contributed appreciably to garment unionization. Positively, he helped create labor unions which improved the lot of immigrant workers. Negatively, through his attitudes and behavior, he failed to offer the rank and file of the union the kind of socialist guidance which might have directed their energies toward real changes in their position. Instead, he supported those aspects of garment unionization which weakened rank-and-file enthusiasms and militancy. He supported an entrenched undemocratic union hierarchy. He contributed to intrafactional strife between socialist and communist and between "radical" and "moderate" which lost sight of common goals and the interests of workers.

Notes

1. Hyman Berman, "Era of the Protocol: A Chapter in the History of the ILGWU, 1910-1916," (Ph.D. dissertation, Columbia University, 1956), p. 24, offers an ethnic breakdown which shows that in 1913 more than 80 percent were Jewish, 15 percent were Italian, and the rest were native-born Americans, mainly of foreign parentage.

2. For a discussion of the Hourwich Affair see John H.M. Laslett, *Labor and the Left: A Study of Socialist and Radical Influences in the American Labor Movement, 1881-1924* (New York, 1970), pp. 98-143.

3. Oneal, *History of the Amalgamated*, pp. 176-77.

4. Isaac Hourwich, "Termination of the Protocol," *New Review* 3, (June 15, 1915), 8:76.

5. Quoted in ibid.

6. Ibid., p. 79.

7. Hourwich, "The Protocol 'On Again'," ibid., 3, (July 15, 1915), 10:129.

8. New York *Der tog*, August 27, 1916.

9. New York *Jewish Daily Forward*, August 20, 1916.

10. J.B. Hardman (Salutsky), "In der arbeter presse," New York *Naye velt*, September 3, 1916. Also see New York *Call*, October 19, 1916, which mentions a sixty-four-page booklet reviewing the union's struggles over the 1914-1916 period. The booklet is written by Schlesinger who thanks the *Naye velt*, *Freie arbeter shtime*, and the *Forward* for help in the strike.

11. B. Levitan, "Vi di cloakmacher agreement vel arbeten: an interview mit Morris Hillquit," New York *Jewish Daily Forward*, September 3, 1916.

12. Epstein, *Jewish Labor*, 2:32.

13. Ludwig Lore, "The New York Mayoralty Campaign," *The Class Struggle* 2, (November-December 1917), 4:100-106.

14. *Proceedings of the Fourteenth Convention of the International Ladies Garment Workers' Union*, May 20, 1918, p. 139.

15. Ibid., "Officer's Report to the Fourteenth Convention of the International Ladies Garment Workers' Union: The Revolution in Russia," (May 1918), pp. 42-43.

16. Ibid., p. 142.

17. Ibid., p. 143.

18. Epstein, *Jewish Labor*, 2:110.

19. Epstein, *Profiles of Eleven*, p. 228.

20. There is a historical literature which deals with the post-World War I garment industry labor movement. Most studies are divided clearly between historians who opposed the Communist influence and those who favored it. However, Melech Epstein's *Jewish Labor* 2 is anti-communist while his earlier work in Yiddish, *Di geschichte fun arbeter-klas in amerika*, is decidedly pro-communist. A widely used anti-communist source is the work by Benjamin Stolberg, *Tailor's Progress: The Story of a Famous Union and the Men Who Made It* (New Jersey, 1944). Sympathetic to the communist position are David Saposs, *Left-Wing Unionism: A Study of Radical Politics and Tactics* (New York, 1926); Lewis Hyman, *Oif di vegn fun kampf* (New York, 1929); Jack Hardy, *The Clothing Workers* (New York, 1935); James R. Prickett, "Communists and the Communist Issue in the American Labor Movement, 1920-1950," (Ph.D. dissertation, University of California, 1975), pp. 43-100. A.J. Muste, "The Communists and the Unions," *Labor Age* 20, (June 1931), 6:5-8 is an important anti-communist article. A more recent account of the period is in Irving Howe, *World of Our Fathers* (New York and London, 1976), pp. 330-38.

21. Quoted in Saposs, *Left-wing Unionism*, p. 57.

22. New York *Women's Wear Daily*, May 8, 1926, Clippings, Hillquit Papers; New York *News-Record*, May 10, 1926, ibid.

23. For example the Communist point of view is presented in the New York *Freiheit*, July 2, 1925. Also see a set of left-wing documents in the Daniel Bell Collection, box 10 (MB 10), Tamiment Library.

24. For Hillquit's comments to the Smith Commission see his *Report*, New York State Governor's Advisory Commission, 1925, Writings, Hillquit Papers. For Sigman's convention remarks see *Proceedings of the Eighteenth Convention of the International Ladies Garment Workers' Union* (1925), p. 236, where he said that "the deterioration of our industry is entirely due to certain industrial changes, for which no human beings can be held reponsible."

25. Ibid., p. 336.

26. Ibid., pp. 281-88.

27. *Final Recommendations*, Governor's Advisory Commission, May 20, 1926, ILGWU Research Library.

28. *Proceedings of the Nineteenth Convention of the International Ladies Garment Workers' Union* (1926), p. 105.

29. Letter from Norman Thomas to Morris Hillquit, December 21, 1926, Correspondence, Hillquit Papers.

30. Letter from Morris Hillquit to Norman Thomas, December 29, 1926, ibid.

31. For the SP's point of view see New York *New Leader*, January 26, 1929. For the extensive Communist coverage of the situation see the New York *Freiheit* between January 22 and March 6, 1929, and the New York *Daily Worker* for the same period.

32. *Proceedings of the Twenty-First Convention of the International Ladies Garment Workers' Union* (1929), p. 132. Also see New York *News-Record*, December 10, 1929, Clippings, Hillquit Papers. Another report of this convention is in New York *Woman's Wear Daily*, December 11, 1929, ibid.

The Last Years

Chapter 18

Hillquit's political behavior in the late 1920s and 1930s had both strengths and weaknesses. On the plus side, he emerged from the intraparty and communist struggles of the previous two decades holding fast to his belief in democratic socialism. He denounced inflexibility and dogma. He lauded the peaceful and parliamentary approach to socialism. Consequently, during the 1920s and 1930s, he continued to oppose the exploitative and undemocratic aspects of American society. His battles were impressive. In the 1920s he ran for Congress and in 1932 for mayor of New York. In these campaigns he was critical of the economic system and of the political corruption of the capitalist candidates, including Roosevelt. In addition, he continued to act as the Party's lawyer in civil liberty cases which had not been concluded with the waning of the early 1920s' Red Scare. For example, he regained the privileges which the Rand School had lost during the Lusk crusade.[1] On several occasions he went to court to do battle against the misuses of injunctions in the garment industry.[2]

However, the experiences of the past decades also accentuated Hillquit's weaknesses. He had lived through the IWW issue and, even more significantly, the Bolshevik split. He had fought the Communists in the needle trades throughout the first half of the 1920s. As an international secretary of the American Party, he had involvement, on an intimate basis, with the exile and imprisonment of Russian Social Democrats (Menshevik). All these experiences reinforced his antipathy toward revolutionary concepts and strengthened his belief that the parliamentary approach to socialism was the only answer. His theoretical acumen, however, was not sharp. In 1921 he published *From Marx to Lenin*, a critique of the non-Marxist nature of the Soviet revolution and Russian society. Other works did not follow. He did not write a theoretical work which integrated the socialist experiences of the past decade with a new Marxist vision. Instead, he spoke in vague generalities about educating workers toward a class consciousness and about evolving democratic institutions which would be a substitute for capitalism.

Furthermore, Hillquit's relationship with labor became more unclear; his attitudes were beset with contradictions. He remained convinced that socialists ought to work within the organized institutions of labor. Yet his attempts between 1921 and 1925 to form a Labor Party left him more critical than ever of the AFL and its leaders whose general orientation favored cooperation with such pro-business groups as the National Civic Federation.[3] On March 9, 1929, Hillquit's *New Leader* article, "AF of L Incredibly Reactionary," attacked the labor federation's leadership for their restrictions on union membership, for their unwillingness to organize new groups of workers, and for their political rewards system which he said made organized labor "doormats in the legislative halls."[4] He also blamed the AFL leaders for keeping the American working class the most backward group of workers in the world.[5]

His attitude toward the more radical wing of the labor movement was equally problematic. In one way he wanted a more militant and industrially organized labor movement. Yet by the middle of the 1920s he had become one of the arch opponents of the communists in the needle trades. The communist position appeared to be one of increased militancy, industrial unionization, and internal democratic reforms within the existing unions. Hillquit supported the old leadership and hence he defended an anti-communist and status quo position.[6]

In the late 1920s the American Socialist Party desperately needed more vigorous leadership. It was Hillquit who in 1928 first proposed Norman Thomas as the Party's presidential candidate. Before the convention, Hillquit suggested that 1928 might be a good year to nominate a virtual unknown. He argued that Thomas would give the Party an opportunity to develop new leadership and to attract new and younger members. Hillquit especially appreciated the Ohio-born Thomas because of the younger man's strong intellectual tastes. As one of Thomas's biographers put it, "Hillquit therefore proposed that the party nominate Norman Thomas, whose ability as a speaker capable of reaching intellectuals impressed him."[7] Although Thomas made a poor showing in the 1928 election, Hillquit continued to admire him. Thomas received less than one percent of the almost 37 million votes cast for Hoover and Smith and he polled the smallest Socialist vote ever recorded by an American Socialist in a presidential election.[8]

By 1929 Hillquit and Thomas were at odds. During the 1929 New York mayoralty campaign, Thomas received considerable support from such anti-Tammany Hall nonpartisan reformers as John Dewey, Rabbi Stephen Wise, the Reverend Harry Emerson Fosdick, columnist Heywood Broun, and Dr. Henry Neumann, leader of the Ethical Culture Society.[9] Thomas's themes during the campaign were in the muckraking tradition. After the election it was suggested by some of the reformers that a federation of Socialists, trade unionists, settlement house workers, independents, and liberals form a coalition with Thomas as its leader. While Thomas was attracted to this idea, Hillquit rejected it.[10] He had returned to his pre-World War I anti-fusionist stand. Hillquit said that he wanted the Party to be open to all reformers but he adamantly objected to a coalition with non-socialists which might result in the abandonment of a specific Socialist Party program and identity.[11]

After 1930 relations between Thomas and Hillquit further deteriorated and their differences merged into a larger party battle (the Old Guard versus the Militants) which embittered Hillquit's last years. This complex controversy ultimately split the Party in 1934, a year after Hillquit's death, the issues being generational tensions and tactical and ideological differences.

The generational issue was clear. The Old Guard, men like Hillquit, Algernon Lee, and James Oneal, were in their fifties and sixties while the Militants were in their twenties and thirties. Many of the Militants were college students who had been attracted into the

Party in the late 1920s. The Old Guard, which held the important bureaucratic positions, had been members for more than two decades.

The tactical and ideological differences were less clear but equally divisive. Tactically, the young Militants wanted the Party to pursue a more aggressive program (that is, special socialist caucuses in labor unions, more mass propaganda, and new Socialist newspapers). The Old Guard, with their experience in the AFL, thought the Militants naïve, especially in regard to a labor policy. They knew that organized labor could not be radicalized by infusing a few socialists into its ranks. The Militants thought the Old Guard labor policy actually protected and condoned the undemocratic craft unionism and stagnant bureaucracy of organized labor. As for propaganda, the oldtimers had devoted their lives to just that. Lee had been the editor of the *Call* and in 1930 was the president of the Rand School. Oneal was the editor of the *New Leader*. At the time of the controversy Hillquit was actively involved in publishing plans related to the "Little Library of Socialism." The library was to include more than twenty books on American Socialist thought, representing works by some of the younger Socialists in the Party, such as Clarence Senior and Heywood Broun.[12]

Ideological conflicts between the Old Guard and the Militants were even more divisive. Actually, the Militants represented two very different ideological positions which were made compatible only by their distaste for the Old Guard. One group, the left-wing Militants, considered themselves Marxists, but in the new style of Lenin. As Louis Stanley noted in the *New Leader*, "As a matter of fact, the militants have something new to offer, new in the sense that they want to apply old principles to new conditions in a new way."[13] The left-wing Militants wanted a working-class party led by a strong centrally organized leadership which would not make a "fetish of democracy."[14] Their model was the Soviet Union and their special quarrel with the Old Guard was centered around Hillquit's and Oneal's anti-Soviet sentiments.

The second group of Militants, whom the historian Shannon calls Progressives, were less "noisy" than their left-wing colleagues but far more pervasive. They were hardly Marxists at all. Shannon aptly characterized them when he wrote that "their goal was a realignment of American politics whereby there would be a party to represent labor and dirt farmers, based upon principles rather than upon thirst for office and political opportunism." Furthermore, "this party once in office would extend democracy and civil liberties, socialize basic industries, and move rapidly in the direction of what is nowadays called the welfare state." However, "if the American electorate should support the Socialist Party and make it such an organization, well and good; if such a party should have to be a new organization, a national farmer-labor party, then the Socialists should go into the new organization."[15]

Hillquit's ideological positions did not please either the left or the Progressive wings of the Militant faction. The left especially disdained his anti-Soviet views. Since 1921 Hillquit had argued that the Bolshevik Revolution was not a truly socialist one and hence he rejected the Soviet experience as a suitable model for American socialists. In a highly publicized debate, "What Shall Be the Attitude of Socialists toward the Soviet Union," in February 1928, he went so far as to assert that "the Soviet regime has been the greatest disaster and calamity that has occurred to the Socialist movement." Despite left-wing Militant insistence that the Soviet Union was a viable experiment and that the Stalin Five-Year Plan promised to show the world that socialism worked, Hillquit maintained that "the experiment has already failed."[16] Hillquit could point to his old mentor Karl Kautsky, whose book *Bolshevism at a Deadlock*, published by the Rand School, corroborated his position.[17]

The left-wing Militants not only disagreed with Hillquit's views on the Soviet Union but objected even more to the fact that under his influence the Party conventions failed to adopt resolutions openly supporting the Russian "dictatorship of the proletariat." For example, at the New York Socialist Party Convention in February 1931, the Militants wanted the Party to recognize that "Soviet Russia is making a fundamental contribution to the realization of Socialism because . . . it is a worker's government . . . [and because] its economic system is founded upon planned production for use." The Militants proclaimed, "The growing success of the Soviet experiment will give an immense impetus to the acceptance of Socialism by workers, failure will set back our propaganda work. . . ."[18]

In contradiction Hillquit supported a resolution advanced by Algernon Lee at the 1931 New York convention which favored United States recognition of Russia but which stressed "that there is a fundamental difference in theory and practice between Socialism and Communism, as exemplified by the Soviet Government." Lee's resolution concluded by noting that:

> The socialist movement . . . opposes all undemocratic tendencies whether in society at large or within the movements of the working class. It specifically rejects the theory that the desired reorganization of society is to be effected through the action of a resolute minority, exercising a dictatorship over the rest of the working class and over society as a whole.

Hillquit added during the debate that "it is absurd to speak of the Bolshevik dictatorship as a workers' government. . . ."[19]

Hillquit was less at odds with the Progressive wing of the Militant faction, or at least the issues were different. Thomas, a Progressive Militant, tended to take a harder line against the Soviets than the left-wingers. But the Progressives were reform-minded and moralistic and their target was not only society at large but also the Socialist Party. While Hillquit agreed with Thomas and the other Militant reformers about the need to criticize the corrupt capitalist system, he did not see this same need for reform applied to the Socialist Party. Thus when his own behavior as a corporation lawyer came under censure by Thomas, he was unwilling to deal with the implications, that is, the accusation that he was involved in capitalistic practices which by definition were inimicable to the interests of the socialist movement.[20]

Hillquit's personal disagreements with the Militants came to a head at the 1932 Milwaukee National Convention. The Militants attempted to unseat him from the National Party chairmanship to which he had been appointed when Victor Berger died in August 1929.[21] The bitterness of the ensuing quarrel was reflected in Nina Hillquit's contention that "for months before the convention was scheduled to take place Norman Thomas, B. Charney Vladeck of New York, and Joseph Bearach of Boston, claiming that they wanted an American party, campaigned secretly and vigorously against Hillquit from Maine to California."[22]

At the convention Militants William Quick and Heywood Broun nominated Milwaukee mayor Daniel W. Hoan for the chairmanship. They argued that the national chairman should not be a New Yorker and that he should be someone unmistakably recognized as "American." Hillquit supporters Louis Waldman, Charles Solomon, and Algernon Lee, all New Yorkers, immediately countercharged the "Thomas alliance" with bringing the issues of race and sectionalism into the Party under the guise of Americanism. The Hillquitites claimed that just before the convention Militants had started a whisper campaign to the effect that Hillquit was a Jew and that the Party should be rid of foreign elements. They also charged that the fight made by Thomas and his followers was really an attempt to destroy "orthodox" socialism in the United States.[23]

The Militants denied both these accusations. B. Charney Vladeck, the manager of the *Jewish Daily Forward*, who described himself as "an internationalist by profession, a Jew by birth and an American by citizenship," defended the Militants against anti-Semitic slurs and against anti-Marxism. The real issue, Vladeck insisted, centered on the Socialist Party's need to change its offical leadership. Hillquit provided the Party "with a radical program with conservative action," while the Milwaukee Socialists "have a conservative program with radical action and that is what we need in the party nationally."[24]

The Hillquit faction, however, refused to leave the "anti-Semitic" question alone. Joseph Sharts, a Hillquit supporter from Ohio and a non-Jew, struck back at Vladeck by saying, "if I had been a Jew instead of a Gentile, it seems to me that the merest intimation that my birth would interfere with my leadership of a party would have brought me at once to the side of my people." In his acceptance speech for the nomination of national chairman, Hillquit also reiterated the anti-Semitic charge. He said he "apologized for having been born abroad, being a Jew and living in New York, a very unpopular place."[25]

Many Jewish socialists suspected that the Hillquit group was emphasizing anti-Jewish feelings in the Party to gain personal sympathy; they perceived the situation as ironic since Hillquit had always intentionally avoided a "Jewish question." Dr. A. Koralnik of *Der tog* succinctly expressed what others thought when he wrote:

> . . .had this happened to a different Jewish socialist, one who lived among Jews or who is an authentic Jew, it would have had some meaning and logic. We could have said: two worlds, separate psychologies. There are too many Jews for the Party to be truly internationalist. But the comic element in this whole thing is that it happened to Morris Hillquit, who guards himself against *Yidishkeit* just like an orthodox Jew avoids a cross. Hillquit will not recognize and will not participate in Jewish matters. He does everything he can so that people should forget he is a Jew. And yet he becomes the victim of whispering Americanists.[26]

At the convention, Hillquit also attacked the Militants' brand of socialism. He said, "I stand for the common, garden variety of socialist," that is, for orthodox Marxism. He claimed there were three other brands represented at the convention which opposed him. "There are the militants, well meaning, immature, effervescent people who will settle down in time, but who for the moment are wild, untamed and dangerous." Then, "there are the Socialists . . . who do not want socialism to be a working class movement. They look to college men and the white collar elements." Lastly, ". . . there is the practical kind of Socialist—like the ones here in Milwaukee—who believe in building modern sewers and showing results right away." Hillquit won the chairmanship by a vote of 105 to 80.[27]

During the 1932 election campaign which followed the Milwaukee Convention, Hillquit seemingly patched up his relations with the Militants. In New York where he ran for mayor on a platform which emphasized municipal reform and especially criticized the Democratic Party, Hillquit backed Norman Thomas's presidential candidacy.[28]

By July 1933 Hillquit again was suffering from tuberculosis. Perhaps this terrible rift between the Old Guard and the Militants weakened him. He had undergone a similar physical breakdown at the time of the Haywood expulsion and again in 1918-1919 during the Communist split. This time it proved fatal.

Until the very end of his life Hillquit remained on active participant in intraparty affairs. He wrote letters and received visits from comrades. He also was in the process of writing an autobiography which was never completed. However, his wife and daughter, later the trustees of his papers, concluded the book with one of his last speeches—one which expressed Hillquit's feelings about his part in the socialist movement. The speech had been originally delivered at the Socialist State Convention of New York in July 1932 where he was surrounded mainly by friends. "I am a Socialist," he said then, "because I cannot be anything else. I cannot accept the ugly world of capitalism, with its brutal struggles and needless sufferings, its archaic and irrational economic structure, its cruel social contrasts, its moral callousness and spiritual degradation." He was very sure of himself. "I am entirely at peace with myself. I have nothing to apolgize for." And he concluded:

> If, forty years ago, I could have foreseen all phases of the tortuous course of the Socialist movement in this country and in the world, I would have done exactly as I did. If I had forty more years of life in me I would continue spending them in the Socialist movement, without regard to its "practical prospects or immediate accomplishments.
>
> To me the Socialist movement with its enthusiasm and idealism, its comradeship and struggles, its hopes and disappointments, its victories and defeats, has been the best that life has had to offer.[29]

In contrast to the thousands of individuals who had left the radical movement in America between 1914-1933, Hillquit's loyalty is commendable. That he felt defensive, as the above speech reveals, is more than understandable. His last ten years, in a party which he had helped to found and for which he had such grand expectations, were difficult. His "garden variety" American socialism no longer appealed to a majority of socialists within the Party nor did his ideas attract new members from without. His career in the Socialist Party of America had come to an end.

Notes

1. See, for example, Albany (N.Y.) *Journal*, May 5 and 6, 1922, Clippings, Hillquit Papers; Brooklyn (N.Y.) *Standard Union*, May 5, 1922, ibid., and New York *Herald*, May 5, 1922, ibid.

2. On the issue of injunctions see New York *Call*, January 12, 1922; New York *New Leader*, November 27, 1926, and December 4, 1928.

3. Hillquit had been critical of the NCF since 1911 for its efforts to "pacify" labor and he had denounced Gompers and the AFL for participating in the organization. He wrote that the NCF was ". . .devised by the cunning mind of the late Senator Hanna, [and] consists of an incongruous mixture of millionaires, labor leaders and 'prominent citizens.' It has for its ostensible object 'the voluntary conciliation between employers and employees as distinguished from arbitration,' but in reality it serves to palliate the aggressive spirit of organized labor without offering any concessions on the part of organized capital." *History of Socialism*, p. 325. For more on the NCF also see Morris Hillquit and Ralph M. Easley, *Socialism and the National Civic Federation* (1911), Writings, Hillquit Papers, which is an exchange of correspondence between Hillquit (dated June 16, 1911) and Easley (dated June 21, 1911).

4. Morris Hillquit, "A.F. of L. Incredibly Reactionary," New York *New Leader*, March 9, 1931.

5. Morris Hillquit, "Paradox of American Labor," New York *New Leader*, November 26, 1932.

6. See Chapter 17.

7. *Minutes of the Socialist Party National Convention of 1928*, p. 11, Tamiment Library. It is important to remember that Thomas joined the SP in 1917 because, in part, he was impressed by Hillquit's New York mayoralty campaign. See, Johnpoll, *Pacifist's Progress*, pp. 27-28, 54.

8. Johnpoll, ibid., p. 58.

9. Ibid., p. 65.

10. See New York *Evening Sun*, November 18, 1929, Clippings, Hillquit Papers; New York *World*, November 18, 1929, ibid.; New York *Herald Tribune*, November 19, 1929, ibid.; New York *Times*, November 19, 1929, ibid., and Des Moines (Iowa) *Register*, November 22, 1929, ibid.

11. See letter from Clarence Senior to the NEC on a motion by Hillquit and Oneal, "The Progressive Revolt," January 15, 1931, Socialist Party Papers, Duke University.

12. Letter from Morris Hillquit to Clarence Senior, April 22, 1931, ibid.

13. Louis Stanley, "A Militant's Program for American Socialists," New York *New Leader*, January 17, 1932.

14. Theodore Shapiro, "The Militant's Point of View," *American*

Socialist Quarterly 1 (April 5, 1932), pp. 29-37.

15. Shannon, *The Socialist Party*, p. 213.

16. New York *New Leader*, February 4, 1928, has a report of this debate which featured Algernon Lee and Morris Hillquit on the anti-Soviet side and Norman Thomas and James Maurer on the pro-Soviet side. For other discussions of Hillquit's stand on Russia and the Old Guard-Militant controversy see, for example, the letter from Murray Baron to *New Leader* editor, New York *New Leader*, November 29, 1930; also issues of January 3, January 31, February 7, 14, 21, and May 9, 1931.

17. Ibid., September 9, 1931. Also see James Oneal, "The Economics of Bolshevism-The Socialist Criticism: Karl Kautsky Sees the Revolution Menaced by Trend of Five Year Plan," June 2, 1931, ibid.

18. The "Militant Resolution B" in ibid., February 7, 1931.

19. Ibid., for Lee's resolution and Hillquit's comments in the debate.

20. The Russian oil scandal is documented in the clippings and letters of the Morris Hillquit Papers, Tamiment Library, which include correspondence with James Oneal, Algernon Lee, and Hillquit among other materials. Also see letters to the *New Leader* from Norman Thomas and Hillquit in the "*New Leader* Mail-Bag" on August 25, 1931.

21. Letter from Morris Hillquit and Vera Hillquit to Meta Berger, August 8, 1929, Correspondence, Hillquit Papers.

22. Nina Hillquit, "Morris Hillquit," p. 53.

23. New York *Times*, May 24, 1932, Clippings, Hillquit Papers.

24. Milwaukee *Journal*, May 24, 1932, ibid. Also see Franklin Jonas, "The Early Life of Charney Vladeck, 1886-1921: The Emergence of an Immigrant Spokesman" (Ph. D. dissertation, New York University, 1972).

25. New York *Times*, May 24, 1932.

26. A. Koralnick, "Roich fun Milwaukee," New York *Der tog*, May 27, 1932. Also see A. Glanz-Leyeles, "Der shtroikhl-shtayn," New York *Yidish*, July 10, 1932, and New York *Der tog*, May 24, 1932.

27. New York *Times*, May 24, 1932. Other accounts of the Milwaukee convention include Columbus (Ohio) *Citizen*, May 24, 1932, Clippings, Hillquit Papers; Reading (Pa.) *Eagle*, May 24, 1932, ibid.; Milwaukee *Sentinel*, May 24, 1932, ibid.; Birmingham (Ala.) *Post*, May 25, 1932, ibid., and New York *Times* May 25, 1932, ibid.

28. New york *Times*, September 8 and 19, 1932, ibid.; Boston *Herald*, September 18, 1932, ibid., and Baltimore *Sun*, September 18, 1932, comment on the reunion. An interesting account of the Socialist Party in the 1930s is Frank A. Warren, *An Alternative Vision: The Socialist Party in the 1930s* (Bloomington, Ind. 1974).

29. *Loose Leaves*, pp. 331-32.

19 Conclusion

Most historians regard Morris Hillquit as an important figure in the American Socialist movement; however, almost without exception he is seen as a one-dimensional figure, that is, as a leader of a New York faction within the Socialist Party of America. This is not so. Hillquit reacted to the American scene with energy and versatility; his activities extended into various levels of intraparty and public politics, into trade unionism, into law, and into the subtle areas of propaganda and immigrant education. In a significant sense, these relationships intermeshed, for socialism in America was an intellectual, emotional, social, and economic phenomenon as well as a political one. Hillquit personified the complex and pervasive nature of the socialist movement in the late nineteenth and early twentieth centuries. He also contributed an exceptional loyalty to American socialism by persevering despite extreme criticism long after the vast majority of his far more militant contemporaries had deserted the radical movement.

Hillquit was the advocate of an often awkward brand of Marxism which called for the radical transformation of capitalist society by means of an established and recognized Socialist Party and socialist-allied trade unions. The independent existence of the Party was one of the basic conditions for revolutionary transformation. These ideals placed him somewhere between the Party's right-wing reformers who were willing to accept the merger of the Socialist Party with reform parties and its revolutionary left-wingers who believed socialists could alter society from outside established institutions. As a centrist, Hillquit exercised a powerful influence over right-wingers from Victor Berger in the pre-World War I period through the Progressive Militants in the late 1920s. The sharp distinctions Hillquit drew between reform and socialist goals as well as the emphasis he placed upon an independent socialist party dissuaded socialist leaders from relying on middle-class alliances and therefore helped keep the Socialist Party from becoming just another reform group. It remained intact.

Hillquit's political flexibility and his activities as a civil rights lawyer and as a practical trade unionist testify against the thesis that American socialists were "otherworldly"—incapable or unwilling to operate within society. Hillquit certainly operated within his society. He worked to establish the Socialist Party and the ILGWU as recognized institutions. Moreover, he exhibited rare courage in his open battles within the so-called practical world of American society. He took unpopular stands by supporting antiwar positions during World War I. He consistently defended freedom of speech and the right to dissent in trials ranging from the Johann Most case in 1901 through the Red Scare of the 1920s.

Despite the various real contributions of high idealism, flexibility, and practicality that leaders such as Hillquit made to the socialist cause, the movement did not flourish in the United States. Although the reasons were many, leadership was neither the only cause nor the most significant. Any explanation for socialism's decline ought to include such varied and interrelated factors as the strength of the American capitalist economy, the structure of the political system, the methods of repression, the heterogeneous nature of the work force, the conservatism of American labor institutions, and the factional problems of the radical parties.

Hillquit was, to a limited extent, personally responsible for the weaknesses of the left in America. His leadership tended to intensify tendencies within the Party which contributed to the weakening of socialism in America and proved detrimental to its continued viability. His ambivalent attitude toward workers—his doubts regarding their capabilities and his blindness to their need for self-reliance—proved to be a most serious failing. The Socialist Party needed to acquire a permanent base of working-class support in order to become a distinct and cohesive political unit within American society. Hillquit did little to contribute to the formation of such support. At times he even discouraged it.

Without entirely realizing it, Hillquit identified personally with the middle class. Economically, he moved out of the working class at an early age. By the time he was in his late twenties, he was a successful lawyer. He could boast of acceptance into the ranks of the educated and prosperous bourgeoisie. He cultivated the social and aesthetic tastes of a middle-class person. His cultural identification made him insensitive toward understanding working-class needs.

He displayed this insensitivity in several concrete ways. First, he did not realize that a workers' party in the United States needed to encourage the idea that workers' efforts could significantly change society. Why else would they join a radical party? But Hillquit's ideological conception of social change was essentially passive and impersonal. His version of orthodox Marxism favored its evolutionary elements. He relied even more heavily upon a belief in the mechanistic development of capitalism than did his pre-1914 German Social Democratic mentors. He thought that advanced industrialization would generate new forms of socioeconomic organization and that somehow socialism would automatically form within the body of the capitalist system. When this transformation did not occur, he explained the failure in terms of impersonal forces. There was little in this theory that could encourage a worker to believe that his or her action—even a strike or a vote—might make a basic difference.

Moreover, Hillquit advocated only legally acceptable action. In effect he substituted legality for militant opposition. He believed that significant alterations were achieved in a procedural manner and could be actualized through American institutions, especially through a recognized political party which did not openly threaten the established order. While he maintained that class interests and class warfare operated within the legal and political systems of American society, he nevertheless saw positive potentialities in these systems. In other words, without ever expressing it in these terms, he was convinced that those political and civil rights which Americans already possessed were viable instruments in the ultimate development of social democracy.

Hillquit's emphasis upon working within the system made it impossible for him to understand why certain radical ideologies (from anarchism to IWWism through communism) appealed to some workers. Therefore, he unqualifiedly rejected every radical ideology which seriously attempted to undermine the established order from outside. Hillquit preferred to think that the question of violence alone divided him from the radical left. He claimed he could not sympathize with militant socialists or trade unionists because they advocated the use of violence as a possible instrument in the class struggle. But the real difference between Hillquit and the radical leftists, like those of the IWW, was not the issue of violence; it was a basic disagreement regarding the potential inherent in the established system.

He did more than just disagree with radicals. From 1913 onward, he was one of the leaders of the movement responsible for creating the impasse between the Party's right and left wings. Specifically, he went along with the measures taken by the Executive Committee which alienated IWW support in 1913 and excommunicated the communists in 1919. In the 1920s he backed the ILGWU leaders in their ouster of the left-wing majority whose demands included democratic reforms within the union and more militant action against the employers. In this way the Party lost a major portion of its rank-and-file support.

Hillquit also contributed to the weakening of the Party, especially in New York, because he discouraged programs which might have attracted and held the loyalty of immigrant workers, particularly Jewish immigrants. Hillquit opposed immigrant-oriented programs which intended to preserve a distinctly Jewish life in America. While he regarded the working-class Jew as forming an oppressed nationality, he did not perceive the need to integrate a religious, nationalist, or culturalist sensibility with a working-class consciousness. He claimed that socialist thinking ought to be secular and internationalist. However, in actuality, his own thinking was nationalistic. As an immigrant to the United States, he underwent a personal process of "Americanization." He transferred his allegiance from the Jewish *folk* to the American people. He wanted to build a unified American Socialist Party and immigrant "cultures" were only a further divisive element in a Party which already suffered from splits along geographical and ideological lines. Consequently, there was no special place for Jews in Hillquit's ideal socialist system in America. He equated socialism with progress. And progress meant a step away from Judaism and from its secularized expression *Yidishkeit*, both of which he considered archaic and inferior forms of culture compared with his own superior brand of socialism.

Hillquit's rejection of a positive role for "ethnicity" within the Party tended to weaken his position as a leader. In part, his was unsuccessful in his candidacies for public office in New York because the Jewish press and the voters distrusted his loyalty. Although he seriously attempted to accommodate special Jewish interests as in the congressional campaign of 1916, these attempts were never wholly convincing. Moreover, he did not provide inspired leadership for the heavily Jewish New York Socialist Party because he was unable to appreciate the concern of the many Jewish leaders and members who belonged to the Jewish Federation, the *Arbeter ring* (Workmen's Circle), wrote or read Yiddish newspapers, and so on. They wanted to continue a separate Jewish socialist identity in America by somehow reconciling that special identity with socialism. It was ironic that for many non-Jewish American socialists, Hillquit's internationalist views as well as his New York Jewish background tended to make him appear foreign and at times inauthentically American. In an important sense, he did not appeal to American socialists outside of his own environment.

Despite his constant battles in the press and in the courts for freedom of speech and other civil liberties, Hillquit also suffered from paternalistic habits of mind which were not always consistent with either democratic practices or tolerance of opposing views. However, unlike European socialists whose parties "came to power," Hillquit's position on such matters was never tested on the American body politic. Yet within the Socialist Party and the ILGWU, he repeatedly failed to support reform measures which would have given the rank and file more power over their organization and more say in regard to policymaking.

Hillquit can be judged a hero, a villain, or some combination of the two. Whatever the judgment, in a real sense his career had tragic dimensions. He observed at first hand the gradual disintegration of the American socialist movement for which he had held such high hopes.

Selected Bibliography

Primary Materials

Manuscript Materials

American Socialist Society Papers. Tamiment Library, New York.
Daniel Bell Collection. Tamiment Library, New York.
Eugene V. Debs Scrapbook Collection. Tamiment Library, New York.
Morris Hillquit Papers. State Historical Society of Wisconsin.
Morris Hillquit Papers. Tamiment Library, New York.
Algernon Lee Papers. Tamiment Library, New York.
Meyer London Papers. Tamiment Library, New York.
Judah Magnes Papers. Hebrew University Archives, Jerusalem.
John P. Mitchel Papers. Municipal Archives, New York.
People's Council Papers. Swarthmore College Archives, Pennsylvania.
Socialist Party Papers. Duke University Archives, North Carolina.
Socialist Party Papers. Tamiment Library, New York.
J. G. Phelps Stokes Papers. Columbia University Archives, New York.

Proceedings and Minutes

"Arbitration Proceedings, The Ladies Dress and Waist Manufacturers Association and the International Ladies Garment Workers' Union" (January 20, 1917). Stenographic report. International Ladies Garment Workers' Union Research Department.

"Council of Conciliation Meetings, Women's Coat and Suit Trade" (July 14 - July 17, 1915). Stenographic reports. International Ladies Garment Workers' Union Research Department.

Governor's Advisory Commission. *Final Recommendation, May 20, 1926.* Typewritten copy. International Ladies Garment Workers' Union Research Department.

International Ladies Garment Workers' Union. *Report of the Proceedings of the Annual Convention, 1916-1929.*

Labour and Socialist International. *Proceedings of the Second Congress of 1925.* Hoover Institute, Stanford University.

———. *Reports and Proceedings of the Fourth Congress of 1931.* Hoover Institute, Stanford University.

Socialist Labor Party. *Proceedings of the 1900 Annual Convention.* Microfilm copy. University of California, Los Angeles.

Socialist Party of America. *Proceedings of the Socialist Unity Convention, 1901.* Typewritten copy. Tamiment Library, New York.

———. *Proceedings of the National Convention of the Socialist Party, 1904, 1910, 1912, 1920,* and *1928.* Tamiment Library, New York.

———. "National Committee, Report of Proceedings at St. Louis," New York *Worker* (February 8, 1903).

———. "Minutes of the Joint Session of the NEC and Campaign Committee, June 16, 1912," *Socialist Party Monthly Bulletin* (July 1912).

———. "Minutes of the Joint Conference of the NEC and State Secretaries, August 10-12, 1918," Socialist Party Papers, Duke University.

Newspapers

Chicago *Social Democratic Herald*

New York *Arbeter zeitung*

New York *Call*

New York *Communist*

New York *Daily Worker*

New York *Der arbeter*

New York *Der tog*

New York *Freiheit*

New York Jewish Daily Forward

New York New Leader

New York *People* (anti-De Leon)

New York *Tageblatt*

New York Times

New York Veker

New York *Warheit*

New York *Weekly People*

New York *Women's Daily Wear*

New York *Worker*

New York *Yidisher kaempher*

Periodicals

American Labor Union Journal
American Socialist Quarterly
Appeal to Reason
Class Struggle
International Socialist Review
Ladies Garment Worker
Liberator
Naye velt
New Review
Socialist (Chicago)
Socialist (Seattle)
Socialistitcheski Vestnik (Paris)
Socialist Party Monthly Bulletin
Yidish
Zukunft

Oral History and Personal Interviews

Columbia University. Oral History Research Project: George Algers, Benjamin McLauren, and John Spargo.

Interview in May 1975 by author: Emil Schlesinger

Primary Books and Articles

Books, lectures, and articles in the Morris Hillquit Papers, State Historical Society of Wisconsin, are not cited below.

American Labor Year Book. New York, 1916.

Bittleman, Alexander. "A Conference of Progressive Reactionaries," *Worker's Monthly* (February 1925), pp. 166-67.

Borochov, Ber. "Socialism un Tammany Hall," New York *Yidisher kaempfer,* November 3, 1916.

Boudin, Louis. "The Emergency National Convention of the Socialist Party," *The Class Struggle* 1, (May-June 1917), 1:41-50.

———. "Immigration at Stuttgart," *International Socialist Review* 8 (February 1908), p. 491.

———. "Let Us Take Ourselves Seriously," *New Review* 3, (January 1915), 1:365.

———. "St Louis - One Year After," *The Class Struggle* 2, (May-June 1918), 2:338-41.

———. *The Theoretical System of Karl Marx.* New York, 1907.

"Boudin Replies to Hillquit," Chicago *Socialist,* January 10, 1912, in Eugene V. Debs Scrapbook, Tamiment Library.

Cahan, Abraham. *Bleter fun mein leben.* 5 vols. New York, 1926-1931.
Chanin, Nathan. "Morris Hillquit," New York *Veker,* October 15, 1943.
Cohen, Julius. *They Builded Better Than They Knew.* New York, 1916.
Debs, Eugene V. "Statement of Presidential Candidates to the Members of the SP," *Appeal to Reason,* July 20, 1912.
———. "Sound Socialist Tactics," *International Socialist Review* 12, (February 1912), 8:483.
De Leon, Daniel. "What Means This Strike?" Published speech delivered in Conn., February 11, 1898.
Eastman, Crystal. "The Socialist Party Convention," *Liberator* 3 (July 1920), p. 28.
Eastman, Max. *Love and Revolution.* New York, 1964.
Epstein, Melech. "Ruthenberg," New York *Freiheit,* March 5, 1927.
Fogelman, L. "Morris Hillquit," New York *Veker,* October 13, 1934.
Fraina, Louis. "The Menace of an American Militarism," *New Review* 3, (March 1915), 3:135.
———. "Problems of American Socialism," *The Class Struggle* 3, (February 1919), 1:24-26.
———. "The Future of Socialism," *New Review* 3, 1 (January 1915), 16.
Freeman, Joseph. *American Testament.* New York , 1926.
Goldman, Emma. *Living My Life.* New York, 1931. One-volume edition published February 1934.
Hardman, J. B. S. "In der arbeter presse," New York *Naye velt,* September 3, 1916.
Hillquit, Morris. " 'Comrade' Bull Moose," Morris Hillquit Papers, Tamiment Library.
———. "Dem onhayb iz der sof," New York *Arbeter zeitung,* December 5, 1890.
———. "Di strik fun di knee pants arbeter," New York *Arbeter zeitung,* April 25, 1890.
———. From Marx to Lenin. New York, 1923.
———. *The History of Socialism in the United States.* New York, 1903. There is a 5th rev. ed. with an introduction by Alfred Fried published in New York, 1971.
———. "In Self Defense," Morris Hillquit Papers, Tamiment Library.
———. "Labor's Progress in Spite of the War," *Ladies Garment Worker* (May 1918).
———. *Loose Leaves from a Busy Life.* New York, 1934.
———. "Marxism: The Basic Philosophy of Socialism," New York *New Leader,* May 2, 1931.
———. *Socialism in Theory and Practice.* New York, 1912.

———. "Statement," June 11, 1931. Morris Hillquit Papers, Tamiment Library.

———. "Sotzializm un anarchizm," New York *Arbeter zeitung*, April 8, 1890.

———. "Ver iz a revolutzionair?," New York *Arbeter zeitung*, September 12, 1890.

———. "Vos iz revolutzie?," New York *Arbeter zeitung*, April 18, 1890.

——— and Ryan, John. *Socialism: Promise or Menace?* New York, 1920.

"Hillquit and Russell on Political Action," Chicago *Socialist*, September 26, 1911, in Eugene V. Debs Scrapbook, Tamiment Library.

"Hillquit Memorial Issue," New York *New Leader*, October 6, 1934.

Hourwich, Isaac. "Termination of the Protocol," *New Review* 3, (June 1915), 7:76.

———. "The Protocol 'On Again'," *New Review* 3, (July 1915), 9:129.

Koralnich, A. "Roich fun Milwaukee," New York *Der tog*, May 27, 1932.

Levitan, B. "Vi di cloakmacher agreement vel arbeten: an interview mit Morris Hillquit," *Jewish Daily Forward*, September 3, 1916.

Liessen, Abraham. "Di yidishe ishue in di itztiche campayn," New York *Jewish Daily Forward*, November 3, 1917.

———. "Campayn notitzen: Morris Hillquit," *Zukunft* 22 (October 1917), pp. 611-13.

———. "Oif frishen kayver fun Morris Hillquit," *Zukunft* 38 (November 1933), p. 622.

Litvak, A. "Fun tsaytungen un journalen," New York *Naye velt*, November 3, 1916.

Lore, Ludwig. "The New York Mayoralty Campaign," *The Class Struggle* 2 (November - December 1917), 4:100-6.

———. "The Elections," *The Class Struggle* 2, (December 1918), 5:621.

Magidoff, Joseph. *Der shpigal fun der East Side*. New York, 1923.

Marshall, Louis. "Morris Hillquit un di yidishe vuters," New York *Tageblatt*, November 14, 1917.

Olgin, Moishe. "Interview mit Morris Hillquit," New York *Jewish Daily Forward*, October 25, 1916.

———. "Morris Hillquit," New York *Jewish Daily Forward*, September 30, 1916.

———. "Vi Morris Hillquit kukt oif di yidishe frage," New York *Jewish Daily Forward*, October 25, 1916.

Oneal, James. "The Economics of Bolshevism," New York *New Leader*, June 2, 1931.

Pinski, David. "Shtimpt far Hillquitn," New York *Yidisher kaempfer*, November 2, 1917.

"Shall Bossism Prevail in the Socialist Party?," *International Socialist Review* 13 (July 1912), pp. 77-78.

Shapiro, Theodore. "The 'Militant's' Point of View," *American Socialist Quarterly* 1 (April 5, 1932), pp. 29-37.

Spargo, John. *The Pro-German Cry of 'No Indemnities.'* New York, n.d.
"Spargo Replies to Debs," Chicago *World*, July 26, 1912, in Eugene V. Debs Scrapbook, Tamiment Library.
Waldman, Louis. *Labor Lawyer*. New York, 1945.
Walling, William English. *Socialism As It Is*. New York, 1912.
Weinstein, Bernard. *Di yidishe yunyons in amerika*. New York, 1929.
Winchevski, Morris. *Gezamelte verk*. 10 vols. New York, 1927.
———. "Morris Hillquit als mentsh," *Zukunft* 22 (November 1917), pp. 614-17.

Secondary Materials

Books and Articles

Antonovski, Aaron. *The Early Jewish Labor Movement in the States*. New York, 1961. A condensation and English translation of Elias Tcherikover (ed.). *YIVO historiche schriften*. 3 vols. Vilna, 1926.
Bell, Daniel. *Marxian Socialism in the United States*. New Jersey, 1967. This essay originally appeared in Donald Egbert and Stow Persons (eds.), *Socialism and American Life*, Princeton Studies in American Civilization, no. 4, 1952.
Borochov, Ber. *Nationalism and the Class Struggle*. New York, 1937.
Braunthal, Julius. *The History of the International*. 2 vols. New York, 1967.
Carpenter, Jesse Thomas. *Competition and Collective Bargaining in the Needle Trades, 1910-1967*. Ithaca, N.Y., 1972.
Cohen, Joseph. *Di yidish-anarchistishe bavegung in amerika*. Philadelphia, 1945.
Draper, Theodore. *The Roots of American Communism*. New York, 1957.
Dubofsky, Melvyn. "Organized Labor and the Immigrant in New York City, 1900-1918," *Labor History* 2 (spring 1961).
———. *When Workers Organize*. Amherst, Mass., 1968.
Epstein, Melech. *Geshichte fun arbeter-klas in amerika*. 2 vols. New York, 1935.
———. *Jewish Labor in USA*. 2 vols. New York, 1950.
———. *Profiles of Eleven*. Detroit, Mich. 1965.
Fainsod, Merle. *International Socialism and the War*. Cambridge, Mass., 1935.
Fine, Nathan. *Labor and Farmer Parties in the United States, 1828-1928*. New York, 1928.
Fox, Richard. "The Paradox of 'Progressive' Socialism: The Case of Morris Hillquit," *American Quarterly* 26 (May 1974), pp. 127-40.
Gay, Peter. *The Dilemma of Democratic Socialism*. New York, 1952.
Ginger, Ray. *The Bending Cross*. New Jersey, 1949.

Goren, Arthur. "A Portrait of Ethnic Politics: The Socialists and the 1908 and 1910 Congressional Elections on the East Side," *Publication of the American Jewish Historical Society* 50 (March 1961), pp. 202-38.

———. *New York Jews and the Quest for Community: The Kehilla Experiment*. New York, 1970.

Hertz, I.S. *Di yidishe sotzialistishe bavegung in amerika*. New York, 1954.

Howe, Irving. *World of Our Fathers*. New York and London, 1976.

Johnpoll, Bernard. *Pacifist's Progress: Norman Thomas and the Decline of American Socialism*. Chicago, 1970.

Joseph, Samuel. *Jewish Immigration in the United States from 1881 to 1910.* New York, 1914.

Karson, Marc. *American Labor Unions and Politics, 1900-1918.* Illinois, 1958

Kipnis, Ira. *The American Socialist Movement: 1897-1912.* New York, 1952.

Kuhn, Henry, and Johnson, Olive M. *The SLP during Four Decades.* New York, 1931.

Kushner, M. *Thirty-Fifth Anniversary Jubilee Book, 1910-1945.* New York, 1945.

Laslett, John H.M. *Labor and the Left: A Study of Socialist and Radical Influences in the American Labor Movement, 1881-1924.* New York, 1970.

Levine, Louis. *The Women's Garment Workers: A History of the International Ladies Garment Workers' Union.* New York, 1924.

Marchand, Roland C. *The American Peace Movement and Social Reform, 1898-1918.* New Jersey, 1972.

Miller, Sally. *Victor Berger and the Promise of Constructive Socialism, 1910-1920.* Westport, Conn. 1973.

———. "Americans and the Second International," *Proceedings of the American Philosophical Society*, 70, (October 1976), 5:372-87.

Morris Hillquit Papers: Guide to a Microfilm Collection. Madison, Wis. 1969.

Nettl, Peter. *Rosa Luxemburg*. London, 1966.

Oneal, James. *A History of the Amalgamated Ladies Garment Cutters' Union Local 10.* New York, 1927.

Quint, Howard. *The Forging of American Socialism*. Columbia, S.C., 1953.

Radosh, Ronald. "American Labor and the Root Commission," *Studies on the Left* 3, 1 (1963).

Reeves, Carl. *The Life and Times of Daniel De Leon*. New York, 1952.

Rischin, Moses. *The Promised City: New York's Jews, 1870-1914.* New York, 1962.

Rogoff, Harry. *An East Side Epic: The Life and Work of Meyer London.* New York, 1930.

Seretan, Glen. "The Personal Style and Political Methods of Daniel De Leon: A Reconsideration," *Labor History* 14 (spring 1973), pp. 163-201.

Shannon, David. *The Socialist Party in America.* New York, 1955.

Szajkowski, Zosa. *Jews, Wars and Communism: The Attitude of American Jews to World War I, the Russian Revolution of 1917 and Communism.* 2 vols. New York, 1972.

Warren, Frank A. *An Alternative Vision: The Socialist Party in the 1930s.* Indiana, 1974.

Weinstein, James. *The Decline of American Socialism, 1912- 1925.* New York, 1967.

Yellowitz, Irwin. *Labor and the Progressive Movement in New York State, 1897-1916.* New York, 1965.

UNPUBLISHED DISSERTATIONS

Berman, Hyman. "Era of the Protocol: A Chapter in the History of the International Ladies Garment Workers' Union 1910-1916." Columbia University, 1956.

Iverson, Robert. "Morris Hillquit, American Social Democrat: A Study of the American Left from Haymarket to the New Deal." State University of Iowa, 1951. This author wishes to thank Iverson for his fine work in dealing with Hillquit's career.

Johnston, Scott Doran. "The Socialist Labor Party, 1890-1903." University of Minnesota, 1952.

Jonas, Franklin. "The Early Life of Charney Vladeck, 1886-1921: The Emergence of an Immigrant Spokesman." New York University, 1972.

Mellon, Knox. "Job Harriman: The Early Years and Middle Years, 1861-1912." Claremont College, 1971.

Musik, Edward. "Victor Berger, a Biography." Northwestern University, 1960

Prickett, James Robert. "Communists and the Communist Issue in the American Labor Movement, 1920-1950." University of California, Los Angeles, 1975.

Index

About the Author

Norma Fain Pratt teaches history at Mt. San Antonio College in Walnut, California. Her article "Transitions in Judaism: Jewish American Women Through the 1930s" will appear in the *American Quarterly*.